FLYING SNAKES AND GRIFFIN CLAWS

"Part miscellany and part detective work, this delightful compendium of folklore combines the spirit of Herodotus and the skepticism of the modern historian. Adrienne Mayor bounds through history dispelling myths and harvesting fascinating insights."

—**CANDIDA MOSS**, author of *The Myth of Persecution: How Early Christians Invented a Story of Martyrdom*

"Adrienne Mayor reminds us in full Technicolor HD why we need to break the academic form to let in the light of brilliant, hypercurious scholars and laypersons from all walks outside it, eventually making terms like 'outside' and 'inside' irrelevant. Mayor's gifts are many, but my favorite is that her writing is immediate, three-dimensional, and inviting. Ancient history is not a black-and-white, linear timeline in her work. Her excitement in her subjects fills me with the same riveted fascination, and I feel like I belong to it as much as any scholar."

—**NEKO CASE**, musician

"Adrienne Mayor is one of our most brilliantly engaging writers on the ancient world, and *Flying Snakes and Griffin Claws* is a delightful cabinet of curiosities. Her inspired detective work reveals the natural-historical and paleontological phenomena that lurk behind the iconic imagery of classical myth, folklore, and history—and much else besides."

—**DANIEL OGDEN**, author of *The Werewolf in the Ancient World*

"Griffins! Dragons! Ghost ships! In her delightful new collection of essays, Adrienne Mayor traces the origin stories of a bevy of irresistible curiosities, from talking mynah birds and musical racing turtles to giants and mermaids. Her impressive scholarship is matched only by her infectious good humor as she plunges into the history behind tattoos and foot fetishes, sifting expertly between mythology and classical sources in pursuit of evidence. A treat to read from cover to cover."

—**NANCY GOLDSTONE**, author of *In the Shadow of the Empress: The Defiant Lives of Maria Theresa, Mother of Marie Antoinette, and Her Daughters*

"This eclectic and fascinating essay collection is Mayor's *Wunderkammer*—the stories from a lifetime of meticulously turning myths into bones."

—**SUSANNA FORREST**, author of *The Age of the Horse: An Equine Journey through Human History*

ABOUT THE AUTHOR

Photo by Gary Wilson

ADRIENNE MAYOR is the author of *The Poison King: The Life and Legend of Mithradates, Rome's Deadliest Enemy,* which was a finalist for the National Book Award, *Gods and Robots: Myths, Machines, and Ancient Dreams of Technology,* and *The Amazons: Lives and Legends of Warrior Women across the Ancient World* (all Princeton). She is a research scholar in classics and the history of science at Stanford University.

FLYING SNAKES AND GRIFFIN CLAWS

FLYING SNAKES & GRIFFIN CLAWS

and Other Classical Myths, Historical Oddities, and Scientific Curiosities

ADRIENNE MAYOR

PRINCETON UNIVERSITY PRESS

PRINCETON AND OXFORD

Published by Princeton University Press
41 William Street, Princeton, New Jersey 08540
99 Banbury Road, Oxford OX2 6JX

press.princeton.edu

Library of Congress Cataloging-in-Publication Data

Names: Mayor, Adrienne, 1946– author.
Title: Flying snakes and griffin claws : and other classical myths, historical oddities, and scientific curiosities / Adrienne Mayor.
Description: First Edition. | Princeton, New Jersey ; Oxford : Princeton University Press, [2022] | Includes bibliographical references and index.
Identifiers: LCCN 2021042475 (print) | LCCN 2021042476 (ebook) | ISBN 9780691217826 (Hardback : acid-free paper) | ISBN 9780691211183 (Paperback : acid-free paper) | ISBN 9780691211190 (eBook)
Subjects: LCSH: Folklore. | Curiosities and wonders. | BISAC: HISTORY / Ancient / General | SOCIAL SCIENCE / Folklore & Mythology
Classification: LCC GR71 .M39 2022 (print) | LCC GR71 (ebook) | DDC 398.09—dc23/eng/20220124
LC record available at https://lccn.loc.gov/2021042475
LC ebook record available at https://lccn.loc.gov/2021042476

British Library Cataloging-in-Publication Data is available

Editorial: Rob Tempio and Chloe Coy
Production Editorial: Lauren Lepow
Text and Cover Design: Chris Ferrante
Production: Erin Suydam
Publicity: Alyssa Sanford and Carmen Jimenez

This book has been composed in Adobe Text Pro and Shackleton

Printed on acid-free paper. ∞

Printed in the United States of America

10 9 8 7 6 5 4 3 2 1

FOR SAMUEL MAYOR ANGEL

Astonish me!

CONTENTS

Acknowledgments   xiii

INTRODUCTION. The Borderlands of Myth,
History, and Science   1

ANIMALS: FABULOUS, REAL, AND EXTINCT

1 The Flying Snakes of Arabia   13

2 Sea Monsters and Mer-People of the Mediterranean   26

3 The Golden Fleece   37

4 Griffin Claws and a Unicorn Horn   41

5 Dolphin Tales   50

6 The Musical Racing Turtles of Greece   59

7 A Little Bird with Poison Poop   68

8 The Roman Army's Vulture Mascots:
The First Banded Birds   75

9 Pet Birds through the Ages   78

10 Your New Puppy in Ancient Times   88

11 Weasels in Classical Myth and History   92

12 Living the Modern Ferret Lifestyle   101

13 Colossal Fossils of Greece   112

14 Hunting Griffins: An Imaginary Letter
to a Paleontologist   117

15 Siegfried and the Dragon   140

16 Tracking the Lucky Rhino in China   143

17 Fake Fossils   147

18 Cuvier and the Mammoth Foot   154

19 Geronimo's Dragon   162

20 Enslaved Africans Were First to Identify
Mammoth Fossils in America   166

FORMIDABLE WOMEN

21 Beauty Secrets of the Ancient Amazons:
Cabbage, Cannabis, and Frankincense   173

22 Arab Warrior Queens   180

23 Chiomara, Courageous Celtic Woman   183

24 Camilla: Why Is There an Amazon in the *Aeneid*?   187

25 Plato and the Amazons   194

26 The Brave Women of Argos   198

27 Cleopatra and Antony Go Fishing   201

CONTENTS

28 The Poetess and the Queen of Amazons 204

29 Proving the Existence of Amazons in 1685 209

30 Wine Goblets and Women's Breasts 213

CURIOUS HISTORY AND SCIENCE

31 Ghost Ships 225

32 Mirages at Sea 236

33 Winds in Ancient Myth and History 250

34 Death by Bronze "Frisbee" 261

35 Could Aristotle Guess Your Personality
from Your Face? 264

36 The First Anti-Vaxxers 267

37 Poison Honey 272

38 Who Was the First Foot Fetishist? 282

39 "Giants" in Ancient Warfare 286

40 Sweating Truth in Ancient Carthage: A New
Appreciation of Flaubert's Punic Fever Dream 306

TRAVELERS, TATTOOS, AND TYRANTS

41 Tourists in Classical Antiquity 323

42 Grand Tourists in Greece, from Lord Byron to
Sigmund Freud 337

CONTENTS

43 Who Were the First Recreational
Mountain Climbers?   349

44 Ancient Tattoos   354

45 Tattoos in Ancient China   363

46 Caligula: Let Them Hate, So Long as They Fear   369

47 A Mountain of a Man: Maximinus Thrax   375

48 King Midas: Gold and Bull's Blood   378

49 Home in a Body Bag: Classical Parallels for a
Persian Gulf Urban Legend   382

50 Perfumes of Power: The Scent of Leaders   386

Notes   391
Credits   395
Index   397

ACKNOWLEDGMENTS

FOR THE DECADES OF CONVERSATIONS, correspondence, and research opportunities represented here, it is impossible to acknowledge all my debts. I'm grateful to the editors of *Sports Afield* for publishing my earliest writing ventures, short pieces on the first artificial fly-fishing lure in classical antiquity (red hackle for Macedonian trout), fireproof salamander wool, hypnotist predators, toads in stone, jewelry (Polycrates's ring) accidentally swallowed by fish and miraculously recovered, ancient puppy chow, and boars with burning tusks in Greek hunting myths. Before the Internet, free-range roaming in libraries was crucial, so I give thanks for access to the Rare Book Room of Princeton's Firestone Library, and to Henry Immerwahr, director of the American School of Classical Studies (ASCS) in Athens, and Zeph Stewart, director at the Center for Hellenic Studies in Washington, DC, for allowing a nonfellow to use their wonderful libraries in the 1980s. Thanks to Cathy Vanderpool, editor of *The Athenian*, who commissioned my first published long-form articles and illustrations, and to other editors who encouraged my work: Elizabeth Boleman-Herring, editor of *Southeast Review* and *Weekly Hubris*; Robert Crowley, editor of *MHQ: Military History Quarterly*; Richard Greenwell, editor of *Cryptozoology*; and Peter Young, editor of *Archaeology*. I was extremely fortunate to have a visionary editor at Princeton University Press, the late Jack Repcheck, who took a chance and published *The First Fossil Hunters* in 2000. Many thanks to Holly Tucker for inviting me to be a regular contributor, from 2011 to 2017, to the award-winning history of science website Wonders and Marvels, "A Community for Curious Minds Who Love History, Its Odd Stories, and Good Reads."

Over the years I have depended on the generosity and expertise of far too many specialists to name here, but I want to express profound gratitude to all the classicists, historians, linguists, curators, paleontologists, archaeologists, and scientists who have shared their knowledge. Heartfelt thanks to Michele Angel, Judith Binder, John Boardman, Taggert Butterfield, Simon Cotton, Lowell Edmunds, Kris Ellingsen, Debbie Felton, Deborah Gordon, William Hansen, Jack Horner, Pamela Johnson, Daniel Loxton, John Ma, Michelle Maskiell, Tom McIver, David Meadows, Marcia Mogelonsky, John Oakley, Josh Ober, Marcia Ober, Severo Perez, Barry Strauss, Philippe Taquet, Eugene Vanderpool, and Margaret Wheeler for encouragement and conversations about curiosities of history and nature. Bill Thayer's website LacusCurtius deserves thanks for making ancient texts and notes available online. Thanks also go to all the curious and helpful people I've interacted with on Facebook and Twitter on all manner of subjects. Over the years I've worn out recordings of Frédéric Chopin's piano nocturnes played by Daniel Barenboim, on endless loop for challenging writing days. Thanks to my excellent agents Sandy Dijkstra and Andrea Cavallaro and their team. Gratitude goes to my sister Michele Angel for superb drawings and the map. I appreciate the constructive comments of the two anonymous readers for Princeton University Press; the thoughtful copyediting by Lauren Lepow; Dimitri

ACKNOWLEDGMENTS

Karetnikov's illustration expertise, and the fabulous cover design by Chris Ferrante. And I simply cannot imagine a better editor for my work than Rob Tempio.

My heart belongs to Josiah Ober, who emboldened and enriched my fascination for enigmas of myth and history.

FLYING SNAKES AND GRIFFIN CLAWS

INTRODUCTION

The Borderlands of Myth, History, and Science

IN MY MEANDERING PATH toward becoming a classical folklorist and historian of ancient science, I've always been drawn to the nooks and crannies and dusty corners of literature, art, and history. Curiosities, mysteries, oddities, outlandish outtakes make my pulse race. When I read classical mythology, it is satyrs, giants, mermaids, witches, nymphs, sea monsters, Amazons, animals, mirages, diverting anecdotes, enigmas, and incongruous details that capture my fancy. I love sifting folklore, myths, legends, and old historical accounts for traces of genuine knowledge embellished with imagination, especially about natural history. Whenever my curiosity is piqued by something that seems out of the ordinary or unaccounted for in ancient writings, I immediately look for explanatory footnotes and commentaries. When they are missing or incomplete, I mark the spot and begin a file, like any other cold-case detective. My battered green and red Loeb volumes of Greek and Latin texts are much scribbled, bristling with Post-it Notes. And my files are unruly thickets of random information that might one day yield worthy patterns—or not.

This kind of work often seems like wandering solo in a landscape shrouded in mist or shadow, along trails rife with forks and false starts. Sometimes there are footprints of previous explorers, but other times there are no traces, no blazes, no way-markers. Sometimes the mosaic of burned-over patches is illuminated by sudden shafts of sunlight and understanding. The word that best describes this sort of marginal territory is the medieval *march*, derived from "edge, boundary, forest, impression, trace." *Marches* are the borderlands or crossroads between realms, deserted or sparsely populated liminal zones on the frontiers of formally recognized centers. In these in-between lands, far from officialdom, different rules apply—or maybe there are no rules at all. In the marcher zones of myth, science, and history, one is free to explore, establish footholds, devise one's own maps.

Each essay in this bundle of fifty has a unique time and place. Together they may serve as dots for tracing the trajectory of my thinking about the intersections of ancient and modern popular lore, nature, history, and science. Recurrent themes, people, and places are cross-referenced. Some essays are new, while some grew out of one-paragraph contributions to *Wonders and Marvels*, a splendid history of science website that flourished until 2017. Some chapters delve into topics that caught my interest in earlier books and are more deeply investigated here. There are also substantially revised, expanded, and updated versions of pieces that appeared in an array of journals and magazines, from *Military History Quarterly*, *Archaeology*, and *Sea Frontiers* to *London Review of Books* and *Sports Afield*. The time span, covering nearly three decades from my earliest publications to the present, and the variety of venues ensures an eclectic, even eccentric selection of topics. For example, I expect that chapter 30, on the age-old relationship between wine goblets and women's breasts in high and low culture, originally published as "Libation Titillation," might provoke justifiable outrage. But it is also evidence for how antiquated popular attitudes persisted into the late twentieth century, and how far things have progressed since 1994.

In that same year, I learned from my tattoo artist friend Phoenix & Arabeth that copies of my Griffin article in *Archaeology* magazine were in tattoo parlors from Vancouver to San Diego, as Scythian-style animal designs were becoming a thing among tattooed folk. Tattoos were just becoming hip but not yet ubiquitous; I had to work hard to convince Peter Young, conservative editor in chief of *Archaeology*, that tattooing in antiquity would be a valid topic for the magazine. We had become friends after he had accepted my 1994 Griffin piece and several other articles. Peter finally published my tattoos article, "People Illustrated," in 1999 (chapter 44). But instead of illustrating it with the beautiful barbarian tattoos lovingly detailed in ancient Greek vase paintings that I had gathered, the editors commissioned insipid, inexpert sketches. I rarely hold a grudge, but I never forgave *Archaeology*'s inexplicable refusal to accompany the piece with real tattoo images from antiquity. I never submitted another article to the magazine. Peter retired in 2011. Jarrett Lobell, at *Archaeology* magazine since 1999, became editor in chief. In 2013, *Archaeology* finally saw the light. "Ancient Tattoos," written by Jarrett Lobell and deputy editor Eric Powell, was lavishly illustrated with color photos of ancient ink on Greek vases and other artifacts.

Other essays are personally more revealing, such as my now rather mortifying imaginary letter to a prominent paleontologist (chapter 14). Mixed emotions also arise from the memoir of our ferret years, chapter 12: What in the world were we thinking when we inflicted the presence of polecats on the good folk of Princeton? "Sweating Truth in Ancient Carthage," chapter 40, is a nostalgic return to Gustave Flaubert's controversial novel of 1862, *Salammbô*. Revisiting that novel now, it was a jolt to realize that, when I first read it at age fourteen, Flaubert's sensational vision was my first introduction to ancient history. Perhaps this explains a lot.

Some essays call up wonderful memories. While researching and writing about the Grand Tours of eighteenth-century travelers to Greece for *The Athenian*, I felt an affinity with some of the early tourists' experiences. Throughout the 1980s, my companion Josh (historian and political theorist Josiah Ober, now my husband) and I hiked over traces of ancient roads to massive stone fortresses built after the Peloponnesian War, the subject of Josh's dissertation. We slept under the stars on the decks of ferryboats and in roofless ruined towers all around the timeless Greek countryside and islands. One summer, after many hot, dry miles on a winding mountain road, we finally reached the isolated, formidable ruins of the fortress of Panakton at dusk, thanks to a lift from a family of *Tsigani* (Romani). We rode in the back of their truck with their dogs, whose collars were heavily encrusted with gold and silver. The family dropped us off at the foot of a rugged peak in the middle of nowhere as night fell, shaking their heads at the crazy foreigners.

We scrambled up the stony slope and marveled at the looming walls of huge limestone blocks that we would measure and draw in the morning. Supper was spartan: one tomato, an onion that had rolled off a passing farm truck, and a pocketful of almonds gathered along the road, cracked with rocks. Brushing aside dry goat droppings, we slept on a flat slab of bedrock—until we were awakened just before dawn by a symphony of tinkling bells and robust farts: a herd of goats had arrived. I'll never forget opening my eyes to the dark silhouettes of curious goats and their mystified guardian standing over us. Josh and the shepherd shared a pipe while we watched a glorious sunrise over the Saronic Gulf far below.

Another time we spent the night in one of the towers of the ancient fort at Messene, in southern Greece. The moon was full, and Athena's owl perched above us in one of the catapult windows. The next morning the air was filled with the sound of buzzing bees tumbling in a field of wind flowers and cyclamen. As we arose, a passing goatherd offered us fresh milk from his pail. It is amazing to realize that any of these vignettes could have taken place when the early travelers ventured on Grand Tours to Greece during the Ottoman Empire.

Living in Athens in 1979–80 and summers for the next decade helping Josh with topographical surveys of ancient roads and towers, I spent many happy hours reading and sketching in the Library of the American School of Classical Studies. I became fascinated with ancient descriptions of bones of enormous size and strange shapes identified as "giants" and "monsters." It occurred to me that the accounts might record discoveries of large vertebrate fossils, if there were any in Greece. I learned about nineteenth-century paleontological excavations not far from Athens at Pikermi from the venerable and kind archaeologist Eugene Vanderpool, who suggested that my intuition was worth pursuing. So I began researching the idea that observations of remarkable remains of extinct species might have played a role in ancient Greek and Roman ideas about some fabulous creatures. What I uncovered led me to pester numerous classicists and archaeologists, trying to convince them that the idea had merit, and that someone should investigate. Eventually, I realized that it would be up to me to gather the scattered evidence from ancient literature and art, history, archaeology, and paleontology and make the case for a link between ancient accounts and fossils. Research into this subject proceeded slowly in library stacks and via stamped, typewritten letters, long before email and the Internet.

Meanwhile, I continued to earn a living as a freelance copyeditor. At first, I worked on medical textbooks, but turned to editing literary, scientific, and historical manuscripts for a dozen trade and university presses. Until the publication of my first book in 2000, I thought of myself as a printmaker rather than a writer. My etchings of mythic subjects were sold in galleries in Washington, DC, Ithaca, New York, and Bozeman, Montana. Some of my original illustrations for articles in *The Athenian*, Greece's English-language magazine, appear in this anthology.

"Colossal Fossils," chapter 13, was my first publication in *The Athenian* (October 1983). After typing it on the old manual Corona at the American School, I drew the illustrations with my precision Rotring rapidograph pen, which I used for cartography and archaeological drawings of fortresses, pottery, and coins. Part 2 of "Colossal Fossils," for the February 1984 *Athenian*, recounted ancient Greek reports of finding giant bones around the Aegean. These illustrated articles represent my plunge into the complicated evidence for what I initially thought of as "paleo-cryptozoology," trying to identify unknown creatures in ancient Greek literature and art. My research into ancient Greek and Roman discoveries and interpretations of fossils continued, with preliminary publications in, for example, *Cryptozoology* (1989, 1991), *Folklore* (1993), *Ar-*

chaeology (1994), and the *Oxford Journal of Archaeology* (2000), culminating in chapter 1 of *The First Fossil Hunters* (2000).

I had become fixated on the Griffin as an ancient cryptid, an unknown creature with four legs and a beak. Each summer in the American School Library I studied thousands of ancient images of bird-headed quadrupeds from Egypt, Crete, Mesopotamia, Greece, and Scythia. The only writings about Griffins were in Greek and Latin literature, however, beginning with fragments of the lost epic by Aristeas in the seventh century BC and culminating with the Roman natural historian Aelian in the third century AD. The texts coincided with an outpouring of artworks depicting Griffins just as they were described by ancient authors. Griffins did not figure in any known Greek myth—instead they were said to be real animals of eastern lands. What might have accounted for a millennium of consistent descriptions and related art? I could come up with only one living four-legged animal with a beak—the turtle. But it occurred to me that some extinct dinosaurs were quadrupeds with beaks.

My obsessive speculation that beaked dinosaur fossils played a role in how Griffins were visualized in classical Greece and Rome began to bug those close to me. Finally, Josh forcefully suggested that I cease talking and write it all down, as a long letter to a paleontologist. Recently settled in Montana, I chose Jack Horner, curator of the new Museum of the Rockies in Bozeman, famous for his discovery of dinosaur eggs and the model for the paleontologist in the 1993 movie *Jurassic Park*.

I never sent Jack Horner my feverish, scattershot letter penned in 1989, "Hunting Griffins," presented here as chapter 14. But a few years later we did meet, thanks to Horner's scientific illustrator, my friend Kris Ellingsen. I showed him ancient Greek vase paintings of Griffins and compared them to the most famous beaked dinosaur in Montana, Mort the Triceratops, mascot of the Museum of the Rockies. Horner nodded, then pointed out my mistaken belief that Triceratops dinosaurs had ever lived in in the Old World. But he encouraged me to forge on with my hypothesis that dinosaurs might be involved. As I left his office, Horner remarked to Kris, "She doesn't know jackshit about paleontology. But she might be onto something." That spurred me to do more homework before trying to explain my ideas to scientists.

Not all the mysteries embedded in myth and folklore and other products of imaginative and collective storytelling over the ages are amenable to scientific explanation or historical solution, of course. Keeping in mind how much information has been garbled or lost over millennia, stumbling into culs-de-sac in the marches of history is inevitable, especially at a far remove in time and space. Franz Kafka's paradox is never far from my mind: "A legend is an attempt to explain the inexplicable. Emerging, as it does, from a basis of truth, it is bound to end in the inexplicable" ("The Rescue Will Begin in Its Own Time," 1917–24). Several essays—I'm thinking of "The Flying Snakes of Arabia" (chapter 1), "Griffin Claws and a Unicorn Horn" (chapter 4), "The Little Bird with Poison Poop" (chapter 7), and "Cuvier and the Mammoth Foot" (chapter 18)—exemplify the impossibility of reaching certainty.

These articles distill a goodly amount of research. Many of the pieces, written for general audiences, do not include references, although some notes at the back of the book indicate ancient sources and further readings. As a footnote and citation devotee myself, I keenly sympathize with readers who feel their absence. For the aficionado of footnotes, I recommend my books and scholarly publications, which are jam-packed with documentation and extensive bibliographies. Meanwhile, I hope you find pleasure in browsing this compilation of my souvenirs from the marches, wondrous hunting grounds for the study of human curiosity.

ANIMALS

FABULOUS, REAL, AND EXTINCT

CHAPTER 1

The Flying Snakes
of Arabia

MY FAVORITE ANCIENT WRITER is Herodotus, the insatiably curious Greek historian from Persian-ruled Halicarnassus (Bodrum, Turkey). Journeying to exotic lands to see the sights, he interviewed non-Greek-speaking peoples about their history and customs, and captivated the Greeks with his *Histories*, written about 460 BC. Herodotus reported what he observed and what locals told him, including contradictory information, and often reserved judgment about veracity, leaving it up to his readers to ponder.

As he traveled around Egypt visiting the famous attractions and marvels, talking with priests and guides at each locale, rumors of "snakes with wings" piqued his curiosity. "I went to try to get more information about the flying snakes," wrote Herodotus.

He learned that the winged serpents lived under fragrant frankincense (*Boswellia*) trees in Arabia. In antiquity, "Arabia" extended from northeastern Egypt across the Sinai Peninsula and Arabia to the Negev Desert. The aromatic trees and shrubs grow in harsh, arid gullies with chalky soil. To gather this valuable resin for incense and perfumes, the Arabians, so Herodotus was told, would burn *styrax* to drive the serpents away. *Styrax* was probably a sweetgum resin gathered from *Liquidambar orientalis* or *L. officinalis* trees, used for incense and insecticide in antiquity.

According to Herodotus's guides, the flying snakes associated with frankincense trees were small with variegated markings. The body resembled a water snake but appeared to have batwing-like membranes.

Later in his discussion of the difficulties of gathering precious spices in Arabia, Herodotus describes the Arabian method of obtaining cassia, another fragrant substance used for incense. Cassia's exact identity is unknown, but it was apparently derived from flag iris roots, related to aromatic orrisroot powder (*rhizoma iridis*). Cassia, noted Herodotus, grows around a shallow lake and was difficult to obtain owing to another sort of fierce winged creature. To gather cassia, the collectors wore thick ox-hide armor to deflect the attack of the aggressive creatures. These creatures resembled small bats, squeaked like bats, and attacked the eyes. I bring this up because, as we saw, Herodotus also likened the flying creatures that dwell around the frankincense trees to bats.

Herodotus's guides told him that the flying snakes would be a plague upon earth but for two reasons. In the first place, the violence of their reproductive life ensures that their population remains small. Not only does the female kill the male after mating by biting through his neck, but the females give birth to live young instead of laying eggs like other snakes. And these young are so vicious that they are born by eating their way out of the womb, thus killing their mother. Some modern commentators speculate that this peculiar detail arose from observations of the empty shed skins of snakes and husks of large insects such as locusts. But it is interesting that scorpions are viviparous, giving birth to live young, and there are anecdotal reports of sexual cannibalism and matriphagy, in which baby scorpions eat and kill the mother. Moreover, at least three types of snakes in Egypt and Arabia give birth to live young instead of laying eggs: rinkhals or "spitting cobras," *Nerodia* water snakes, and sand boas. The scorpion and snake embryos develop in eggs but hatch inside the mother's body and emerge alive. This unusual fact could be the origin of the folk notion that the young "ate" their way out.

The other curb on the numbers of flying serpents depended on a special predator. In the early spring when the winged snakes migrate from Arabia to Egypt, they must travel through a mountain pass to reach a wide valley. As the winged snakes emerge from the narrow pass, "ibis birds" gobble them up. "Entirely jet black with legs like a crane and a very hooked beak," says Herodotus, "these birds are about the size of a Greek *krex.*" If only we knew the identity of the *krex* bird! Zoologists have suggested that the *krex* was a wading bird such as the Black-winged Stilt, *Himantopus himantopus* or *rufipes*; the Corncrake *Rallus crex*; or the Avocet, *Recurvirostra avosetta*.

Happily, we can make good guesses about the identity of the snake-eating bird. Both Herodotus and the natural historian Aelian (third century AD) specified that black ibises devour the "flying snakes." Solinus (also third century) remarked that black ibises dwelled around Pelusium. In antiquity, the black Glossy Ibis (*Plegadis falcinellus*) frequented the brackish region of salt valleys and shallow lakes and marshes between Egypt and the Sinai Peninsula. This region no longer exists as it did in antiquity, now bisected by the Suez Canal and the adjacent Great Bitter Lake. Flocks of Glossy Ibises were migratory, and they fed on dragonflies and other flying insects and small snakes. Another likely candidate would be the now nearly extinct Waldrapp (*Geronticus eremita*), the Northern Bald Ibis. These migratory, black desert ibises were once widespread across North Africa and the Middle East, making their nests and breeding in arid, rocky cliff ledges in deserts, rather than in salty wetlands like their cousins. The black ibises also eat insects and reptiles, including snakes. The black ibises in Herodotus and Aelian appear to be a genuine and consistent detail of local natural history, which suggests that the winged serpents might be some sort of real creatures, mistaken for or described as flying snakes.

In his investigation of the flying snakes, Herodotus traveled to the vicinity of Buto, in northeast Egypt. Somewhere in this vicinity he was taken to a narrow mountain pass that led to a broad plain contiguous with the plain of Egypt. Here his guides showed him skeletons and vertebrae heaped up in incalculable numbers. Without giving any dimensions, Herodotus observed that the skeletons ranged from large and medium to small. Although Herodotus does not clearly state it, the guides' implication was that these were the remains of the "flying snakes" killed by flocks of ibises as the flying snakes migrated in hordes from Arabia to Egypt.

These passages are among the most cryptic in Herodotus. Classicists, natural historians, and zoologists have long puzzled over what Herodotus observed. Where exactly was the narrow valley with the heaps of bones? And what kind of creatures' bones were heaped in the pass?

At least we can identify his setting-off point, Buto (modern Tell el-Farein, "Hill of the Pharaohs"). Buto was an important ancient city on the southern shore of the shallow, brackish Butic Lake about sixty miles east of Alexandria near the edge of the Arabian Desert (Sinai Peninsula). Today, Burullus Lagoon is a vestige of Butic Lake. In antiquity "Buto" also referred to the larger region around the city of that name. The city of Buto was occupied through the Roman era. The ruins of the city, royal palace, pottery, statues, and other artifacts now lie by the shores of the dry lake bed.

East or southeast of the area of Buto, Herodotus was shown piles of bones in a pass. Some modern commentators believe that the narrow pass into the plain was on the El-Kantareh (El Qantara) road between Manzala Lake and the Abbasiyah Canal (of 1863), south of Tell el-Defennah. This makes sense—the ancient Egyptian road, the *via maris* (coastal road) also known as the Way of Horus, went from Tanis to El Qantara to Gaza. The route crossed sand ridges threading coastal lagoons and salt marshes and desert. It was the main route for armies and travelers between Egypt and the Near East in antiquity.

Remarkably, we have two accounts of flying snakes in Arabia that predate Herodotus's description, biblical and Assyrian. In the Old Testament, a passage by the eighth-century BC prophet Isaiah says that the desert is a dangerous place of lions, adders, and flying vipers. The Assyrian king Esarhaddon's military expedition to conquer Egypt in 671 BC is recorded on fragments of clay tablets found in Nineveh. As his army traversed the Negev and Arabian deserts, Esarhaddon identified landmarks by their natural features on the arduous overland route. Instead of taking the coastal Way of Horus, Esarhaddon followed the ancient Spice and Frankincense Route from Rafah, near Gaza, south to Mehktesh Ramon in the Negev Desert and then west across Arabia. One of the places was described by Esarhaddon as "yellow snakes spreading wings."

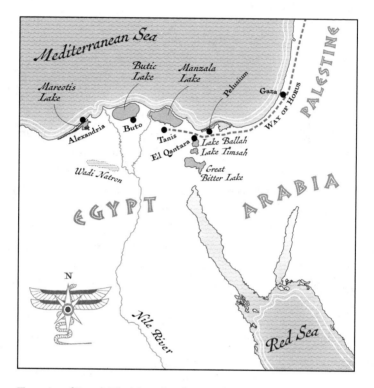

The region of Egypt's Nile delta and Arabia. Map by Michele Angel.

What might account for the flying snakes?

Some commentators have wondered whether there might have been a now-extinct population of "parachuting" lizards or "gliding" snakes in the Sinai. This is the most common "solution" proposed for this zoological mystery, but it is the least plausible. The gliding snake of Southeast Asia, *Chrysopelea*, flares its ribs to glide through the air. But this "flying" snake's habitat only extends to western India. The parachuting lizard *Draco volans* has elongated ribs with bat-like membranes, allowing it to glide through the air. But this lizard's habitat is also Southeast Asia. These were likely the "reptiles with membranous wings like bats" mentioned by Strabo in his list of creatures of India in the first century BC. The parachuting lizards and gliding snakes glide from tree to tree in tropical rainforests and do not form swarms; they can be eliminated as candidates for the winged snakes of Arabia.

A more viable clue might lie in the comparison to bats. Herodotus likened the flying creatures in the region of frankincense and cassia to bats. A species of small vesper bat, the desert long-eared bat, inhabits extremely arid, hot, barren, deserts and shrublands of Arabia and the Negev Desert (now southern Israel). About two to three inches in size, the gray-and-white microbats (*Otonycteris hemprichii*) feed on poisonous scorpions and spiders on the ground. The tiny bats roost in rocky crevices. Their flight is described as awkward, slow, and "floppy." Ibises eat insects and small mammals, and so might attack microbats hunting on the ground. There are also reports that birds and bats compete for similar prey in some locales. Could misunderstood descriptions of swarms of desert microbats help explain tales of small bat-winged snakes with variegated markings?

The locale, Buto, provides an important clue. Herodotus tells us that Buto was famous for its temple and the oracle of the winged cobra goddess Wadjet. Wadjet was known to the Greeks as "Buto," and in Herodotus's day the region was called the "land of Wadjet or Buto." The temple of Buto was known to the Egyptians as Per-Wadjet, "House of Wadjet." Notably, Wadjet's symbol was a cobra, typically pictured with wings. The winged cobra symbol can be seen on the Uraeus crown worn by Egyptian gods and rulers. Many fabulous golden

Top left, winged serpent symbol of goddess Wadjet, golden collar, Tutankhamun's tomb, New Kingdom Eighteenth Dynasty, Egypt 1332–1323 BC; top right, four-winged snake, sarcophagus of Seti I, Nineteenth Dynasty, 1370 BC, Soane's Museum, London; bottom, typical Uraeus winged cobra, symbol of Wadjet. Drawings by Michele Angel.

neckpieces and other artifacts depicting winged cobras have been found in Egyptian tombs, and the image appears widely in paintings, reliefs, amulets, and ornaments. The ubiquitous iconography of snakes with wings would be quite striking to visitors in ancient Egypt. It seems safe to assume that Herodotus decided to travel to Buto to ask about flying snakes because the region was the sacred abode of the winged cobra goddess.

The winged Uraeus, an image of a rearing cobra with two, sometimes four, wings, was a popular motif in Egypt, but it also appeared in the Near East in the Bronze Age. The four-winged version is featured on numerous seals in eighth-century BC Judah. Notably, cobras spread their neck ribs as a defensive posture, perhaps giving rise to an idea of "wings." Herpetologists note that the horned viper (*Cerastes cerastes*) of Egypt and Arabia sometimes flings itself into the air to attack. Strabo mentioned that in southern Arabia where frankincense is gathered, dark-red venomous snakes (identified as the saw-scale or painted carpet viper) can spring up a few feet in the air to strike. These activities could also fuel the notion of "airborne" snakes. It is easy to see how Egyptian and Near Eastern iconography of cobras with wings may have combined with the very real threat of deadly snakes in ancient allusions to "flying serpents."

As noted, snakes and scorpions in the Arabian Desert give birth to live young, which matches some details that were related to Herodotus. Could scorpions have influenced the tales of small flying snakes? Scorpions do not fly, but many ancient authors consistently referred to winged varieties of scorpions, and winged scorpions are also depicted in ancient artifacts. The natural historian Pliny explained the error. Scorpions are given the power of flight by very strong desert winds, he said, and when they are airborne, the arthropods extend their legs, which makes them appear to have wings. A swarm of wind-blown scorpions in a dust storm might give an impression of flying snakes. Some ibises prey on scorpions.

Another appealing explanation is that the creatures referred to as small "flying serpents" in Herodotus's account were really some sort of large-winged insect, such as dragonflies or locusts, which have long bodies and four membranous wings (as depicted on some Uraeus serpents and Hebrew seals). This explanation could also account for the behavior of and sounds made by the flying creatures that frequented the lake where cassia grew. Herodotus's "flying snakes" story might well have originated as garbled or exaggerated lore based on hearsay or observations of large swarms of flying insects. In fact, periodically, millions of desert locusts (*Schistocerca gregaria* or *Gryllus gregarius*) migrate across the Sinai, and the hordes of locusts would be prey for birds, especially flocks of ibises. The flying locusts are just over two inches long, but they migrate in massive clouds covering hundreds of miles.

Several other ancient authors writing in the centuries after Herodotus also described "flying snakes" devoured by ibises in the region, and their accounts strongly evoke invasions of clouds of locusts. For example, Cicero (in the first century BC) mentioned that ibises kill and eat snakes (*anguis*) with wings that arrive in clouds carried by Libyan wind from the African desert toward Egypt. The Jewish historian Josephus (first century AD) related an apocryphal account of Moses using ibises to repel snakes, and Josephus further commented, like Herodotus, that some Egyptian snakes could fly. Another author, Pomponius Mela (first century AD), reported that venomous snakes with wings from the Arabian marshes are eaten by ibises. In the third century AD, Aelian wrote that black ibises prevent snakes (*opheis*) with wings from entering Egypt. Around the same time, Solinus (third century AD) stated that black and white ibises devour the swarms of venomous, winged snakes (*anguium*) from the marshes of Arabia. Finally, Ammianus Marcellinus (fourth century AD) stated that when flocks of venomous, winged snakes (*anguium*) migrate from the marshes of Arabia, ibises overcome them in the air and eat them. All these reports confirm that ibises preyed on periodic swarms of small, flying creatures that behaved like migrating insects.

What can we say about the piles of bones and vertebrae viewed by Herodotus? No other author mentions unusual bones in northern Egypt or Arabia in relation to flying snakes. Egypt does have conspicuous and rich deposits of fossilized bones of dinosaurs and prehistoric mammals. Phlegon of Tralles, writing in the second century AD, was the first to describe some of these remarkable fossil remains at Wadi Natron, dry soda lake beds about sixty miles south of Alexandria. This is far from Herodotus's location east of Buto, but the Nile delta's silt overlies a Pleistocene foundation, so erosion might expose fossils in certain areas.

In 2007, the Assyrian scholar Karen Radner took up my brief suggestion (in *The First Fossil Hunters*, 2000) that fossils might account for what Herodotus observed. She proposed that both Esarhaddon and Herodotus got the impression of winged snakes at a rich fossil deposit of elongated vertebrae of prehistoric reptiles and amphibians at Makhtesh Ramon, in the Negev Desert between Beersheba and Eilat. Abundant fossils are conspicuous in the cliffs of the eroded crater at Makhtesh Ramon, the world's largest erosion cirque. The *wadi* was a station on the Spice and Frankincense route between southern Arabia and Gaza. Radner's proposal is worth considering. The location matches the itinerary of Esarhaddon as he set out across the Negev for Egypt, and it may be the place of "yellow snakes spreading wings." But the unique landform in the center of Palestine lies about four hundred miles east of Buto, where Herodotus sought information about flying snakes. Herodotus clearly states that he personally observed heaps of vertebrae. As enticing as Radner's proposal is, unfortunately the geography makes it implausible that Herodotus trekked across the daunting Arabian and Negev deserts and back.

Note that in his investigation of the tale of flying snakes, Herodotus was never shown live specimens, only heaps of jumbled skeletons and spines of different sizes. One might suggest the following scenario. Egyptian and Arabic tales of "flying serpents" may have been a popular way of alluding to swarms of microbats, windborne scorpions, or periodic locust hordes. The allusion might have been taken literally when it was retold and translated in antiquity. When Herodotus asked his Egyptian guides about these creatures, the guides took him to view some mysterious deposits of bones, implying a link to the "winged snakes." The jumbled bones may have been a fossil bed of unknown extinct creatures, like the sites at Wadi Natron and Makhtesh Ramon. Another possibility is that Herodotus saw a large deposit of skeletal remains of present-day birds and other creatures, perhaps preserved over the years by desert minerals, such as natron, weathering out of the edges of the salt marshes, which are now obliterated by the Suez Canal.

Without further information, the true identity of the winged snakes of ancient Arabia remains a tantalizing enigma. But it seems likely that the idea of flying snakes arose from folk descriptions of microbats, scorpions, and/or migrating locusts as "flying serpents," elaborated with natural oddities of desert creatures. These details may have been elaborated in tall tales told by Arabian spice traders to discourage others from trying to gather costly perfumes. (For more on ancient perfumes, see chapters 21 and 50.) Exaggerated or garbled stories about little-known desert denizens, plus traders' stories, merged with the very real prevalence of dangerous snakes in Egypt and Arabia and conflated with the widespread images of winged cobras sacred to the goddess Wadjet in jewelry and art and pictured on pharaohs' Uraeus crowns. Heaps of extraordinary vertebrae, displayed to visitors like Herodotus, would serve to confirm a story of bizarre fauna in the region. Herodotus was persuaded that the rumor of flying snakes was worth investigating. But he kept his own counsel about whether he believed that the evidence he was shown confirmed the tale.

Sea Monsters and Mer-People of the Mediterranean

TRITONS AND MER-PEOPLE

"TRITONS ARE ALWAYS QUITE A SIGHT," wrote Pausanias, "but this one would really make you gasp!" An enthusiastic travel writer of the second century AD who recorded legends about famous places all around the ancient world, Pausanias had once viewed a merman, or Triton, preserved in Rome. But he found the Greek specimen displayed in Tanagra, Boeotia, much larger and more impressive. The creature's sleek hair was the color of "frogs in a stagnant pond," and its body was covered with fine scales. Gills were visible behind the ears, and the wide mouth was studded with large, sharp teeth. Pausanias also described the merman's greenish-gray eyes, shell-encrusted fingernails, almost-human nose, and scaly dolphin's tail.

According to the ancient Boeotians, this particular Triton had menaced women bathing in the sea and even attacked boats along the coast. The merman was finally lured into a trap baited with a bucket of wine set out on the beach. While it was in a drunken stupor, the villagers killed it and then pickled for posterity. About a century after Pausanias wrote his account, a Greek expert on marine monsters named Damostratos also investigated the Tanagra Triton.

Mediterranean mer-people were still a spectacle in Europe more than a thousand years later. I found an advertising flyer for a cabinet of curiosities in London in 1774 that promoted a "merman from Greece." About fifty years later, in 1822, the American sea captain Samuel Barrett Edes purchased a "ningyo"—a "mermaid"—from Japanese fishermen. This mermaid was displayed in London and acquired by the Boston Museum in 1842. The museum later leased it to the showman P. T. Barnum, who publicized it as the "Fiji Mermaid." Many other Fiji mermaids and mermen have fascinated audiences ever since. What were these creatures?

Examination of "mermaids" and "mermen," like Barnum's specimen preserved in Harvard's Peabody Museum, reveals that sailors stitched monkey's heads and torsos to fishtails to fool landlubbers. From Pausanias's description, it appears that the Triton of Tanagra may have been one of the earliest fabricated curiosities of this type. (See chapter 17 for other faked composites.)

In classical antiquity, Tritons, who were believed to speak in human voices, were not invariably malevolent beings. A helpful merman guided Jason and the Argonauts through the lagoon at Lake Tritonis in North Africa during their epic quest for the Golden Fleece (see chapter 3). On the other hand, Tritons jealously guarded the superiority of their conch-blowing abilities. One ancient legend told of a Triton who drowned a mortal man who dared challenge him to a conch-trumpeting contest.

SEA MONSTERS

Tritons were just one of the many types of extraordinary marine creatures described in the lost treatise by the sea-monster expert Damostratos. Luckily, however, there are enough artistic depictions and literary descriptions to satisfy the most demanding sea-monster fan. The first eyewitness account of a sea serpent in the Mediterranean was recorded in the eighth century BC by the Assyrian king Sargon, who observed an unidentifiable marine creature near Cyprus. In the fifth century BC, when the Persians invaded Greece, their fleet met with a violent storm between the Aegean island of Thasos and Athos on the northern Greek mainland. Those who were not drowned, according to the historian Herodotus, were devoured by the "sea monsters" that infested the sea around Athos. These monsters were probably sharks.

A century later, Aristotle noted that experienced Greek fishermen and sailors occasionally encountered unknown sea

Sea monster, after vase painting on Caeretan black-figure hydria, 530 BC. Drawing by Daniel Loxton.

animals that pursued and capsized their boats. Aristotle had interviewed seamen and learned that some monsters resembled massive beams of black wood, while others were round like giant red shields, with many fins. A few centuries later, the Roman naturalist Pliny the Elder mentioned thirty-foot "dragons" that swam with their heads raised like periscopes, in the classic Loch Ness sea-serpent pose. Another ancient text referred to "crested sea monsters" in the Mediterranean.

For sheer drama, it is hard to match the Roman poet Virgil's vivid description of the pair of monsters that swam across the Aegean near Lesbos to strangle Laocoön and his sons. "I shudder to think of it," Virgil wrote in the *Aeneid*. "The two giant snakes swim over the peaceful sea unwinding their huge coils. . . . Their necks rise above the billows, their blood-red crests tower over the waves . . . vast tails curve in sinuous coils . . . burning eyes shine red . . . tongues dart and flicker."

It is interesting that red crests on long sinuous bodies appear in ancient Greek vase paintings of sea monsters. They look suspiciously like oarfish, real but mysterious denizens of the deep. Oarfish can grow twenty feet long, and they sport distinctive red crests along their backs. Because they dwell in the deepest parts of the Mediterranean, oarfish are rarely viewed except when they wash up on beaches. The strange carcasses could have inspired sea-monster stories.

The presence of aquatic monsters was a trial for the ancient inhabitants of Aegean shores. Travelers between Athens and Corinth had to worry about a serial killer named Sciron, who used to throw his victims over the cliffs near Megara, into the jaws of a gigantic, savage sea turtle lurking below. The largest of the three marine turtle species in the Mediterranean, the leatherback, can grow ten feet long, weigh as much as a thousand pounds, and live up to one hundred years (see chapter 6 for more turtles). Leatherbacks eat jellyfish, crustaceans, and fish. They are now rare in the Aegean, but one venerable leatherback may have inspired the stories recounted around Megara in antiquity.

Pausanias also mentioned that swimming in the sea off Troezen was dangerous because of the "large numbers of marine monsters there, including sharks." He also claimed that so many sea monsters inhabited the Adriatic that "their smell hung thick in the air." The nineteeenth-century folklorist J. G. Frazer, intrigued by Pausanias's comment, sailed those waters three times but never caught a whiff of anything untoward.

Since Phoenician times Rhodes had been known as "the isle of serpents." During the Punic Wars, a Roman soldier named Attilius Regulus killed one of the Rhodian monsters—and its skin was said to be over a hundred feet long. In the Middle Ages, it was said that ferocious crocodile-dragons harassed Rhodians living around the marshes below Mount Saint Etienne. In 1329 the grand master of the Knights of Rhodes forbade any of his men to attempt to destroy the current marauder. Already several had lost their lives trying to kill the legendary dragon, whose scales seemed totally impervious to their weapons. However, a young knight named Gozon de Dieu-Donné secretly vowed to exterminate the marsh beast. For some weeks he observed the monster from a safe distance, then returned to his château to meditate upon his strategy. Gozon constructed a wooden model of the dragon, covering the belly with leather. He spent months training a team of large and fearless dogs to dash under the life-size model and attack the leather underbelly.

At last, Gozon and his dogs were ready. The knight donned his armor and rode his charger to the marshes. The Rhodian chronicle relates that his lance "shivered on the hide of the serpent as though it had struck a stone wall." Gozon's horse was so unnerved by the "wide-open slavering jaws, terrible burning eyes, and foul odor" of the monster that it threw Gozon to the ground. The knight gave the signal, and his hounds rushed in and fastened their teeth in the dragon's belly. Instantly Gozon was on his feet, plunging his sword into the monster's exposed vitals.

The heroic knight was given a triumphal parade, after a mild scolding by the grand master for disobedience. The hideous head of the last dragon of Rhodes was displayed for many years on one of the city gates. What was that head? Could it have been the fossil skull of some unfamiliar prehistoric creature? I also note that Rhodes has two dozen types of lizard, some rather large. But my guess is that the dragon of Rhodes was a Nile crocodile, either living or skeletal, that had been transported to the island from Egypt, as an exotic gift.

Sightings of monsters in the Mediterranean were not confined to antiquity and the Middle Ages. In 1742, tuna fishermen in the Ionian Sea reported that prodigious eels were wrecking their nets. Giant eels were seen in those waters again in 1907, 1924, and 1958. In 1877 officers of the royal British yacht *Osbourne* sighted a multifinned monster; some twenty years later another British crew described a 150-foot "giant centipede" propelled by "an immense number of fins." That same year a pair of sea serpents whose heads resembled those of "greyhounds without ears" kept pace with a ship sailing at eight knots. A ship's log of 1924 noted the appearance of a 100-foot "serpentine animal with raised head" rolling in the waves in "vertical undulations."

On a spring day in 1916, Lieutenant Edouard Plessis and a party of sailors set out from Thessaloniki in a Greek fishing boat, headed for Thasos. Just west of the island, the crew was startled to see what looked like a periscope traveling in the opposite direction. The object projected about six feet out of the water and moved quite swiftly—at about fifteen knots, they estimated. At a loss to identify the thing, Plessis sounded the "submarine warning," even though he knew no submarine could go that fast submerged. Upon his return to Thessaloniki, he was reprimanded by his superior for giving such an absurd warning. Years later Edouard Plessis was still wondering what manner of beast he had seen.

Plessis would have been interested to know that in 1912, off Cape Matapan at the tip of the Mani, the crew of the steamer *Queen Eleanor* had observed a twenty-five-foot mottled sea serpent swimming alongside at the same speed as their ship. Captain A. F. Rodger described the incident for a 1961 BBC program on sea monsters. He noted that the eel-like creature "had two coils or humps behind the neck," and explained the coloring as "camouflage." The creature disappeared after the chief engineer took a shot at it with his rifle.

Sir Arthur Conan Doyle, who maintained a keen interest in prehistoric animals, found his experience with mysterious Greek marine life more fascinating than threatening. The creator of the unflappable fictional detective Sherlock Homes was on a voyage to the island of Aegina with his wife and children in 1928. Standing on the deck of the steamer, gazing at the Temple of Poseidon on Cape Sounion, the family was suddenly distracted by something swimming parallel to the ship. Conan Doyle recalled that "the curious creature had a long neck and large flippers. I believe, as did my wife, that it was a young Plesiosaurus." Large marine reptiles of the Jurassic period, 150 million years ago, plesiosaurs went extinct about 65 million years ago and are known only from fossil remains. Their shape strongly resembles the reported forms of typical sea monsters in the popular imagination. Perhaps it was this incident that inspired Conan Doyle to write the novel *The Lost World*, in which extinct animals are brought back alive to London.

MERMAIDS

In ancient times, the Old Man of the Sea, Nereus, lived in the ocean with his daughters, the Nereids. The eldest of Nereus's daughters, Thetis, used her inherited ability to change shape to elude the embrace of the mortal man Peleus. Thetis transformed herself into fire, water, wind, a tree, a bird, a tiger, a lion, a serpent, and finally a cuttlefish, in which form she was finally seized by the determined Peleus. Thetis then assumed human form and became the young man's bride. Their son was Achilles, the great warrior of Homer's *Iliad*. In antiquity, the people of Phocis, near Delphi, believed that they had originated from a similar courtship between the mortal man Aeacus and a Nereid (water nymph) named Psamathe.

Legends of love between Nereids and men persist in Greece. Several modern Greek families claimed to be "Nereid-born." The renowned Maniot clan, the Mavromichalis, traced their lineage to the day one George Mavromichalis found a Nereid sitting on a rock on the Mani shore, the southern tip of Greece. The adventurous admiral Lazaros Kondouriotis, born in 1769 on the island of Hydra, was said to have captured a

Nereid when he was shipwrecked; descendants of their union still told the tale in 1900. Around the same time, a family in Menidi, near Athens, boasted a Nereid great-grandmother, and everyone knew of the three Nereid sisters who lived in the gardens along the Kephissos River in Patissia. Nereids were endowed with great beauty, yet romantic liaisons with them were destined to end unhappily. Sooner or later, every Nereid tired of earthly life and returned to her watery home.

Nereids share the attributes of Sirens and other water spirits. They dwell near wells, streams, fountains, grottoes, and springs, as well as the seashore. All authorities agree on their appearance and character: dangerously beautiful and willfully capricious. Being struck blind or dumb was often the penalty for interrupting a bevy of Nereids at play. Falling in love with one was even more dangerous. Young men under the spell of Nereids became melancholy and prone to seizures or wasting illnesses. Only rarely was a "Nereid-doctor" able to cure the Nereid-struck with charms or potions. Besides their fickle and not entirely benign nature, Nereids were known as wonderful cooks and skillful spinners of delicate cloth. Strangely, they are not immortal—their life span was fabled to be only about a thousand years, but their beauty never fades.

Lonely young shepherds, especially flute players, were apparently the most susceptible to a Nereid's wiles. One old island song warned, "Do not play your flute by the lovely river, lest the Nereids, finding you alone, gather round you in a throng." The youth is liable to be whisked away to a secret grotto and wrapped in a passionate embrace, only to find that the nymph disappears at cockcrow.

According to legend, there were ways to capture a Nereid for a bride. The tale told in Crete in the 1860s is typical. A young man used to play his flute for the nymphs who danced at an isolated spring. They wore pearls and coral in their sea-green hair and garlands of flowers. Inevitably he fell in love with one of them. He sought the advice of an old woman, who told him to seize the girl's hair just before sunrise and to hold fast no matter what happened. He did this, and watched in amazement as his beloved changed into a dog, a snake, a camel, and finally fire in his arms. At dawn her companions had vanished. She returned to her original form and followed him home to his village. They married, had a son, and lived happily until, true to her nature, she deserted her husband and child. Some say the trick to keeping a Nereid is to hide a piece of her clothing. It must be well hidden because she will search for it and disappear when she finds it.

While the sisters of Thetis haunt seashores and grottoes, the oceans are home to fish-tailed lovelies who make life interesting for fishermen and sailors. Mermaids, known as *gorgones*, are often painted on the walls of seaside tavernas, or used as figureheads for boats, or tattooed on the arms of old mariners, who say that the mermaids are most commonly encountered in the eastern Aegean. A well-known sea yarn claims that during dreadful storms in those waters, a dazzling *gorgona* might suddenly surface and grab the bowsprit of the tossing boat. She demands of the captain, "Where is Alexander the Great?" If he responds properly, at the top of his lungs, "Alexander the Great lives and reigns!" the mermaid will calm the waves and vanish. A wrong answer causes the tempest to intensify, and the boat is plunged to the bottom of the sea. The modern Greek writer Ilias Venezis recounted this legend in the memoirs of his childhood in Anatolia, and George Seferis mentioned the tale in his poem "The Argonauts." The novelist

Stratis Mirivilis also referred to the story, and in his book *The Gorgon Madonna* he tells of an island fishing village in whose church the Virgin is portrayed as a mermaid.

The popular song "Delphinokoritso" (The dolphin girl), based on a poem by Nobel Prize winner Odysseas Elytis and set to music in the 1970s by Linos Kokotos, reminds us that the idea of mermaids continues to enchant:

Just off the islands of Hydra and Spetsae
There you were before me, a dolphin-girl
She dived into the waves and disappeared
Then she arose and held onto my boat
God forgive me! I bent down to have a look
And the wicked creature gave me a kiss!

CHAPTER 3

The Golden Fleece

THE ORIGINS OF THE TRADITIONS about the quest for the Golden Fleece are uncertain. The precious object was sought by Jason and the Argonauts, on their voyage across the Black Sea to the land of golden treasure (ancient Colchis, modern Georgia). The story is one of the oldest Greek myths, believed to have evolved into an oral epic form sometime before Homer (eighth to seventh centuries BC). A written version, the *Argonautica* by Apollonius of Rhodes, is from the third century BC, but scenes from the oral tradition are illustrated on early vase paintings from the fifth century BC.

The exciting sailing expedition to find the Golden Fleece was set in the Mycenean era of the Bronze Age and features several magical and mythical episodes drawn from storytellers' imaginations. But the narrative also contains many nuggets of historical, ethnographic, geographic, and natural realities. Ancient Greek travelers reached the far shores of the Black Sea at an early date, and hearsay preceded their contact. Proper names from the Circassian and Abkhazian languages of Colchis and the Caucasus region are preserved in several archaic Greek myths. For example, Apsyrtos, the brother of the Colchian witch Medea, who became Jason's lover, has an Abkhazian name. The name of the seductive sorceress in Homer's *Odyssey*, Circe, means "The Circassian."

Some modern scholars interpret the Golden Fleece of the Argonauts' quest as a symbol for the wealth of Colchis, known for its gold. But the true identity and meaning of the Golden Fleece was already recognized in Roman times, by the natural historian Pliny and by the geographer Strabo, a native of Pontus on the southern Black Sea coast who had traveled to neighboring Colchis. "It is said," wrote Strabo, "that in their country gold is carried down by the mountain torrents, and that the barbarians obtain it by means of perforated troughs and fleecy skins, and that this is the origin of the myth of the golden fleece."

Appian (Roman historian, born ca. AD 95) gives the fullest explanation of the local tradition that explains the Golden Fleece. People of Svaneti, western Colchis, would submerge a sheep's hide or lamb's fleece in streams and rivers as an efficient way to collect gold grains and flakes carried down from the mountains. The fleeces would be hung on branches to dry. This ancient technique is still used by local mountain villagers in Svaneti. It is certainly plausible that the method was employed in the Bronze Age. Geologists today describe gold dust suspended in the rivers of western Colchis. The fact that gold particles adhere to the fleece would have been discovered serendipitously when people washed new lambskins in rushing streams that contained plentiful gold grains.

When Greek adventurers first sailed to Colchis and reported on its golden wealth in archaic times, they may have repeated vague rumors about the mysterious "Golden Fleece," as something unknown associated with the fabulous gold of Colchis. It was pictured as a ram's hide of gold suspended on a tree branch and protected by a serpent. Later Greek travelers heard explanations of the technique, and then some observed it firsthand. By the seventh century BC, Greeks had established trade colonies along the coast of Colchis in order to obtain precious Scythian and Caucasian gold. Archaic Greeks were fascinated by the romance and mystery of the "golden fleece" before they understood the technology that would have made the ram's hide golden.

This fleece technique would have been a mystery to the Greeks because it was unknown in Greece, which imported gold from other lands. The practice works only in certain geographic areas and under special geological conditions, where rivers and streams are laden with gold sand. The sand erodes out from high mountains bearing igneous rock with rich veins of gold. Panning for placer gold in rivers and streams in the Gold Rush days of the old American West was based on this geological situation. In the famous Scythian gold fields of the arid Central Asian deserts, however, Bronze Age prospectors could not use the fleece method. Instead, they sifted dry sand for placer gold, brought down by erosion into barren gullies along the Silk Route below the Altai ("gold") Mountains.

Among the small gold and bronze artifacts of rams excavated in ancient Colchis are curious figures that the archaeologists describe as "ram-birds," supposedly combining a ram's head with a bird's tail. But now that we know how gold was collected in that region, it seems plausible that the figure is not meant to depict a composite "ram-bird."

Instead, it resembles a ram's hide with the head and horns attached. This is a common way to display and identify the species of animal skins: think bearskin rugs with head attached. Several ancient Greek vase paintings show the Golden Fleece, indicated by a ram's hide with head and horns, either hanging in a tree or in Jason's hands. The texture on the

Colchian figurine might indicate gold particles. Although it cannot be proved, it seems safe to guess that the so-called ram-bird figurines of Colchis represented the Golden Fleece.

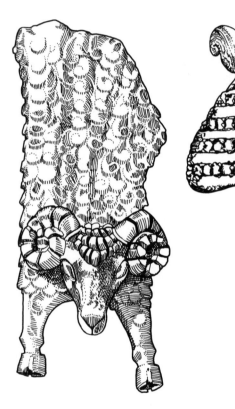

Typical representation of the Golden Fleece, statue, Batumi, Republic of Georgia; "ram-bird" figurine. Drawings by Michele Angel.

CHAPTER 4

Griffin Claws and a
Unicorn Horn

HOW DID THE VENERATED SAINT CUTHBERT, born about AD 634 in northern England, happen to possess not one but *two* claws of a fabled Griffin? And it turns out that Cuthbert's were not the only Griffin talons in medieval Europe—Charlemagne the Great also had one, said to be from Persia. I set out to discover the stories behind these relics.

Since classical Greek and Roman times, the legendary Griffin had been described as a creature with a lion-like body and a head and curved beak like an eagle. Griffins were believed to dwell in Central Asia along the Silk Routes where they guarded gold. By the Middle Ages, travelers' tales conflated the earthbound Griffin with the giant Roc bird of Arabian myth, capable of carrying off sheep and people in its talons. It was said that Griffins laid eggs in nests on the ground in the deserts of Asia. Notably, Cuthbert's treasures included a pair of Griffin eggs as well as a pair of Griffin talons, according to the 1383 inventory of the saint's shrine at Durham Cathedral. The eggs have long since vanished, but one of Cuthbert's Griffin claws can be admired in the British Museum, along with other Griffin-related relics of the Middle Ages.

Saint Cuthbert's Griffin claw, British Museum, OA24, donated by Sir John Cotton, acquired in 1753.

Cuthbert, the most renowned Celtic holy man of the medieval era, traveled, preached, and worked miracles in northern England and southeastern Scotland. In later life, Cuthbert lived as a hermit on a rocky island near Lindisfarne monastery, founded in about 634 on the Holy Island of Lindisfarne, off the Northumberland coast. Cuthbert died in 687, soon after becoming the bishop of Lindisfarne. His body was buried there in an oak coffin. When his coffin was opened in 698, it was observed that his body had not decomposed—a typical sign of sainthood. His tomb became a pilgrimage site. Cuthbert's many miracles were reported by the Venerable Bede, and the beautiful illuminated Lindisfarne Gospel books were created in about 710 in his honor.

As his fame grew, Cuthbert's cult accumulated costly dedications. In 793, the era of violent Viking invasions began with an attack on Lindisfarne monastery. After another raid at

Lindisfarne, the monks removed the saint's remains for safe-keeping in 875. His body and his treasures traveled around northeast England, disinterred and reburied by monks in several different coffins. We know that Cuthbert's body (and relics) were laid to rest in Durham in about 882–83, then removed to Ripon in 995. After more travels, in 1104 Cuthbert was finally reburied again in Durham Cathedral.

Almost three hundred years later, Durham Cathedral's inventory of 1383 lists two "Gryphon claws" and two "Gryphon eggs" among Cuthbert's treasures. In the Middle Ages, Griffin eggs were believed to protect against venomous snakes. Griffin claws were particularly sought after because they were believed to detect or neutralize poison in one's drink.

How did Cuthbert come by such exotic treasures? Alive and as a corpse, Cuthbert was certainly well-traveled. But he never left the British Isles. Over the centuries, Cuthbert accumulated valuable objects of gold, silver, ivory, and gems, fine embroidered vestments of Byzantine silk, rare manuscripts, curios from far-flung lands, and other costly treasures. We might guess that the precious Griffin claws and eggs were donated to his shrine in Durham centuries after his death, by wealthy followers who obtained them during the Crusades of the eleventh to fourteenth centuries.

Indeed, Griffin relics became highly prized in Europe in the later Middle Ages. Such wonders were obtained by early travelers to Asia and pilgrims and crusaders in the Holy Land. Many of the objects labeled "Griffin eggs" in medieval cabinets of curiosity and churches were in fact ostrich eggs, unfamiliar to Europeans. The 1442 inventory of Holy Trinity church in Coventry lists "a white egg of a Griffin"; York Minster had one too, and a John Hill of Spaxton bequeathed a Griffin egg cup to his son in 1434. Other more rare "Griffin eggs" were large fossilized dinosaur eggs from the Junggar and Gobi deserts, gathered along the Silk Route. Another favorite souvenir was a Griffin feather—actually raffia palm fronds from Madagascar painted to resemble giant feathers. "Griffin claws" became wildly popular. Gerard Leigh, a chronicler of heraldry, wrote in 1563, "I have a *clawe* of one of their pawes, whiche should shewe them [Griffins] to be as bigge as two lyons." Corpus Christi College, Cambridge, and Queen's College, Oxford, each owned a Griffin claw. And in France, the treasury of Bayeux Cathedral displayed three Griffin talons on the altar on festival days. In 1716, while she was touring the Danube, Lady Mary Wortley Montague observed a "prodigious claw set in gold which they called the claw of a griffin."

I found that the emperor Charlemagne (748–814) also possessed a Griffin claw. In the Basilica of Saint-Denis outside Paris, France, the monastery's inventories of 1505 and 1534 mention a Griffin claw and an intricately carved ivory chess piece belonging to Charlemagne. The Dutch traveler Arnold Van Buchel wrote that he observed both objects in 1585. The claw was described in detail in the inventories of 1625, 1634, 1746, and 1915. Charlemagne's Griffin claw was set in a gilded copper mount fashioned like a raptor's leg and talon with a small eagle on the spherical ball at the point. The claw is a bovid horn of unknown age and provenance. The style of the copper mount suggests that it was made in about 1200.

Charlemagne's Griffin claw cup was taken from Saint-Denis during the turmoil of the French Revolution in 1789. In 1794, it was found and deposited in the Cabinet des Médailles, Bibliothèque nationale, where it still resides with other fabulous relics of Saint-Denis. In 1813, Sir John Reresby visited

Charlemagne's Griffin claw drinking cup. Trésor de Saint-Denis, Bibliothèque nationale de France, Monnaies, Médailles et Antiques, Saint-Denis 1794.4, acquired in 1794.

Saint-Denis and marveled at the claw of a Griffin "as big as a cow's horn" belonging to Charlemagne. The antiquarian Edward Peacock noted in 1884 that the Griffin's talon had been presented to "the Emperor Charles the Great by a monarch of Persia."

In fact, Charlemagne did receive gifts from the caliph of Baghdad, Harun al-Rashid, during the Carolingian-Abbasid alliance, between 797 and 801. Among the magnificent gifts sent by Harun al-Rashid to Charlemagne were gorgeous silks, exotic perfumes, an ivory chess set, a live elephant named Abdul, an enormous deluxe tent, an intricate mechanical clock, and a "carved ivory horn." It seems plausible that an object identified as the claw of a Griffin was one of Charlemagne's earliest relics, perhaps one of the gifts from the caliph. Griffins had been featured in Persian art since antiquity. We know that the Saint-Denis church was completed under Charlemagne and that he attended its consecration in 775. He may have donated some precious items from the caliph himself at that time. It is recorded that his grandson Charles the Bald (823–77) presented the major collection of Charlemagne's treasures and relics to Saint-Denis.

Most so-called Griffin claws were fashioned into ornate drinking cups like Charlemagne's. Examination of numerous examples in the British Museum reveals that the claw cups were the horns of cape or water buffalo from Africa and India, embellished with gold and silver fittings. Another very early Griffin claw drinking cup is in Kornelimünster, in Aachen, Germany, Charlemagne's headquarters. The church was established in 814–17 by Charlemagne's son Louis. According to legend, this claw belonged to Saint Cornelius, martyred in AD 253. Cornelius received the claw after healing a Griffin of epilepsy and was always pictured with his special drinking horn. The cup, the horn of an Asian water buffalo, may have been acquired in the ninth century when Cornelius's head was transferred from his shrine in Italy to the monastery in Aachen. It was later embellished with silver and engraved with a likeness of Cornelius in the fifteenth century. The coincidence of two very early, similar Griffin claw drinking cups associated with Charlemagne and with Cornelius, around the same time and in the same place, is striking.

Compared to the profusion of bovine horn Griffin drinking cups like those of Charlemagne and Cornelius, Cuthbert's long, curved Griffin claw is quite rare. The Griffin claw of Saint Cuthbert in the British Museum is just over two feet long. It is identified as the horn of an Alpine ibex. Ibex horns are dark gray, thick, and heavily ridged, however, and this horn is smooth, slender, and resembles old ivory. It transpires that the outer ridged keratin sheath has been removed, and one can still discern traces of the growth ridges.

I have been able to locate only one other long, curved Griffin claw similar to Cuthbert's. It also has a fairly early date. Displayed in Brunswick Cathedral, Braunschweig, Germany, it was donated by Henry the Lion (1129–95). Henry obtained the marvel during his pilgrimage to Jerusalem in 1172. John Vinycomb wrote in 1906 that the claw was some sort of antelope horn, so it must have resembled Cuthbert's long claw. Its fate is unknown, since the dispersal of the cathedral's treasures during the Nazi era.

The peregrinations of Cuthbert's relic are easier to track. The silver band at the base of the horn is inscribed "GRYPHI UNGUIS DIVO CUTHBERTO DUNELMENSI SACER" (The claw of a Griffin sacred to the blessed Cuthbert of Durham). According to medieval lore a holy person who, like Saint Cornelius, offered medical aid to a Griffin, would receive a claw in gratitude. Possibly a story once circulated claiming that Cuthbert the miracle worker had treated a wounded Griffin and was rewarded with a pair of its claws and two eggs.

The Durham inventory of 1383 mentions a simple "silver hoop" on one of Cuthbert's Griffin claws, probably for ease of display. The inscribed silver band was added later, sometime between 1575 and 1625, after the relic was acquired by Sir Robert Bruce Cotton (1571–1631), an avid collector of fossils, Roman coins, antiquarian curios, and rare, precious manuscripts.

But how did the claw come into Cotton's hands? During the upheavals of the Reformation, when Henry VIII broke with the Catholic Church and ordered the dissolution of the monasteries in 1536–40, church treasuries, saints' shrines, and valuable manuscripts were plundered and sold for royal profit. Durham Cathedral and Cuthbert's treasures were stripped in 1537–38. Cotton made it his mission to recover the precious Lindisfarne Gospel and related texts dedicated to Cuthbert, so it seems plausible that the Griffin claw had also survived the despoliation of the shrine and was acquired at the same time by Cotton. In 1631 we know that the Griffin claw was inherited by his son Sir Thomas Cotton, who died in 1662 and passed it on to his son Sir John Cotton, who donated it to the English Parliament in 1701. Parliament placed the relic in the British Museum at its founding in 1753.

Like Brunswick and Durham cathedrals, Saint-Denis and Charlemagne's possessions also passed through turbulent times, and many of the venerable objects were destroyed or stolen, during the French Wars of Religion (1562–98) and the French Revolution (1789–99). Some of the treasures were placed for safekeeping in the National Library of Paris in 1791, others in the Louvre in 1793; much of Charlemagne's valuable collection is now in the Cabinet des Médailles, including his Griffin claw cup.

While reading the inventory of the surviving treasures of Saint-Denis, compiled in 1915 by Martin Conway, I noticed that Charlemagne's fabulous trove donated by his grandson Charles the Bald included, besides the Griffin claw, some elephant teeth and the horn of a Unicorn. The Unicorn horn was displayed on feast days up through the sixteenth century in Saint-Denis. Today one can admire the spiral horn in the Museum of the Middle Ages in Paris: it measures six feet, seven inches long. Like the Griffin claw, the horn was a gift to Charlemagne from "Aaron, King of Persia"—namely, Harun al-Rashid—in 807. What is the story of this relic?

Unicorn horns were often given as diplomatic gifts, and they became as popular as Griffin relics in cabinets of curiosity and sacred treasuries. The horns were believed to have magical and medicinal powers. So-called Unicorn horns actually came from narwhals, a small Arctic whale with a single, long spiral tusk. These were brought to Europe from the seas around Greenland and Russia, so it is difficult to imagine that a narwhal tusk was a gift from the caliph of Baghdad. But were there European whalers in the early Middle Ages? I learned that Norsemen were whaling at an early date, and Basque whalers set out from Bayonne as early as the eleventh century. Were there any Carolingian whalers? Intrigued, I delved deeper.

To my surprise, I found that the abbey at Saint-Denis itself was involved in early medieval whaling. The monks operated a whale fishery and flensing port on the Normandy peninsula beginning in 832. At some point in a whaling voyage from the icy whale-hunting waters to Normandy, it appears that a ninth-century sailor's souvenir narwhal tusk became enshrined as a Unicorn horn belonging to Charlemagne.

CHAPTER 5

Dolphin Tales

DOLPHINS, THE PLAYFUL CHARMERS of the ocean, have long held a special place in the hearts of Greeks—the dolphin is honored as the national animal. Myths and legends tell of their friendship with humans and gods alike. Spotting a school of dolphins frolicking in the waves is thrilling. They've been described as "beautiful abstractions of speed, energy, power, and ecstasy." Greek sailors say sighting dolphins brings good luck—and some claim that all dolphins answer to the name of Vasili (Billy in English).

I had a chance to test this claim when my husband, Josh, and I guided a tour group on the splendid vintage yacht *Sea Cloud* sailing from Istanbul around the Aegean islands, and on to Athens. One fine day between Santorini and Samos, as I recounted myths and legends about dolphins, I concluded with a gesture to the navy-blue waves, jokingly calling out, "Vasili! Billy!" like the sailors of yore. Suddenly they appeared, a troupe of silvery dolphins leaping alongside our ship. The group was delighted, so I hid my own astonishment.

But if calling dolphins by name doesn't work, you might try playing a tune on a flute. The dolphin's passion for music was recognized over two thousand years ago by the ancient Greeks. The classical playwrights Euripides and Aristophanes referred to the allure of flute melodies for dolphins, while

Young flute player riding a dolphin, red-figure jar, Alcestis Group, Etruria, ca. 350 BC, National Archaeological Museum, Athens, © Marie-Lan Nguyen / Wikimedia Commons.

other writers mentioned their appreciation for shepherd's pipes.

Dolphins were admired in antiquity for their sociable and compassionate nature. Aristotle had observed dolphins coming to the aid of their injured young, and he described a group of dolphins flocking to a harbor to beg fishermen to release a netted companion. Dolphins were known to rescue drowning people too. Many writers extolled the amiable, intelligent cetaceans' remarkable affinity for humankind, for extending friendship and expecting nothing in return.

One Greek myth attributed dolphins' "human" qualities to the fact that they were once human themselves. According to the story, the purple-robed god of wine Dionysos was captured by pirates on his way to Naxos. Believing they were kidnapping a member of a royal family, the pirates chained the god to the mast and rowed away with him, dreaming of great ransom. Unobserved, Dionysos managed to break his chains and took out his flute. As he played a magical song, thick grapevines entwined the ship's mast, the oars became writhing serpents, and the god himself changed into a panther. The terrified pirates threw themselves overboard and were instantly transformed into dolphins. Ancient Greek vase paintings illustrate the diving pirates in midtransformation. To this day, says the myth, dolphins are drawn to humans, boats, and music.

A distinguished ancient musician, Arion of Lesbos, bet his life on dolphins' love of music. In 625 BC, Arion was returning from a successful concert tour in Italy. Halfway to Greece, the ship's crew conspired to relieve Arion of his tour profits. They were about to throw him overboard when Arion requested that he be permitted to play one last song on his lyre. According to the historian Herodotus, the sailors acquiesced, eager to hear such a world-famous star for free. Arion put on his professional costume, and the crew assembled for the musician's farewell concert. As the music drifted over the water, dolphins drew near the boat. As the song ended, Arion leaped overboard and was carried safely to the shores of southern Greece by one of the dolphins. Upon his safe landing at Cape Matapan at the tip of the Peloponnese, the musician wrung out his singing robes and commissioned a bronze statue of a man riding on the back of a dolphin. Just such a figurine was discovered in the ruins of the ancient town of Taenarum, on Cape Matapan. And Arion's hometown of Methymna issued coins depicting Arion dressed in a long chiton and seated on a dolphin, holding his lyre.

According to ancient tradition, Tarentum, the town in Italy where Arion had set sail, was founded by Taras, a Greek who had been saved from a shipwreck by a dolphin sent by his father, the god Poseidon. Tarentum, whose founding was predicted by the Delphic Oracle in the eighth century BC, issued several coins depicting Taras riding a dolphin.

Scores of Greek legends feature dolphin lifeguards. Centuries after Taras and Arion were rescued at sea, Alexander the Great happened to be on a beach when a boy named Dionysius was brought safely ashore by a dolphin. Alexander took the boy into his circle, and he became a priest of Poseidon, god of the sea. According to Greek myth, when Ino was driven mad by the jealous goddess Hera, she leaped off the Moulourian Rocks into the sea (the site is on the old road between Eleusis and Megara) with her infant son Melikertes in her arms. A dolphin rescued them and carried mother and son to the Isthmus of Corinth, where the Isthmian Games were established in Melikertes's honor. Isthmian coins show Ino and her son on the cliff with an alert dolphin waiting below, and Melikertes on the dolphin's back. At Isthmia today one can see the ruins of the circular temple built over Melikertes's tomb. According to illustrations on bronze coins, its domed roof was decorated with dolphins, and there was a statue of the boy riding on the dolphin inside.

In Arion's hometown of Methymna, legend told of a youth named Enalus who snatched up the daughter of Smintheus as she was about to be sacrificed to the sea goddess Amphitrite. He leaped over a cliff into the sea with her in his arms. The two were saved by dolphins. In a ninth-century romance, once described as a "rather tasteless love story in eleven volumes," a mysterious winged boy on a dolphin rescues the maiden

Hysmire from a shipwreck. In another myth, vigilant dolphins nudged Odysseus's little son Telemachus back to shore at Zakynthos when he strayed into deep water. In gratitude Odysseus decorated his shield and signet ring with the image of a dolphin. An inscription cut into rock on the island Santorini has been interpreted as a commemoration of a man's rescue by a dolphin.

It seems that in antiquity dolphins zealously patrolled the sea for human swimmers in trouble. The notion that should one fall into the sea, a dolphin might come along was proverbial by Plato's time. A humorous twist on the theme appears in one of Aesop's fables: a cruising dolphin scoops up a shipwrecked monkey near Sounion thinking it is a small Greek man. As they approach Athens's harbor Pireaus, the dolphin inquires whether his passenger is Athenian. The money indicates he is. But when the dolphin asks, "So, do you know Piraeus well?" the monkey replies, "Oh yes, we're good friends," whereupon the dolphin realizes his mistake and flips the monkey into the water to swim the rest of the way.

Dolphins were said to remember kindnesses. A favorite example was the sailor Coeranus, a native of Paros. Coeranus once paid a group of fishermen at Byzantium to release some dolphins caught in a net. Years later Coeranus was washed overboard in a storm between Naxos and Paros and would have perished had not grateful dolphins carried him to a cave on the island of Sikinos. When Coeranus died as an old man, it was said that scores of dolphins assembled offshore to pay tribute at his funeral.

An anecdote of the second century AD tells of an old couple who rescued a young dolphin injured by fishermen. It became the companion of their grandchild, and when the dolphin grew up, it helped the old couple by catching fish. Mediterranean fishermen exploited the fish-catching abilities of dolphins after they noticed that small fish fled before pursuing dolphins. Several ancient writers describe how dolphins would come when fishermen called them, to herd schools of mullet into nets. The fishermen rewarded their finny helpers with a share of the catch and a bonus of bread soaked in wine.

Sometimes dolphins brought drowned bodies to shore for burial. The eighth-century BC poet Hesiod was a well-known example. According to tradition, after Hesiod was murdered in the Nemean Grove in Locria and thrown into the sea near Euboea, dolphins transported his body to the beach. When Saint Lucian was lost at sea in the fourth century AD, his friends were amazed to see his body carried gently to land on the slippery back of a dolphin, "as if resting upon a bed." A song about this marvel was still current centuries later: "Upon its back the dolphin carried him / and breathed its last upon the shore."

It became a poetic cliché that a dolphin inevitably perished of exhaustion upon depositing a drowning victim on the beach or died of a broken heart upon the death of a human companion. By Roman times nearly every story of human-dolphin friendship ended with an obligatory double-death scene. Some accounts added the detail that during the dolphin's death throes on the sand the creature turned every hue of the rainbow. Lord Byron (see chapter 42) compared the dolphin's death to sunset: "Parting day / dies like the dolphin, whom each pang imbues / With a new color as it gasps away. / The last still loveliest, till—'tis gone, and all is grey."

The best-known tragic tale from antiquity is that of the tame dolphin Simo ("Snub-Nose") and Hyacinthus. Simo was hand-fed, came when called, and gave the young boy Hyacinthus a ride to and from school each day. When Hyacinthus fell ill and died, Simo waited forlornly at the accustomed places. At last Simo passed away from grief and was buried at the boy's grave. In a similar legend, Hermias of Iasus used to plunge into the sea each day after training at the gymnasium. Waiting faithfully was a dolphin who gave the boy rides far out to sea and back. One day Hermias drowned. The dolphin rushed him back to shore, then expired from sorrow. Their friendship was memorialized in a statue of the two, and ancient coins from Iasus show Hermias swimming with one arm over the dolphin's back.

Some cities became renowned for their trained dolphins. Pausanias, the travel writer of the second century AD (chapter 41), saw the famous tame dolphin of Poroselene, an island near Lesbos, which gave children rides and performed tricks. The town charged admission to the show and featured the creature's likeness on its coins. Another performing dolphin was described about a hundred years earlier by the natural historian Pliny. One day a dolphin made friends with an adventurous child swimming far out to sea; the next day the whole town turned out to see whether the dolphin would reappear. This time the dolphin was coaxed to shore, where everyone patted its head and children took turns riding on its back. One day an official poured perfume on the town's aquatic mascot during a ceremony—a gesture the dolphin did not appreciate, for it seemed to faint from the "strange sensation and smell" and disappeared for several days. This tale had an unhappy ending: after enduring several years of unruly tourist hordes, the village fathers decided to quietly do away with the famous attraction.

Today's dolphins are just as playful, friendly, and music loving as their ancestors. There are modern accounts of musicians performing well-received concerts for dolphins, children befriending them, and exhausted swimmers being pushed to safety by them. The adventure of a Greek sailor who fell overboard between Crete and Thera-Santorini in the 1950s is typical. He was not a strong swimmer; just when he thought he was done for, he felt something large and smooth under his tired legs. A dolphin swam right between his knees and carried the sailor at a gentle pace until he could wade ashore. Even this modern example ends with the demise of the dolphin, whose blowhole was inadvertently blocked by the exhausted sailor. I heard that two American archaeologists bathing in the Corinthian Gulf off Porto Germano were playfully nudged by a dolphin, an experience reported by other swimmers there.

Writer Patrick Fermor recalled a memorable sunset in the Cyclades. He and some friends were on a yacht between Folegandros and Sikinos (where Coeranus had been rescued by dolphins) listening to a recording of Handel's *Water Music*. As the melody wafted over the calm sea, they saw a dolphin leap not far away, then another and another, until the boat was surrounded by dolphins gracefully "gamboling and pirouetting" to the music. A friend of Fermor's, poet-psychiatrist Andreas Embirikos, remembered the day he was listening to a symphony on a portable radio in a small rowboat in the bay of Batsi, on the island of Andros. Soon six or seven dolphins began to leap and dive, becoming quite boisterous as the music reached a crescendo. Fearing that his little dinghy would capsize in the waves made by the dancing dolphins, he switched off the radio and quickly rowed to shore. Safe on the beach, Embirikos turned the radio back on and enjoyed the rest of the concert while the dolphins continued to cavort nearby.

Ferryboat passengers in the Aegean lucky enough to hear the delighted cry "Delphinia!" are in for an exhilarating sight, as dolphins surge and leap in the wake or off the prow, or race alongside. One writer has described the breathtaking experience of watching dolphins playing at dusk in phosphorescent waves. "Flames seemed to whirl from them"; as they leaped, they shook off "a million fiery diamonds and when they plunged it was a fall of comets." Streaming away together, each trailed a wake of glowing bubbles until they became a "far-away constellation on the sea's floor." At a moment like this, one must agree with the Greek poet Oppian: "Diviner than the dolphin is nothing yet created."

CHAPTER 6

The Musical Racing Turtles of Greece

Sacred to Pan, lethal to Aeschylus, and possessed of an indescribable voice, the lovesick tortoise of Greece has been around since before the Ice Age.

MUSIC AND RACING are two activities that fail to leap to mind when one considers land tortoises. But in antiquity, the unassuming tortoise won races against the hare and the great warrior of Greek myth Achilles. And the most noble musical instrument of antiquity, the lyre, was fashioned from the carapace of the lowly turtle. Technically, *tortoise* refers to the land creature as distinct from the aquatic *turtle*, although the words are often used interchangeably, as in this article.

Remember Aesop's fable, in which the land tortoise, slow and steady, wins the race with the overconfident hare who dawdles on the way to the finish line? The Greek philosopher Zeno of Elea (born about 490 BC) put a twist on the story when he pitted a tortoise against swift-footed Achilles in a theoretical race. Because proud Achilles can run ten times as fast as the turtle, he gives the turtle a head start of one hundred yards. But, in Zeno's famous paradox, Achilles will never win, because as he runs those first hundred yards the tortoise covers ten more, and while Achilles runs those ten yards, the tortoise advances one more yard, and while Achilles runs that one yard, the tortoise moves forward one-tenth of a yard, and so on ad infinitum.

In real life, land tortoises plod slowly over fields, through the golden stubble under olive trees, and across the rocky hills and mountains of mainland Greece and the islands. During our fieldwork measuring ancient stone forts and towers, we often encountered them in isolated valleys and on high ridges, laboriously making their way over outcroppings and through thorny underbrush. In the hot, arid summer, you can hear them noisily approaching through the crackling dry weeds. Once, on the Road of the Ancient Towers, in the Megalo Vathychori, a valley below the slopes of Mount Pateras in western Attica, I observed two turtles bashing one another like miniature tanks among the windflowers and poppies. I assumed they were disputing territory.

Three species of land tortoises inhabit Greece, *Testudo graeca, T. hermanni*, and *T. marginata*. The distribution of these terrestrial turtles helps scientists determine the history of changes in sea level and land masses in the Aegean. The *T. graeca* tortoises, for example, live on Cos, Thasos, Samothrace, Limnos, and Samos, where they were stranded, along with the lesser mole-rat and some lizard species, when the last glaciers melted. The *T. hermanni* species prefers lower altitudes, such as Euboea. Naxos, Kythira, and Skyros are home to the *T. marginata*, which are also found in the mountains of the Peloponnese and south of Mount Olympus. On the islands of Patnos, Kythira, and Chios, terrestrial tortoises are quite rare. In classical antiquity, Aegina was famous for minting silver coins with the image of a sea turtle in the sixth century BC, when it was a great sea power (see chapter 2 for a man-eating sea turtle of myth). The island was taken over by Athens and lost its trading status in the fifth century BC. After that, Aegina's coins featured a land tortoise instead. No tortoises have been sighted on the island since the nineteenth century.

In antiquity the tortoises of Mount Parthenion (in the Peloponnese) were sacred to Pan, god of the woodlands. This is where Pan promised the powerful runner Pheidippides that he would help the Athenians beat back the Persians at the Battle of Marathon in 490 BC. When the Persians landed, Pheidippides was dispatched to Sparta to ask for help. He ran about 150 miles in two days. After the Greek victory, footraces were held in Pan's honor. Perhaps the tortoise was honored as well, in memory of its own improbable racing victories. Or perhaps Pan's tortoise mascot was chosen in the same ironic spirit that led the basketball team at the University of California–Santa Cruz to call themselves the "Slugs."

In the second century AD, the Greek travel writer Pausanias visited the cave where Pan had made his promise. Pausanias remarked that the area had lots of tortoises, "which are excellent for making lyres. But the people are terrified to kill them and forbid strangers to take them, for they believe the creatures are protected by Pan." Pan was known as the avenger of cruelty to animals. The young girl playing with a hapless turtle as a yo-yo, depicted in an ancient Greek vase painting, would seem to be courting disaster.

The tortoise's determination and simple, effective means of self-defense was much admired. The Romans named their defensive military formation the *testudo* (Latin for tortoise): the soldiers advanced slowly under a "shell" of interlocking

Girl with turtle yo-yo, after Greek red-figure vase painting in British Museum, 360 BC. Drawing by Adrienne Mayor.

shields. A folklorist traveling in Macedonia around 1900 heard that it was considered very lucky to come across a tortoise, and very bad karma to kill one. Moreover, anyone who found a tortoise upside down had a duty to help it—and anyone malicious enough to flip one onto its back committed a dire sin. The villagers said that the very sight of a turtle upside down is "an insult to the Deity," and one should hasten to its aid. Notably, the 1982 science fiction movie *Blade Runner* featured empathy for an upside-down turtle in a "Turing test" to ferret out emotionless android replicants.

Oddly enough, the Original Tortoise once insulted Zeus. According to an ancient Greek tale, Zeus invited all the animals to his wedding. Only the turtle, Chelone, stayed home, and Zeus demanded to know why. Chelone replied that her house was too dear to her to leave it even for a grand party. Miffed, Zeus decreed that such a homebody should have to

carry her precious home with her ever after. Chelone's name
is commemorated in the scientific name for the order of turtles: Chelonia.

Eagles were companions of Zeus and therefore no friends
of tortoises. Ancient naturalists told how eagles would seize
tortoises and drop them on rocks to smash the shell and eat
the flesh. The great tragic playwright Aeschylus perished in
456 BC, killed instantly when an eagle dropped a tortoise on
his bald head, mistaken by the eagle for a rock. This shocking
accident must have reminded many Greeks of the cautionary
fable about the Turtle who learned to fly.

Once a Turtle told the Swallows, "Would that I too had
wings to fly!"

An Eagle overheard this exchange and said, "How much
would you give if I enabled you to rise effortlessly high up
in the sky?"

The gullible Turtle answered, "I'd give all the riches
of the East!"

"You're on," said the Eagle, "I'll teach you to fly!" He
carried the turtle aloft upside down until they reached
the clouds. Then the cruel eagle dropped the tortoise on a
mountainside, dashing his hard shell to smithereens.

As he fell, the Turtle was heartily sorry: "What possessed me to wish for clouds or wings when even on the
ground I could not move with ease?"

Although tortoises are certainly easy for humans to catch
and kill, there is not much evidence that anyone ate land turtles in classical times, except during famines. Archaeological
excavations, for example at Nichoria in southern Greece, reveal

that in Byzantine times, when food was very scarce, small tortoises were cooked for supper. But tortoises were highly esteemed for medicinal uses in antiquity. Pliny the Elder listed sixty-six remedies based on tortoises.

As noted, the shells of turtles were in great demand for making musical instruments. An ancient riddle asks, "What lifeless thing can produce a beautiful living sound?" Answer: a lyre made of a tortoiseshell. The legend of the lyre's origin goes like this. The messenger god Hermes, when he was a boy living near his birthplace in a cave on Mount Kyllene, slaughtered some oxen owned by his older brother Apollo. Then he saw a tortoise by the cave. He killed it too, stretched some ox hide over the concave carapace, and fixed seven ox-gut strings across the sound box. The boy assuaged Apollo's anger about the dead oxen by plucking a tune on this simple instrument. In inventing the first lyre (called a *chelys*, or turtle), Hermes, it was said, "created endless delight, because it was he who first made a turtle sing."

Greek with tortoiseshell lyre. Drawing by Adrienne Mayor.

The traditional lyre was made of a turtle shell with two horns of a wild goat extending as parallel arms from the sound box. Ox gut or sinews of various thicknesses were strung from the crossbar between the horns to the shell. The instrument produced music described as "noble, serene, and virile." In skilled hands, a lyre was liable to make stones dance, rivers stop flowing, and wild animals turn tame.

Hermes taught Orpheus to play the lyre so sweetly that he could soothe even the god of the Underworld with his songs. When Orpheus was killed by maenads, his lyre fell in the sea and washed up on the island of Lesbos. A fisherman brought the instrument to the poet Terpander. This composer of the sixth century BC is renowned as the founder of classical Greek music. Terpander won many contests in Sparta with his compositions for the *chelys*.

Orpheus had taught the poet Linus to play the lyre. His mournful songs became famous enough to be called "linuses." Like Aeschylus, Linus discovered that when poet's skull meets turtle shell, it's Turtles 2, Poets 0. According to myth, when Heracles was a boy, he took music lessons from old Linus. When he was reprimanded for his poor playing, he bashed his music master over the head with his heavy tortoiseshell lyre, killing him.

Plodding so patiently over the landscape in search of morsels and dewdrops, this low-profile homebody, this master of passive self-defense, the modest tortoise seems utterly removed from the kinds of ruckus associated with its name in antiquity, not to mention lyrical music.

And yet . . . Picture zoologist George E. Watson of the Peabody Museum, binoculars around his neck, notebook in hand, stepping through thickets of thorny burnet on the island of Cos. It's a fine day in May 1961. Watson cocks his ear, startled by a peculiar knocking sound. Ten meters away in a little clearing he spots a "female *Testudo graeca* being pursued by an ardent male *T. graeca*." Riveted by the spectacle, Professor

Watson sits down and observes the tryst through his eight-power binoculars, furiously scribbling notes. The Roman naturalist Aelian had remarked in the third century AD that the tortoise was "a most lustful creature." Aelian speculated that "since the males couldn't sing they must charm the females by means of an herb." But Watson's monograph, "Notes on the Copulation of Aegean Land Tortoises," is the first scientific eyewitness account of the courtship of the Greek species. Hermes may have been the first to make a lifeless turtle shell sing, but it was George E. Watson who told the world about the mating call and lively courting dance of the lovesick Greek tortoise.

The rhythmic knocking sound that Watson heard was the suitor bumping his sweetheart's carapace with his own to get her attention. His crashing and bashing kept up for nearly half an hour. She kept on moving up the hill in the underbrush, pausing flirtatiously and starting forward again. The male tortoise was thrown off balance, tumbled down the incline, and landed upside down. Watson observed that the turtle finally righted himself and "recommenced his pursuit and bumping." Again and again he rolled downhill, got right-side up, and began his bumping anew.

Then the tortoise began to sing! Watson knew of some earlier reports of turtle mating calls in other parts of the world, but all previous scientific studies concerned captive turtles, and no one had described any vocalizations by native wild Greek species. A German zoologist once maintained that the European land turtle's cry was "very like a cat's miaow." Louis Leakey claimed that a tortoise in a zoo in Uganda gave a "loud husky cry" when courting. A pet South American tortoise bobbed his head and emitted a sound "like a mother hen teaching her chicks to scratch for food." Another turtle native to an island in the Indian Ocean "gave a deep trumpeting call." The two species of giant Galapagos tortoises have rather different courting styles. One is quite taciturn—the male skips the shell-bumping ritual altogether and manages to "roar with his mouth closed." The male of the other species sways his head, bumps a bit, and then opens his mouth wide to give a "light and gasping call."

The mating call of the wild tortoise of Cos was "audible for a least 20 meters" (about 21 yards). Watson saw him open his mouth and heard a "high nasal whine, somewhat resembling a complaining puppy's voice." He also noted that the song was short, lasting about half a minute.

No ancient author ever mentioned the call of the live turtle, preferring to dwell on the beauty of the music produced by the hollow tortoiseshell lyre. But thanks to George Watson of the Peabody Museum, whenever I walk through hillocks of oregano and thorny burnet in Greece, I listen for crashing carapaces in the underbrush and a live version of the wild tortoise song.

A Little Bird with Poison Poop

AMONG THE POISONOUS CREATURES reported in classical antiquity, one of the most mysterious is the *Dikairon* bird, whose droppings were said to be deadly to humans. This exotic avian biotoxin was deliberately collected in the high mountains of India. Note that in antiquity, "India" referred to the remote lands east of Persia (Iran).

Ctesias, a Greek physician living in Persia in the late fifth century BC, was the first writer to describe the bird, followed by the Roman naturalist Aelian in the third century AD. They reported that a powerful poison was excreted by a tiny orange bird called the *Dikairon*. A minuscule amount of the little bird's droppings could bring death in a few hours. This rare substance was one of the most precious and rare gifts exported from the rulers of India to the kings of Persia. It was kept as a poison in the royal pharmacy—a valuable drug for assassination or suicide.

What sort of bird was it, and what was the secret of its poison?

The Dikairon was said to be the size of a partridge egg, about one and a half inches long. The excreta of such a small bird would be exiguous, but one clue to consider is that bird feces are known to carry more than sixty diseases. Dried bird droppings can harbor pathogens that attack the lungs and central nervous system, including *Salmonella* and *E. coli* bacteria, and the fungus that causes histoplasmosis, a fatal respiratory disease. Perhaps the dried droppings of the unknown Dikairon bird contained a particularly virulent lethal pathogen.

Some classical scholars have suggested that the exotic poison was betel nuts or cannabis. But cannabis of the steppes was known to Herodotus and is not deadly (chapter 21); chewing the berries of South Asian areca palm with betel leaf is carcinogenic but not a fast-acting poison. Others speculate that the Dikairon was not a bird but a winged dung beetle whose droppings were confused with opium. The creature's small size does match that of a dung beetle. Dung beetles have long wings and are strong fliers. Certain types of dung beetles are even found in birds' nests. The notion that the little orange bird was actually a dung beetle is attractive, except for the fact that dung beetles are not toxic, and the source of opium—poppies—was well known in antiquity.

Beetles could be involved, however. Some large, winged beetles might be mistaken for small birds. Many species of highly toxic beetles have been used to make poison weapons. For example, the San people of the Kalahari Desert in Africa have used the insides of *Diamphidia* beetle larvae to poison arrows for thousands of years. Could "droppings" have been a Greek translation for insect excretions or insides? Perhaps the ancient account of the little "droppings" of the mysterious Dikairon originated in a garbled report of a similar beetle toxin gathered in India. Some species of poisonous beetles were recognized in classical antiquity. For example, Aristotle and the toxicologist Nicander described deadly substances obtained from blister and *Staphylinus* beetles, whose poisons are strong enough to kill cattle that accidentally munch them.

A recent discovery by entomological pharmacologists might help solve the mystery of the fabled Dikairon. In the 1980s, scientists began investigating the toxic properties of the *Paederus* beetles of the large Staphylinidae family (rove beetles), found in many areas of the world, including northern India. These predatory flying insects are orange and black, or entirely orange, and about an inch long. Some species inhabit birds' nests. These features—flight, color, and nests—could account for a confusion with tiny birds as folklore traveled west. It transpires that this beetle was known to Chinese medicine twelve hundred years ago. A pharmacopoeia written by Ch'en in AD 739 accurately described the *Paederus* beetle, called *ch'ing yao ch'ung*, and stated that its "strong poison" could be used to remove boils, polyps, and unwanted tattoos from the skin.

These blister beetles secrete a virulent poison, and in their insides, or hemolymph, is found pederin, one of the most powerful animal toxins in the world, more potent than cobra venom. On the skin, pederin raises angry, suppurating sores, and in the eyes it can cause blindness. If pederin is ingested, as Dikairon droppings were said to be, severe internal damage ensues.

There is one other possible solution to the riddle of the Dikairon bird. Could the Dikairon story have arisen from a rare example of avian toxicity, achieved by birds dining on toxic plants or beetles containing neurotoxins?

Strangely enough, the Dikairon is not the only poisonous bird described in antiquity. Mithradates VI of Pontus (northern Turkey), Rome's enemy during the Mithradatic Wars

(89–63 BC), was an experimental toxicologist (see chapter 36). He cultivated poison plants in his gardens in his quest to create a "universal antidote." He also raised Pontic ducks, whose flesh was known to be poisonous. According to Pliny the Elder, who read Mithradates's handwritten notes on toxicology after his death in 63 BC, Mithradates hoped to exploit the ducks' ability to live on poisons. He fed them the baneful plants they preferred and harvested the ducks' eggs, blood, and flesh for his experiments. Pliny stated that Mithradates mixed the blood of the Pontic ducks into his special antidote. In the second century AD, Aulus Gellius remarked that the ducks of Pontus had the "power to expel poisons," and that Mithradates found that the ducks' blood was the most potent agent in their bodies.

Several other ancient Greek and Roman writers knew of other creatures that could eat things poisonous to humans without experiencing ill effects. It was recognized that bees of Pontus, for example, safely gathered nectar from toxic rhododendron flowers, but that their honey was baneful to mammals, including humans (see chapter 37). Like the ducks of Pontus, goats and quail were said to thrive on toxic plants that rendered their meat deadly to predators and humans. This principle was discussed in the fourth century BC by Aristotle (*On Plants* 820.6–7), and later by Philo (*Geoponics* 14.24 and *Special Laws* 4.120–31), Lucretius (*On the Nature of Things* 4.639–40), Galen (*De temperamentis* 3.4), and Sextus Empiricus (*Outlines of Pyrrhonism* 1.57). The quail were believed to eat toxic hemlock seeds, hellebore, or henbane, plants common around the Mediterranean and in Anatolia.

The Old Testament tells of what appears to be an episode of mass poisoning by quail on the Israelites' journey to the

Promised Land. According to Exodus (16.11–12), when the Israelites were starving as they crossed the Sinai Desert, a multitude of quail miraculously descended on their encampment at twilight. The book of Numbers (11.31–34) relates that winds carried immense flocks of quail from the sea to the camp. The birds were so concentrated on the ground that the people gathered them up by the hundreds that night, and the next day they feasted on the roasted meat. As soon as they devoured the birds, a severe plague decimated the Israelites. Historians of science speculate that the "plague" was an outbreak of quail poisoning, a condition called coturnism. Eating toxic quail can cause rhabdomyolysis, destruction of muscle tissue, leading to shock and lethal kidney failure.

As early as the second century AD, the physician and medical writer Galen observed that quail poisonings occurred in autumn, when flocks of European quail migrate south across the Mediterranean, Anatolia, and the Arabian Desert, on their way to Egypt and East Africa where they spend the winter. Galen surmised that the quail fed on hemlock seeds as they migrated and became poisonous. Hemlock seeds contain the neurotoxin coniine, causing paralysis and asphyxia. Modern scientific studies confirm that European migrating quail (*Coturnix coturnix coturnix*) become toxic only on their southern flights in the autumn. The multitudes of quail fly in the dark and rest by day, which matches the details in the biblical account. The seasonal toxicity hints at the ingestion of something widely available on their journey south. Hemlock is a prolific producer of seeds in the fall.

A recent incident of quail poisoning was reported in the autumn of 2007 in Turkey, afflicting four of ten people who had enjoyed a dinner of roasted migrating quail. Coturnism incidents have been reported in Algeria, France, Spain, Italy, and the island of Lesbos, Greece, all stopping points for the migrating game birds. It is interesting that the Palestinians of Gaza (see map in chapter 1) eagerly await the annual arrival of quail in September and October, catching them by the hundreds at dawn in fine nets, to roast or make traditional quail soup. The small bird is an important food source, the only meat in their diet. Yet there appear to be no reports of coturnism in Gaza. Scientific studies show that susceptibility to quail poisoning depends on genetic mutations of human liver enzymes. The ancient Israelites may have been especially genetically susceptible; the Turkish diners less so; and the Palestinians perhaps even less so.

Given the number of ancient and medieval reports of poisonous ducks and quail, it is surprising that the phenomenon of avian toxicity began to attract scientific attention only after the Pitohui, an orange-and-black songbird of Australia and New Guinea, was "discovered" in 1989. It is now classified as the world's most poisonous bird. The Pitohui, the Blue-Capped Ifrita, and the Little Shrike-thrush were long recognized as toxic by indigenous peoples. Touching them causes unpleasant numbness and tingling, and eating them can be fatal. Scientists found that these and other poisonous birds sequester batrachotoxins, the family of chemicals secreted by poison-dart frogs, in their skin, feathers, and flesh. Presumably the droppings also contain batrachotoxins. These birds eat poisonous Choresine beetles, little-studied members of the Melyridae family. In Africa, the Spur-Winged Goose eats blister beetles, which produce cantharidin, making the cooked goose lethal to humans. The orange-and-black Hoopoes of East Africa and Asia are now known to harbor toxic bacteria in their feather-preening glands. So far, about a hundred avian species, from quail, grouse, and geese to smaller birds, have been identified as unpalatable, malodorous, or dangerously toxic to humans.

Avian toxicity remains a little-studied field, and the empoisoning process is not completely understood. It appears to be an evolved chemical defense trait acquired by ingesting plant or beetle toxins or somehow absorbing insect toxins. But the exact mechanism by which the birds become poisonous is as yet unknown.

Nevertheless, we can now ponder several possibilities for identifying the cryptic Dikairon bird and its deadly droppings deliberately collected as a potent drug for murder or suicide, described by Ctesias and Aelian. The tale could have been based on a hypervirulent bacterium or fungus in the dried excreta of an unknown bird of the mountains of India. Alternatively, the story could be the result of popular misidentification of a large, highly toxic, orange beetle as a small, poisonous orange bird in garbled travelers' tales. Another plausible explanation is that the Dikairon is a yet-to-be-discovered example of avian toxicity, a tiny orange bird still flitting and shitting batrachotoxins in the unexplored, forested slopes of the Pamir, Hindu Kush, or Himalayan mountains.

The Roman Army's Vulture Mascots

THE FIRST BANDED BIRDS

VULTURES WERE OFTEN the first responders to the carnage of war. The large birds of prey were commonly observed wheeling over battlefields to feast on the dead and dying. Scavenging vultures learned to follow ancient armies on the march in anticipation of a banquet of carcasses.

When the great Roman commander Marius (157–86 BC) was leading campaigns against the Germanic tribes (the Cimbri, Teutons, and Ambrones) in Europe, the soldiers noticed that a pair of vultures made a habit of hovering over his army as they marched (see chapter 39 for more on these tribes). The troop's blacksmith forged two bronze collars, and the legionnaires managed to capture the two vultures with nets, probably while they were feeding. The men placed the bands around the raptors' necks and released their new mascots.

Ever after, when the Roman soldiers caught sight of the vulture pair and saw their bronze collars flashing in the sun, their spirits rose and they would cheer their soaring escorts. Vultures had been considered good omens since the founding of Rome. The vulture pair boosted the army's morale, for their

Pair of cinereous vultures with engraved bronze collars. Drawing by Michele Angel.

sighting was taken as a sure sign that the Romans would be victorious and their vulture mascots would soon feed on the corpses of the enemy.

This anecdote describing the earliest documented bird banding (known as ringing in England) was originally reported in the first century AD by Alexander of Myndus, whose works on animals are now lost except for fragments, and by the biographer Plutarch (AD 46–119) in his *Life of Marius*.

There were several species of vultures in Europe during the Roman period. Possibilities include the griffon vulture (*Gyps fulvus*), the cinereous or black vulture (*Aegypius monachus*), and the bearded vulture or lammergeier (*Gypaetus barbatus*). European vultures live solitary or in pairs. They are very intelligent and monogamous; they mate for life as equal companions. We can guess that the vultures banded by Marius's men were probably a male and female couple. Vultures can live forty years; their wingspans range from seven to ten feet. The legion's raptors were not described as tame pets, but it is easy to imagine the Roman soldiers setting out food near camp or while on the march to seal a bond between the army and the vultures (see chapter 9 for pet birds).

The soldiers serving Marius would have known stories about pigeons and crows that delivered letters, requests for reinforcements, and military intelligence, via messages tied to a foot or neck during sieges and between armies. One of the earliest examples occurred during the Second Punic War (218–201 BC), when a swallow was fitted with a string knotted to indicate how many days until help would arrive to aid a besieged Roman position. There were also many anecdotes about swallows, pigeons, and ravens conveying news about sports victories, by knotted threads or dyed cloth attached to their feet or dabs of paint signifying the winning team. Such accounts of temporary banding of birds for communicating messages can be traced back to the fifth century BC. In the medieval era, falconers banded their raptors to show ownership. It was reported that a peregrine falcon with the French king Henry IV's band turned up in Malta in about 1595.

As far as we know, Marius's vultures, banded more than two thousand years ago, were the first birds to carry permanent collars so that they could be identified, and their movements tracked.

Pet Birds through the Ages

THIS ARTICLE IS DEDICATED to the memory of two talking birds of my acquaintance. When I was eleven, I received a green parakeet for my birthday. We named him Bebop because we had heard that "b" and "p" sounds were the easiest for birds to replicate. Bebop could say his name, and my mother taught him to declare, "Birds can't talk!" All on his own, Bebop learned the first lines of the "Liechtensteiner Polka" ("Ja, das ist die Liechtensteiner Polka mein Schatz!"). The record was number sixteen on the US pop chart in 1957, incessantly played on the radio and our hi-fi. The other talking bird I knew was a large Amazon parrot kept in the lobby of the National Geographic building in Washington, DC. I used to stop in to visit on my lunch breaks when I worked near the White House in 1968. This parrot knew only one poignant phrase, squawked to everyone who came by: "Say something! Say Something!"

Pet birds have brought joy to the lives of famous—and infamous—people over centuries. Ancient Greek vase paintings show children holding doves and ibises as household pets in women's quarters. In Roman times, Catullus wrote erotic verses (2 and 3) playing on the affection that his lover lavished on her pet sparrow, and Ovid penned a satiric elegy for his mistress Corinna's parrot (*Amores* 2.6).

Modern poets, too, immortalized parrots in their verse. "I would not give my Paroquet for all the Doves that ever flew," wrote poet Matthew Prior in 1718. William Cowper's poem, "Parrot," of the same era, describes a typical interchange between parrot and owner: "Sweet Poll! His doting mistress cries / Sweet Poll! the mimic bird replies."

Tame bird, from Greek vase painting, 420 BC. Drawing by Michele Angel.

Bird owners of Restoration England were quite attached to their pets, as these classified advertisements in the *London Gazette* attest:

> A Little Parakeet with a red Head, a green, red and black Tail flew out of my Window on Sunday last. (1688)

> A Green Parraketto with a black and red Ring about his Neck, lost. (1675)

Readers of the *Tatler* journal (founded in 1709, sometimes called the first social media platform) came across complaints from one young man that his sweetheart paid too much attention to her parrot and ignored his endearments.

Canaries, too, had become wildly popular. A notice in a London newspaper of 1685 announced the availability of "700 canary-birds, lately of the Canaries." Some years later, curious crowds flocked to Regent Street to hear a canary with impressive speaking abilities. Besides "Kissie, kissie," accompanied by appropriate sound effects, the bird could say, "Dear sweet Titchie, Pretty little Titchie," and "Kiss me then, dear Minnie." This canary's repertoire also included the first bar of "God Save the Queen."

The East India Company imported a great many exotic birds in the seventeenth century, and several were presented to British royalty. The Duke of York, for example, received a Bengal mynah from the company in 1664. This bird, which knew many phrases and could neigh like a horse, is believed to have been the first mynah in England. A favorite London pastime in those days was strolling in fashionable St. James Park, to view the hundreds of rare and beautiful birds in the public aviary. The name Birdcage Walk, still used for that part of the park, memorializes the grand aviaries, which were filled by the East India Company during the reign of Charles II.

In 1662, Charles II married Catherine of Portugal, whose dowry included the cities of Tangier and Bombay. But instead of a rare bird from one of these tropical ports, King Charles preferred to keep his tame English starling in his bedchamber. This royal starling was later given to Samuel Pepys, the great diarist who wrote about the daily life of the British upper classes in the 1660s. Pepys exclaimed in his journal that the king's starling "doth talk and whistle finely, which I am mighty proud of." Pepys also owned some canaries, gifts from a sea captain friend. Pepys described a pleasant shopping trip for canary cages and recorded his sorrow at the death of a bird that he had kept for four years. He also admired his wife's parrot, remarking that "for talking and singing I never heard the like!"

Pepys was amazed when a friend's parrot immediately recognized Mingo, an African servant it had known from another household. Another parrot nearly put out the eye of an acquaintance who was paying a social visit in Pepys's neighborhood. Pepys's diary entry in June 1662 describes a merry dinner party with entertainment provided by a parrot that Lord Batten "hath brought from the sea." Although Pepys remarked that it "speaks very well and cries 'Poll' so pleasantly," he noticed that Lady Batten and her mother were less than enthusiastic about the bird. Perhaps its days at sea among sailors had influenced its vocabulary—a long-standing problem with talking birds.

The Reverend Mr. Wesley of Epworth tells the story of a parrot who lived in a cage hanging in Billingsgate Street. This was a neighborhood of fish markets frequented by sailors and fishermen notorious for the foul language that could be heard in the lane day and night. Naturally, this parrot developed quite a repertoire of vulgar slang. In an attempt to reform it, the owners sent the bird away to live in a genteel tearoom on another street. In less than six months, the parrot's collection of bawdy expressions had been replaced by inoffensive tearoom chatter, along the lines of "What's new?" and "Kindly bring another cup of coffee." Thus converted, the parrot was allowed to return home to Billingsgate. Alas, reported Reverend Wesley, "Within a week it had got all its wicked cursing and swearings down as pat as ever."

Another cursing parrot was featured in a poem by George Crabbe in 1809. In this tragic tale, a parrot named Poll lost his mistress's favor—and his life—when he "was heard to speak / such frightful words as tinged his lady's cheek." The poor parrot, now stuffed, was replaced by a "clipped French puppy" in the lady's affections.

A seafaring parrot named Popeye caused the same sort of stir in 1938 in New York City, where a radio contest was held to find the best talking bird. The twelve hundred contestants were to be judged on diction, vocabulary, and originality of expression. Entrants included a fruit vendor's African grey parrot who called out the names of fruits in English for his Italian-speaking owner. There was an Omaha parrot named Theodore Metcalf (after the Nebraska lieutenant governor elected in 1931) who barked, mooed, mewed, groaned, and gurgled. A ninety-year-old Boston bird recited the Lord's Prayer. Popeye, who was sponsored by the New York Seamen's Church Institute, was immediately disqualified for his salty language, despite his impressive vocabulary, good diction, and originality.

An amusing account of other talking birds with minds of their own comes from ancient Roman times. The story is told by Aelian, the natural historian who collected curious incidents to entertain his readers in the third century AD. It seems that Hanno, a famous and arrogant lion tamer from Carthage in North Africa, purchased a large number of captive songbirds and kept them in a dark room. For months he rehearsed the birds to repeat one phrase: "Hanno is a god." When the birds had learned to repeat this sentence, Hanno released them in all directions, hoping to broadcast his superiority far and wide. But the birds simply returned to their "native haunts, sang their natural song and made music as birds do, without the slightest regard for Hanno or the lessons they had been forced to learn in captivity."

Birds with spectacular speaking abilities and plumage have been favorites of royalty since the time of the Incas and Aztecs. Christopher Columbus presented a collection of colorful parrots from the New World to King Ferdinand and Queen Isabella in 1493. Several of these parrots escaped from the royal palace in Granada to the nearby forest and fields. Their brilliant feathers were much admired by the peasants, who were further amazed when the birds parroted Spanish phrases.

An African grey parrot was an honorary member of the royal court in England. At age twelve, the future king George V (1865–1936) became a cadet in the British Navy, voyaging around the world until 1892 (see chapter 31 for his sighting of the legendary ghost ship the *Flying Dutchman*). In Japan in 1881, sixteen-year-old George got a red-and-blue dragon tattoo. At Port Said, Egypt, he acquired a parrot, Charlotte, whose companionship he enjoyed the rest of his life. When he was king, meeting with the Privy Council, Charlotte perched on his shoulder and cocked her head to view state and confidential documents. Every now and then she would call out in a loud seafaring voice, "What about it?" When King George fell ill, Charlotte spent hours muttering, "Where's the Captain?" During the king's convalescence, she was the first visitor admitted. Dancing with delight, she flew to his shoulder, exclaiming, "Bless my buttons! Bless my buttons! All's well!" According to witnesses, breakfasting with the king was made hazardous by the presence of Charlotte, who was fond of digging heartily into other guests' boiled eggs. When the bird dropped crumbs on the tablecloth, King George would slide a saucer over them so the queen would not notice. A charming family photograph in the Royal Archives shows the two-year-old future queen Elizabeth with Charlotte at Balmoral Castle.

Another famous "bird of state" was a valiant French pigeon who saw action in the World War I Battle of Verdun in 1916. During horrendous fighting on the Western Front, the French commander at Fort Vaux dispatched his last homing pigeon with a desperate message requesting reinforcements. Still suffering from the effects of a recent poison gas attack, the pigeon fluttered weakly away. It managed to reach the headquarters at Verdun and deliver its message just before it died. The pigeon was awarded the Legion of Honor for its brave feat. Its stuffed form may be seen today in Les Invalides, the military museum of Paris that also contains Napoleon's tomb.

Other notable birds have been commemorated by the taxidermist's art. Houdini's pet parrot's remains are kept in the American Museum of Natural History in New York City, and Charles Dickens's pet raven is preserved in the Free Library in Philadelphia. The great French novelist Gustave Flaubert (chapter 40) kept a stuffed parrot on his desk for inspiration. Its whereabouts are unknown, but at least two dozen contenders have been curated in two municipal museums in France.

Among the illustrious dead honored at Westminster Abbey is the beloved parrot of the Duchess of Richmond, Frances Theresa Stuart, known as "La Belle Stuart" for her remarkable beauty. The parrot, companion to the duchess for forty years, died of grief a few days after her passing in 1702. The bird won a place at the side of the effigy of the duchess in the abbey, where wax figures of monarchs and royalty are displayed. La Belle Stuart's companion is believed to be the oldest stuffed parrot in existence.

Everyone has heard stories of eccentric millionaires who leave their fortunes to their pets. One such fortunate bird was Louis, a macaw born in 1863. Louis lived with the prominent spinster Victoria Wilson on her British Columbian estate until she died in 1949. It was soon learned that Miss Wilson had willed to Louis, who was then eighty-six years old, her mansion and grounds and half a million dollars. She also provided for a servant to look after Louis. In 1963, on the macaw's one hundredth birthday, *Life* magazine published a photograph of Louis with his caretaker and speculated that the wealthy heir might live to be three hundred years old. This news dismayed the already-frustrated real estate developers who hoped to establish condominiums on the Wilson estate.

Perhaps the bird with the most impressive lifestyle was the parrot that belonged to the maharajah of Nawanagar (1872–1933). This parrot, said to be 115 years old, had its own passport so that it could accompany the maharajah on diplomatic missions. While the maharajah was busy with state affairs or cricket matches, his parrot went for rides in its own chauffeured Rolls Royce.

Other birds have had to work for a living. A mynah named Raffles was the highest-paid bird in the 1940s. Raffles, who affected an Oxford accent, received five hundred dollars per radio performance. Raffles was heard on *Duffy's Tavern* and *The Fred Allen Program*, and in Hollywood Raffles met Walt Disney, the popular ventriloquist Edgar Bergen and his dummy Charlie McCarthy, and the great producer David O. Selznick. The celebrated hostess of the day Elsa Maxwell threw a party for Raffles, and Paramount Pictures signed Raffles to play opposite Dorothy Lamour in the 1944 film *Rainbow Island*. The celebrity mynah had his own dressing room with a nest of hot water bottles and a good supply of grapes. Raffles summoned stagehands by loudly imitating the sound of a buzzer.

Special birds have performed in many other motion pictures: all the *Treasure Island* movies (1934–2012), *The Birdman of Alcatraz* (1962), *The Pigeon That Took Rome* (1962), and *The Birds* (1963) are only a few examples. But one of the most unusual dramatic opportunities for avian actors must have been

Bill and Coo, released by Republic Pictures in 1948. This avian romance was set in the town of Chirpendale; it featured a cast of 273 trained birds in little human costumes and was shot on a miniature set on a tabletop. The lovebirds Bill Singer and Coo were terrorized by the Black Menace, a large crow bent on destroying Chirpendale. *Time* magazine gave the movie a good review despite its "laborious cuteness."

Novelists have included parrots as characters in their sea adventures. Long John Silver of Robert Louis Stevenson's *Treasure Island* was never without his parrot, and another well-known fictional parrot is Poll in Daniel Defoe's *Robinson Crusoe* (1719). After two years alone, shipwrecked on his desert island, the napping Crusoe is awakened by a voice calling, "Robin, Robin, Robin Crusoe! How did you come here? Where have you been? Why are you here?" The startled sailor finally realizes it is Poll, whom he had not seen since the shipwreck. The parrot is repeating Robinson Crusoe's own solitary lamentations. Parrot and sailor are overjoyed to be reunited, and Poll provides Crusoe with his only society until Man Friday appears two decades later.

In Defoe's novel, Crusoe tames two other wild parrots native to "the Brazils" and teaches them to talk, although they never equal Poll's conversational powers. Crusoe always remains grateful for Poll's company, and his tribute to his avian companion strikes a timeless chord: Poll spoke "so familiarly and so articulately that it was very pleasant to me."

Historians, anthropologists, and linguists are intrigued by the South American parrots described by the German naturalist Baron Alexander von Humboldt (1769–1859). On his expeditions, he admired the great flocks of purple, blue, and yellow macaws, and remarked that many villagers kept tame macaws that could speak. In a Maypure village on the Orinoco River Humboldt met a venerable old talking macaw. The people told him that no one could understand what it said, however, for this macaw was the only surviving speaker of a language once spoken by an extinct tribe of Indians. There were other old macaws who were the sole speakers of lost languages. In 1799, Humboldt brought one of these back to Europe and transcribed the macaw's vocabulary by phonetics, thus honoring the last words spoken by a long-lost people.

Your New Puppy in Ancient Times

IMAGINE YOU LIVE IN ANCIENT GREECE OR ROME. You are about to choose a new puppy. What should you call it? There was a science to choosing and naming a dog in classical antiquity.

First, how should you select your puppy? Which is the finest puppy in a litter? Like moderns, the ancients looked for an adventurous and friendly nature. But one test for determining the pick of the litter seems shockingly heartless today. Let the mother choose for you, advises Nemesianus, a Roman expert on hunting dogs. Take away her puppies, surround them with an oil-soaked string, and set it on fire. The mother will jump over the ring of flames and rescue each puppy, one by one, in order of their merit.

Other signs of an excellent hound, according to the ancients, were large, soft ears, instead of small and stiff ones. Upright ears are fine, but the best ears should flop over just a bit. A long, supple neck adapts well to a collar. The chest should be broad, the shoulder blades wide apart, and the hind legs slightly longer than the front, for chasing rabbits uphill. The dog's coat, whether long or short, can be any color, but the fur ought to be shiny, dense, and soft.

Training a young dog begins at twenty months, but a puppy needs a good name right away. Xenophon, the Greek historian who wrote about hounds in the fourth century BC, maintained that the best names are short, one or two syllables, so they can be called easily. No Greek hounds were saddled with monikers like Thrasybulus or Thucydides! Xenophon

Pet dog portrait, Greek pyxis, fourth century BC, Walters Art Museum, 48.82.

maintained that the meaning of the name was also important for the morale of both master and dog: names that express speed, courage, strength, appearance, and other qualities were favored. Xenophon named his favorite dog Horme (Eager).

Argos was the name of the faithful dog of the Greek hero Odysseus. Atalanta, the famous huntress of Greek myth, called her dog Aura (Breeze). An ancient Greek vase painting of 560 BC shows Atalanta and other heroes and their hunting hounds killing the terrible Calydonian Boar. Seven dogs' names are inscribed on the vase, some of which violate Xenophon's brevity rule: Hormenos (Impulse), Methepon (Pursuer), Egertes (Vigilant), Korax (Raven), Marpsas (Seizer, Snatcher), Labros (Fierce), and Eubolous (Shooter).

The Roman poet Ovid gives us the Greek names of the thirty-six dogs that belonged to Actaeon, the unlucky hunter of Greek myth who was torn apart by his pack. The names include Tigris (after the river), Laelaps (Storm), Aello (Whirlwind), and Arcas (Bear). The Roman writers Pollux and Columella listed several canine names, but by far the longest list of suitable names for ancient Greek dogs—forty-six in all—was compiled by the dog whisperer Xenophon. Popular names for dogs in antiquity, translated by earlier commentators from Greek, include Lurcher, Whitey, Blackie, Tawny, Blue, Blossom, Keeper, Fencer, Butcher, Spoiler, Hasty, Hurry, Stubborn, Yelp, Tracker, Dash, Happy, Jolly, Trooper, Rockdove, Growler, Fury, Riot, Lance, Pell-Mell, Plucky, Killer, Crafty, Swift, and Dagger.

Notably, the names of ancient Mesopotamian dogs were multisyllabic mouthfuls. A pack of five small but lovingly detailed clay figurines of mastiffs in the British Museum, discovered in the Neo-Assyrian palace at Nineveh, was made in about 650 BC. Each has its name inscribed in cuneiform. They were called "Expeller of evil" (*mušēṣu lemnūti*); "Catcher of the enemy" (*kāšid ayyāb*); "Don't think, bite!" (*ē tamtallik epuš pāka*); "Biter of his foe!" (*munaššiku gārîšu*); and "Loud is his bark!" (*dan rigiššu*).

Alexander the Great honored his faithful dog Peritas by naming a city after him. Greek and Roman writers reminded their readers to praise their canine companions. Arrian, a biographer of Alexander the Great who also wrote a treatise on hunting, says one should pat one's dog, caress its head, pulling gently on the ears, and speak its name along with a hearty word or two—"Well done!" "Good girl!"—by way of encouragement. After all, remarks Arrian, "dogs enjoy being praised, just as noble men do."

Now, what should you feed your new companion?

Most ordinary pups in antiquity would get barley bread softened with cow's milk or whey. But more valuable hunting puppies would enjoy their bread soaked in sheep's or goat's milk. You might add a little blood from the animal you expect your puppy to track and kill when it grows up.

Then, at dinner with your family, you might scoop a few soft chunks of bread from the center of a loaf to wipe grease or oil from your fingers—and toss those chunks to your dog. This could be supplemented with bones and other table scraps, perhaps even a basin of meat broth. After an animal sacrifice or a fancy banquet, you could make a special treat: a lump of ox liver dredged in barley meal and roasted in the coals. Naturally, as a matter of professional courtesy, you would certainly share any rabbits, stags, or boars with your faithful hunting partners.

Was such a diet nutritious? The idea that dogs' principal sustenance must consist of only red, raw meat is a popular misconception. In the wild, canines hunt plant- and grain-eating animals. At the kill, wolves and wild dogs often first devour the stomach filled with predigested grass and cereals, and then the organs, before turning to the flesh. They often gnaw the bones, thus assuring a balanced meal with vitamins and minerals. That Greek dogs thrived on their grain-and-meat diet is confirmed by Aristotle (b. 384 BC). He remarked that a hardworking Laconian hound usually lived to be ten or twelve years old, and that other breeds reached the age of fourteen or fifteen. Today's average fifty-pound dog can expect the same life span as Laconian hounds.

Should your dog suffer from worms, wheat awns (whiskers) are recommended. But a more aggressive treatment would be *Artemesia*, wormwood, a natural antihelmintic to expel parasitic worms. And what if your neighbors complain that your hound keeps them awake at night? Why, you resort to the ancient Greek cure for excessive barking and conceal a live frog in a lump of his or her food.

Weasels in Classical Myth and History

Before the housecat, there was the weasel. No stranger to Athenians in classical antiquity, this fierce little mouser was also the subject of fable and myth. Aristotle, Aristophanes, and Aesop immortalized the fascinating ferret.

IN THE ATHENIAN AGORA (the ancient marketplace below the Acropolis) in the fifth century BC, the peddler of household goods called out his wares: "I've got pennyroyal and dittany, fans and lantern wicks! Ducklings and goslings, delicious eels fresh from Lake Copais! Whisk brooms, talking birds, partridges, weasels! . . ." Weasels? Why would a Greek housewife want to buy a weasel? Superstitious people considered it bad luck to have a *nifitsa* or *kounavi* cross their path, and everyone knew that male polecats had a smell that could knock your sandals off.

But weasels are mousers par excellence, and house cats were very rare in classical Greece. Until late Roman times it was forbidden to export cats from Egypt, where they were considered sacred animals. From literature, history, and art we know that the ferret—the domesticated weasel or polecat—was a common pet for households and farms until the "wave-tail" (*ailouros*, cat) later eclipsed it in popularity.

Ferrets earned their keep by decimating the hordes of moles, mice, and rats that nibbled away grain and other food supplies. The naturalist Aelian (third century AD) noted that hens, roosters, and mice were instinctively terrified by the peculiar chattering sound made by a weasel. Ferrets (whose name means "wily one" in Greek, and "little thief" in Latin) occasionally overstepped their duties and stole poultry and eggs for themselves. Farmers kept fowl in pens to discourage such ferret moonlighting. One ancient writer blamed the demise of his son's three pet goldfinches on the household ferret. Perhaps sympathetic magic accounted for the notion that thieves could sneak up on guard dogs if they approached holding forth the tail of a noxious-smelling "little thief."

Aristotle described the house ferret this way: it was about the size of a Maltese dog, with thick fur, a white belly, an elongated body, and short legs. The ferret was just like the weasel "in craftiness of its manners, but could become very mild and tame." Aristotle cautioned that the ferret "delights in honey and steals from beehives," and noted that "ferrets will also catch birds."

Aristophanes, whose plays are treasuries of details about Athenian households of the fifth century BC, refers often to ferrets. In his comedies, people purchased ferrets in the marketplace, and these pets did catch mice but they also stole meat at night. Several of his jokes allude to the well-known fact that the males (like their North American cousins, the skunks) release a terrible stench when alarmed.

Wild weasels were distrusted in antiquity, and even the household ferret's reputation was dubious—unflattering connotations of "weasel" and "ferret" are still apparent in our modern figures of speech. Not as faithful or affectionate as a dog (already "man's best friend" in antiquity), the ferret was considered at best a mischief-maker with insatiable curiosity; at worst, its name was synonymous with relentless bloodthirstiness.

Certainly this pet was less amenable to "persuasion" than traditional domestic animals like the dog and horse. As a ferret owner I can confirm the ancient reports that these sinuous little carnivores have sharp teeth and claws, a distinctive, happy-sounding chatter, a notorious sweet tooth for honey and ice cream, a compulsion to "steal" things, a fetish for investigating any dark nook, a rambunctious temperament, and none of the "restraint or remorse" we expect of other pets (see chapter 12). On the other hand, ferrets appeal to people who find dogs too servile and cats too snobbish—the independent little ferret never outgrows its boisterous playfulness.

Weasels and ferrets found a niche very early in Greek folklore. The notoriously misogynistic poet Simonides of Samos (seventh century BC) wrote a disagreeable verse comparing women's personality types to various animals. One of the worst was the ferret-woman, a "miserable wretched creature, neither beautiful nor desirable" yet filled with lust and prone to thievery. One had to be vigilant lest she even abscond with unburned parts of animal sacrifices!

Several of Aesop's fables feature weasels. One, "The Battle of the Weasels and Mice," became the subject of popular tavern paintings. In this tale, and army of weasels routs a panicked crowd of mice whose ostentatiously decorated generals become stuck in the narrow mouse holes. In another fable, an old weasel no longer able to chase agile mice tricks them by "rolling in flour and throwing herself carelessly in a dark corner." After the weasel has devoured several young mice who scamper near the "heap of flour," an elderly but wise mouse, veteran of many mousetraps and predators, happens by. Perceiving the ruse, he calls out, "I wish you luck—just as sincerely as I believe that you are a pile of flour!"

The story of the weasel-bride is another very old legend. Aphrodite, the goddess of love, takes pity on a female weasel who has fallen in love with a handsome young man. Venus changes her into a beautiful girl, and the young man's heart is captured. At the wedding feast, however, his bride's true nature is revealed when a mouse skitters across the floor. His beloved bride leaps from the marriage couch to pursue it! Modern Greek folklore echoes part of this ancient story. To see a weasel near the house of a woman about to be wed is a bad omen because it is said that the *nifitsa* ("little bride") was once a young woman who was about to marry but "somehow was robbed of her happiness" and transformed into a weasel. Now the jealous little creature is believed to destroy wedding dresses unless honey and sweets (called "the necessary spoonfuls") are set out for her before the wedding and songs are sung to appease the disappointed "little weasel bride."

In ancient Greek myth, Heracles set up an altar to honor a weasel-woman of Thebes, Galinthias, who had originally been a fair-haired friend of his mother, Alcmene. Hera had attempted to prevent the birth of Heracles by means of a magic spell, but Galinthias thwarted the hex by tricking the goddess into thinking that Alcmene had already given birth to Zeus's son. The incensed goddess changed the golden-haired Galinthias into a weasel. Later, Hecate, goddess of witchcraft, invited Galinthias to become her assistant. The grateful Alcmene claimed that she felt comforted whenever she glimpsed her friend around her house in Thebes, "as active and energetic as ever," and still blonde! Domestic ferrets often have light-colored fur. One writer in the Middle Ages described the color of tame ferrets' fur as "wool stained with urine."

The Athenians mocked the Thebans for believing this version of Galinthias's fate. In Athens, they told a different story. In their version, Galinthias was a Theban harlot who had been turned into a weasel by the witch Hecate because of her unbridled lust. The Athenians insisted that the weasel had simply frightened Alcmene into labor by suddenly dashing across the floor. The Greek travel writer Pausanias visited Thebes in the second century BC and admired a carved stone relief of the witches sent by Hera to delay the delivery. He was also shown the chamber where Alcmene gave birth to Heracles, which had become a tourist attraction (see chapter 41).

Ever since Hecate invited Galinthias to be her assistant, weasels have been associated with witches and shape-shifting, the same role that cats later came to play in the Middle Ages. Some ancient Greek horror stories describe sorceresses who could transform themselves into weasels and engage in dire activities, such as biting off the ears and noses of sleeping men or corpses.

In ancient Athens, an assembly had to be canceled if a weasel was spotted on the Pnyx, where citizens gathered to make laws. And it was bad luck for a weasel to cross one's path—though one could break the jinx by throwing three pebbles across the road. In Macedonia, on the other hand, it was considered a good omen to see a weasel, although Macedonians did blame the *nifitsa* for destroying clothing stored in closets. Some people believed that if they got a headache after washing their hair, it meant that a weasel had glanced into the basin of water.

Weasels in Greek myth were usually depicted as female and were often connected with marriage, birth, and magic spells having to do with sex. The Roman naturalist Aelian pointed out that the Thebans worshipped the weasel because it had helped Alcmene in labor. But Aelian had also heard that the weasel was once a human sorceress who was punished for her "extreme sexual desires." Aelian considered the slender predator a "malicious" animal and claimed that a magical weasel amulet could prevent conception or break up a friendship.

Aelian also reported that the chattering of weasels was supposed to predict a rainstorm, and if mice and weasels were seen leaving a house or a village together, it presaged certain disaster. This latter phenomenon was observed in 373 BC just before an earthquake and tsunami devastated the town of Helike on the Gulf of Corinth. Weasels, along with their enemies, snakes, and mice, and accompanied by beetles and centipedes, were seen fleeing on the road out of town before the quake struck.

Several ancient writers mention weasels' antipathy for snakes. One of Aesop's fables tells of a tame ferret fighting a snake that invaded its household—but the battle abruptly ends when they both spot a mouse. Aesop's moral is that even political adversaries will quit arguing to destroy a weaker common enemy. Aelian calls both the snake and the weasel "evil creatures," but he declares that the weasel is bolder, probably because it chews rue before attacking snakes, which detest that bitter herb.

Besides the polecat and ferret, the weasel's relatives include the ermine (winter weasel), marten, sable, badger, fisher, mongoose, mink, and wolverine. Today the small brown-and-white weasel in Greece is called *nifitsa*, and the larger pine marten is known as the *kounavi*. I can report that both have been spotted in the yard of a friend who lives in Euboea. In antiquity, several species of polecat were recognized: the North African/Spanish, the Steppe, and the European polecats, along with the smaller and lighter-colored domesticated ferret.

In ancient Greece, the pelts of the wild *Mustela* and martens were prized, and vase painters used ferret and sable fur brushes. The use of ferrets to hunt rabbits spread from North Africa to the Mediterranean in antiquity. The naturalist Pliny the Elder reported that in the first century AD, the residents of the Balearic Islands sent a desperate request for military aid to the Roman emperor Augustus because millions of rabbits were overrunning the island. The practical-minded emperor quickly dispatched a troop of Roman legionnaires armed with ferrets on leashes.

By medieval times, weasels were credited with the ability to kill evil Basilisks, and they were said to know how to use a magical life-restoring herb, rue, with which they could overcome their enemy the snake. The weasel in its winter coat—the ermine—became a symbol of purity and royalty in European heraldry.

Archaeological excavations have turned up some remains of members of the weasel family at ancient Greek sites. Prehistoric ancestors of *Mustela* have been excavated in the fossil beds of Pikermi, on the road to Marathon (see chapter 13). A ferret skull was found at the Early Bronze Age site (occupied in about 2750 BC) of Thermi on Lesbos, and weasel bones were discovered at sites in Anatolia settled by Greeks. It is

Domesticated weasels, from Greek vase paintings, fifth century BC. Drawings by Adrienne Mayor.

only recently that zooarchaeologists have begun to collect and identify small bones found in ancient domestic sites. Further study is needed to determine whether such remains are of domesticated or wild animals.

Depictions of ferrets in ancient art are fairly rare compared to portrayals of other animals. A charming red-figure vase by the Eucharides Painter depicts a tame weasel climbing up a knobby staff held by a youth. Another vase, by the Euphronios Painter (about 500 BC), shows a seated man playing with a ferret. A red-figure bowl (from Attica, fifth century BC) has a comic household scene: a man shakes a stick at a small ferret pouncing at a candlestick. Some Etruscan wall paintings done in the Greek red-figure style (fifth century BC) show a marten stalking some birds, and two ferrets apparently ignoring a rabbit and birds.

The dog may have been humans' best friend in ancient Greece, and cats later became our other favorite companion. The so-called Dog and Cat Painter immortalized these two pets in vase paintings, and many of their names have been preserved. One hunting hound was even named "Weasel" (see chapter 10 for other dogs' names). But before the widespread availability of cats, the feisty little ferret won a place in many hearts as it worked and played in Greek homes. A tiny silver charm made in the fourth century BC, less than an inch high, must have been made by someone who knew ferrets well. The lovingly detailed little trinket shows a *nifitsa* in a typically alert pose. I like to imagine that the amulet represented the owner's beloved pet polecat and brought luck.

CHAPTER 12

Living the Modern Ferret Lifestyle

DENISE CAME TO LIVE WITH US when we moved from Athens, Greece, to Montana in the summer of 1980. Born in the stable of the renowned classical guitarist Christopher Parkening, Denise turned up for sale (twenty dollars) at the Bozeman Farmer's Market. Josh and I had never seen a little ferret kit before. We were enchanted by the tiny black-masked creature's habit of hopping sideways while chattering happily, and awed by her ability to slip under doors like a furry snake. Ferrets were virtually unknown in American households at that time, and I think Josh and I were among the first to have a ferret as a house pet. We named her Denise, after the 1963 song by Randy and the Rainbows, covered in 1978 as "Denis" by the New Wave band Blondie, and crooned by Deborah Harry: "Denis, Denis / Oh Denis, scooby do / I'm in love with you."

Josh built a spacious wooden cage for her, with a sleeping loft and a beefcake photo of Arnold Schwarzenegger in his 1970s pumping-iron phase. Denise lovingly clawed the future governor's pinup picture to shreds. (Schwarzenegger would later costar with a ferret in the 1990 movie *Kindergarten Cop*.) For several hours each day, we let Denise scamper around the house, exploring, and sometimes leaving a few modest

Portrait of Denise. Drawing by Adrienne Mayor.

poop pellets in corners. We learned that close supervision was required: her slinky body and short legs could wriggle through knotholes in walls and incredibly small openings around pipes and wires, allowing her access to mysterious—and otherwise inaccessible—passageways of the house.

In Montana, we became avid fly fisherpeople, so Denise feasted on raw trout hearts fresh from the Yellowstone River. Her favorite treat was honey, licked from a spoon, eyes closed in ecstasy. Ferrets have a sweet tooth, a trait that proved indispensable in coaxing Denise out from behind furniture and under sinks when it was time to return to her cage. Honey also allowed manicures; just a tiny dab on her tummy distracted her long enough for us to clip all twenty wolverine-sharp claws. Before we hit upon this method, Josh and I often sported bandaged fingers. Many years later, we learned that sweets are not good for ferrets, being hard to digest.

Ferrets' sharp teeth are much larger than those of domestic cats. A ferret's vise-like grip is notorious, and, like many wild ferrets, Denise tended to bite when in doubt. Later, after owning four ferrets, we finally discovered the secret of getting a biting ferret to release its jaws. Instinctively pulling away only tightens the grip, so one must—against all reason—push one's hand even farther into the razor-toothed maw to make the ferret let go. Moreover, unlike cats, which can play with their claws pulled in, ferrets are more like tiny grizzly bears, with wicked, nonretractable claws. Just the thing for burrowing after wild rabbits in warrens, but they do need trimming for playing with humans.

Like all ferrets, after a burst of manic energy—chirping in the distinctive happy chatter of polecats and stoats and performing wild dances of pure joy—Denise tended to take sudden naps, invariably totally flat, usually under a carpet. On several occasions when Denise was young, Josh and I were terrified that she had perished in her sleep, but all ferrets sleep extremely soundly, going dead limp, mimicking a coma-like state. When they finally do emerge from sleep, they come back to life very slowly, yawning, blinking, stretching, and lolling about until fully alert. This bipolar feature of activity/ deep sleep posed a great danger—we learned to look carefully wherever we stepped when she was out and about.

Until the mid-1990s, most US veterinarians were clueless about ferret care. Were ferrets canine or feline? Our Montana vet decided to give Denise all the routine shots for both cats and dogs, just to be safe. Should we feed her dog food or cat food? Denise preferred feline kibble, supplemented by raw beef and trout.

The first time that young Denise went into heat, she became so weak she nearly died. At that time, no one understood that puberty could be fatal for female ferrets. Her puzzled vet said he could only recommend TLC. So we placed Denise on a heating pad and hand-fed her simple gruel and water for ten days. To our great relief, she survived.

In the wild, ferrets have a short life span, three or four years. Fighting males defending territory often inflict fatal wounds on each other, and even the mating behavior of males and females is remarkably violent. Nature's orders are shockingly cruel for jills (female ferrets): "Mate or die!" A few years later, Denise's doctor learned that jills in heat who fail to mate may not survive the rigors of long-term, unsatisfied estrus. Since we did not plan on breeding ferrets, we opted to have Denise spayed, another learning experience for her vet. No one knew how long she would live in domesticity.

In the 1980s, second-home Californians and New Agers had not yet discovered unspoiled Montana. Friends and family in other states were appalled that in our new home in the far Rockies we were cosseting such a strange wild animal. Many people assumed that Denise was a species of large rat, while others worried that we lived with a treacherous weasel, feared for vicious sneak attacks.

Ferrets are not rodents but European polecats, in the mustelid family. Mustelids include weasels, minks, fisher cats, pine martens, badgers, and wolverines: a family of fierce, extremely strong for their size, determined alpha predators that hunt prey much larger than themselves. Oh, and mustelids do have a distinctive odor—Denise's two-tone black-and-tan fur gave off a strong, musky-sweet scent. Like their cousins the skunks, both male and female ferrets release a powerful spray when startled or angry, though later we were made aware that the male version is about ten times more eye-watering than the female.

Sadly, ferrets do have a vicious reputation in folklore and literature, a result of their use in rabbit hunting in the British Isles, where ferrets were deliberately kept untamed by owners and not coddled as pets. Many literary friends reminded us of the murderous fictional ferret named Shredni Vashtar in the horror story of the same name by the witty and macabre Edwardian writer Saki. Others sent us descriptions of an obscure British endurance sport called "ferret-legging," in which pub patrons bet on how long contestants can tolerate a ferret scrabbling curiously inside a pair of belted, baggy woolen trousers with tight cuffs.

To counter our friends' and relatives' terror and to reveal the charms of our beloved Denise, we typed and mailed out an irregular series of newsletters titled "Denise's Diary," recounting her adventures and musings on life. Decades before the Internet and the Blogosphere, Denise was the first Ferret Blogger. Well traveled, she crisscrossed the country with us several times. In Minnesota, she learned to swim in my mother's goldfish pond, and she escaped from a flimsy cardboard enclosure to surprise my father in the bathroom at midnight. In North Carolina, Denise was involved in setting off a false fire alarm, as we tried to sneak her into a motel that frowned on pets of any kind. She lived in an outdoor cage filled with straw for a year as an illegal alien in New Hampshire (ferrets were banned by law in that state). In New Hampshire, Denise tasted maple syrup, licked from the finger of our three-year-old niece Katy. Denise also accompanied us to Ann Arbor, Michigan, for a year. She was allowed to dwell in our apartment only because the landlady was under the false impression that we owned a "small animal something like a hamster."

Denise enjoyed an adventure-filled life of six years, double the span of her wild relatives. By the time she passed away in 1986, ferrets were just beginning to enter American popular culture. We fancy that Denise's widely disseminated "Diary" played some small part in making ferrets more acceptable. In 1986, ferrets were declared "Pet of the Year" on the front page of the *Wall Street Journal*. About a decade later, celebrities like Madonna and Paris Hilton were joining the fad for ferrets as fashion accessories. Paris Hilton's first ferret (2005) was named Cinderella; her two ferrets Dolce and Gabbana were confiscated by the state of California.

In 1988, missing Denise's lively, fierce presence, we found Spike, a male ferret with a gentle personality so different from Denise's. White, fluffy, innocent-faced ferrets like Spike were often more "domesticated"—they made eye contact and rarely nipped. Ferrets like Denise, with black tails and legs, slender and sleek physiques, pointed noses, and raccoon-like black masks, more closely resembled their wild relatives, the nearly extinct black-footed ferret of the high prairies. Along with being sneakier and more feral in behavior, it's fair to say that Denise and her kind also seemed more intelligent than their fluffy white cousins.

Like all ferrets, Spike was a thief, stealing anything he could drag with his powerful little jaws. He was attracted to houseguests' wallets, scattering credit cards and cash under beds and dressers. And he often horrified visitors who witnessed him scuttling backward into the dark recess under the sofa with his favorite toy: a naked Barbie doll.

Spike accompanied us when we moved to Princeton, New Jersey, in 1990. One day, our good friends Marcia and Ronna brought their very proper mother, visiting from Montreal, to tea. Mrs. M—well aware of the nefarious literary reputation of ferrets—was taken aback to find Shredni Vashtar's cousin cavorting on the carpet next to the coffee table. Before we could stop him, Spike ran up her white linen trouser leg. Luckily, before he reached her knee, he was awkwardly extricated without snagging flesh or fabric. Profuse apologies were sincerely proffered. Mrs. M was quite gracious about this unannounced bout of ferret-legging, but she left the tea party as soon as good manners allowed.

Known for his unusually sweet disposition, Spike was also distinguished by his extra stinkiness. As noted, ferrets often release their musk glands when threatened or taken by surprise. Spike was especially sensitive. He was routinely startled upon simply awakening from an ordinary nap. Apparently, momentary disorientation caused him to immediately let loose a spray of overpowering polecat perfume, a stench especially intense in the close quarters of our car when we drove across the country between Montana and New Jersey. Rolling down the windows was the only recourse, even in winter. We take this opportunity to apologize to the countless toll-takers on the Pennsylvania, Ohio, Indiana, and Illinois Turnpikes who recoiled from the skunky blast suddenly emanating from an otherwise normal-appearing car.

In 1993, Spike was featured in *Life Blood*, a best-selling mystery novel by the late writer Caroline Champlin, who had met him on many occasions in Princeton. In the novel, the fictional Spike helps a young boy to solve a murder in the Cotswolds.

The real Spike was utterly fearless, leaping from high places with all four short paws splayed, and he had a naïve, unbounded curiosity. We once searched for him for hours, finally detecting the faint sounds of his attempts to burrow out through a wall in the basement behind the laundry basket next to the washing machine. He had slid down the space *behind* an old-fashioned laundry chute on the first floor and landed in a sealed-off space in the basement. He had to be rescued through careful carpentry, because while Josh drilled and sawed an opening in the wall big enough for his escape, Spike was also trying to help enlarge the hole from the other side. As soon as he was released from the trap, the intrepid creature bounded up the stairs and attempted to slide down the same hatch to the basement again.

Spike had other, more sensual pleasures. On the long road trips between our new home in Princeton, where Josh taught Ancient Greek History, and our old place in Montana each summer, we chose lodgings that accepted pets. Spike was enamored of 1950s-era mom-and-pop motels equipped with shag carpets and those vintage Magic Fingers vibrating beds. I will never forget the sight of a fluffy white ball of fur chattering and skittering like a mad thing across the shaggy rug and bouncing on the vibrating chenille bedspread. Wherever we traveled together, Spike's unexpected habit of licking the hands of friends and strangers alike endeared him to everyone who met him.

The next year, we went abroad and were compelled to leave Spike in the care of our house sitter, a serious Brahmin philosopher from India, Professor Arindam C. We hoped that Spike's delightful personality and vague physical resemblance to a mongoose might facilitate their relationship. Professor C assured us that he and his charge got along famously.

Denise and Spike inspired me to delve into the history of ferrets, weasels, polecats, and ermines. I learned that domestic ferrets were featured in ancient Greek myths and comedies and depicted at play on Greek vase paintings and Roman frescoes. Long before cats became available outside of Egypt (as sacred animals, cats were not permitted to be exported), Greeks and Romans prized ferrets as mousers and pets. My article originally titled "Grecian Weasels" (chapter 11), tracing the ancient history of ferret domestication and published in Athens, was dedicated to Spike and Denise. Josh and I admired Leonardo da Vinci's portrait of a girl with her tame "ermine," and learned that ferrets were pets in the Middle Ages and Renaissance. Fitches—ferrets—were raised for their fur and for rabbit hunting in nineteenth-century America (as the many towns named "Fitchburg" attest).

Yet in the United States ferrets are outlawed in Manhattan, California, New Hampshire, and other locales, labeled as "dangerous, undomesticated wildlife." In 1999, we heard Rudy Giuliani, then mayor of New York City, deliver his infamous "ferret rant" on the radio, comparing ferrets to "wild tigers," and advising psychiatric interventions for "crazy weasel-lovers." Ferret owners responded with ferret rallies in Central Park, and *Modern Ferret: The Ferret Lifestyle Magazine*, founded in New York in 1995, joined the protest. We were among the first subscribers to *Modern Ferret*, named one of the fifty most notable magazine launches of 1995. The *Los Angeles Times* wrote, "*Modern Ferret* is must reading for the dedicated owner"; *Entrepreneur*'s Business Start-Ups called it "the hip and humorous bimonthly which has been dubbed the *Rolling Stone* of pet magazines."

Spike passed away at age eight. We buried him in our backyard in Bozeman, Montana, his birthplace. Back in Princeton, missing Spike, in 1996 we decided to double the fun with twin ferret kits. We named the sisters Blanche and Stella. They loved to chase each other, chuckling wildly, creating a maze of tunnels underneath our Turkish carpets. The twins had wildly different personalities: Blanche, fluffy, white, and chubby like Spike, also possessed his trusting, innocent personality. Her sister, lean, black-masked Stella, was more feral, like Denise. Stella's first impulse was to bite and never let go. Stella could be vindictive, too, especially when we retrieved the TV remotes that she stole and hid under the couch. For revenge, she would sneak up behind whoever had grabbed her treasure and sink her sharp incisors into an ankle. Yet as we gazed at Stella and Blanche sleeping cozily together in their little blue-striped hammock, we knew we loved them equally.

Like Spike, Stella and Blanche also traveled by car back and forth between Montana and Princeton each summer. Though Magic Fingers vibrating beds had by now disappeared from motels, the twins enjoyed squirming up inside the box springs of mattresses, and there they remained until our departures—delayed until a dab of honey could be procured.

During our time in Princeton, we often entertained with dinners for eight. Sometimes, after dessert, guests, in devil-may-care moods or out of genuine curiosity, would ask to meet Stella and Blanche. We were reluctant, since an encounter between people who have indulged in wine and a pair of exuberant, wriggling ferrets can create a dynamic difficult to control but all too easy to predict. Sometimes we would comply, however, and privileged guests were treated to the charming spectacle—and true peril—of excited, clumsy little furry creatures frolicking up and down the table among the wine goblets, candlesticks, silverware, and fruit and cheese rinds. Blanche never nipped, but Stella always did. We warned our guests not to extend fingers or try to pet Stella—but it was not easy to tell the twins apart by candlelight. Sometimes the evening ended calmly, but other times chaos threatened, and Josh would scoop up the ferrets and put them away. Then Band-Aids—considered badges of honor by colleagues and graduate students—were dispensed, as Blanche and Stella snuggled peacefully into their hammock.

Stella lived to the ripe old age of nine and a half, and her companion Blanche died a month later. They are recalled fondly by all who were lucky enough to attend their legendary dinner parties in staid old Princeton.

After two decades of living the twentieth-century "modern ferret lifestyle" with Denise, Spike, Stella, and Blanche, for the new millennium we welcomed a different sort of exotic creature into our lives. We found our Bengal kitten named Bindi, with soft, spotted fur like the Asian Leopard Cats he descended from, on a ranch in Montana, the home of two wildlife biologists. They had weaned Bindi and his siblings from their mother's milk to raw meat from their own bison herd. Our beloved Bindi ("spot" or "dot" in Hindi) was a piece of work, filling our lives with joyful aggravation in a hundred different ways. But that's another story.

Colossal Fossils
of Greece

IN 1838 A BAVARIAN SOLDIER serving the German king Otto of Greece discovered a skull and some weathered bones in a gulley in the Megalorhevma, a valley near Pikermi, northeast of Athens. The skull appeared to be of human shape and size, but the soldier was most impressed with the "diamonds" he saw sparkling in the crevices of the bones. Back in Bavaria on furlough, the soldier could not resist boasting in taverns about the exotic treasure he had brought home from Greece. News of the man's good fortune reached the authorities—the soldier was arrested and the pilfered "human" bones confiscated.

The German paleontologist Andreas Wagner (b. 1797) examined the "diamond-encrusted" bones and was able to exonerate the soldier. The gems turned out to be mere calcite crystals, which sometimes form on mineralized fossils. Moreover, to Wagner's amazement, the skull belonged not to a man but to a Late Tertiary period ape. Until then it had been believed that men and apes had appeared together and in a more recent geological age. *Mesopithecus pentelicus*, or the Pikermi Ape as the specimen came to be called, revealed the error of this assumption and stimulated a search for a transitional primate link between monkeys and *Homo sapiens*.

Some three years earlier the British historian George Finlay had come across some fossil bones while looking for antiquities in the same Pikermi ravine. But the Bavarian soldier's discovery in 1838 set off a rush to unearth more paleontological finds in the region. Pikermi became a Mecca for flocks of British, French, Greek, German, Swiss, and Austrian fossil

The Pikermi Skull. Drawing by Adrienne Mayor.

collectors, who, says one author, "made the pleasant pilgrimage to Attica year after year" (see also chapter 42). The red limonite banks of the ravine proved to be a real treasure trove of prehistoric mammal remains from the geological period of 66 to 2.6 million years ago, whose special scientific significance was to help clarify climatic and geographical influences on animal migration patterns in an age long before humans inhabited the Mediterranean area.

From the mass grave of extinct animals that roamed Attica between five and ten million years ago came the remains of apes, ostriches, great bears, lions, hyenas, saber-toothed tigers, the giant ancestors of elephants, giraffes, rhinoceroses, and porcupines, and the distant relatives of zebras, horses, goats, and antelope. By the mid-nineteenth century, scientists, among them Jean Albert Gaudry, Édouard Lartet, Wilhelm Dames, Melchior Neumayr, Arthur Smith Woodward, Hercules Mitsopoulos, and Theodore Skouphos, were able to piece together a picture of Miocene and Pliocene Greece, which began as forest and swamplands and was slowly transformed by climatic change into grasslands similar to the savannas of Africa today.

Some of the creatures found at Pikermi were of bizarre appearance and bear no resemblance to animals living today. Ancylotherium, for example, a type of chalicothere whose name means "beast with hooked claws" in Greek, was a huge and grotesque herbivore with feet that confounded scientists of the day. Unlike modern hoofed herbivores, this chalicothere was equipped with enormous wickedly curved claws, which defied the accepted dictum that grass-eaters must have hooves.

Another animal, Dinotherium, was the second-largest mammal that ever existed. Standing over fifteen feet tall, it carried tremendous lower tusks that arched down and back rather than up and forward like those of other elephant types. Paleontologists were at a loss to classify this strange beast—it was variously assigned to the hippopotamus, walrus, tapir, giant sloth, and sea cow families until it was at last recognized as a specialized swamp elephant, adept at using its backward tusks as a kind of hoe. Dinotheres were apparently the first victims in the Pikermi mass grave. As their favorite swamps of the Miocene era gradually dwindled to a few oases in the drier grasslands typical of the Pliocene and early Pleistocene, they became extinct owing to overspecialization, giving way to the so-called Pikermi fauna, more like that of central Africa.

In the Pliocene epoch, great rolling plains extended from Greece all the way to India. The vast cemetery of prehistoric mammals at Pikermi provided nineteenth-century scientists with enough evidence to advance the bold theory that, before the Mediterranean Sea appeared, there had once been a land connection between Asia and Africa, and that Greece was an important crossroads in the mass migrations of many animal groups across southern Europe. Many of the characteristic savanna animals, such as antelope and giraffes, were originally from southern Europe and Asia, and migrated to Africa by way of Greece. Others, like the elephant and perhaps anthropoid apes, originated in Africa and traveled to Asia. One strong connection between Greek and African fauna was established by the Helladotherium ("Greek animal"), a common fossil in the Pikermi digs. This strange cryptid creature puzzled scientists for fifty years; it appeared to be an improbable combination of a zebra, an antelope, and a giraffe. Remarkably, in 1901 a smaller relative of the Helladotherium, a "living fossil" called the okapi, was discovered alive and thriving in central Africa.

The reason for the demise of so many different animals at the Pikermi site remains a mystery. Several scientists maintain that heavy rains and floods over the course of time washed the bones of innumerable animals into the gorge. Some blame a great drought; others blame wildfires. A few hold that saber-toothed tigers, lions, and other carnivores habitually carried their prey to that particular valley, leaving an accumulation of bones to be found millions of years later.

Although the Pikermi remains were the first to attract scientific attention, other parts of Greece proved equally fossiliferous. In 1872 excavations by Charles I. Forsyth Major on the island of Samos produced a monstrous mammal skull belonging to Samotherium, a large but apparently harmless giraffe-type beast that once grazed the wooded plains now occupied by the Aegean Sea. Continued digging brought up the remains of double-horned rhinos, mastodons, hyenas, horse and aardvark relatives, and other Miocene-Pliocene fauna. According to paleontologists at the University of Athens, the fossil beds of Samos may have been watering holes in prehistoric times. A severe drought might have finished off the animals.

The soft lignite or peat deposits around Megalopolis in the Peloponnese abound in darkened fossil bones of mastodons and other Pleistocene megafauna of the Ice Age. Another area of paleontological interest is Crete. There in the early 1900s Miss Dorothea Bate of the British Museum found prehistoric elephant, wildcat, and other mammal fossils. Euboea, Naxos, Delos, Karpathos, Rhodes, Chios, Kythera, and Cos have also yielded fossils of extinct animals of past ages.

Toward the very end of the Pliocene period, perhaps during some of the last great animal migrations and thousands of years before the last great ice sheets retreated from Europe, humans appeared in Greece. The oldest entire human skeleton found so far in Greece came from the Franchthi Cave in southern Greece, excavated in the 1960s and '70s. Evidence of human occupation beginning in 20,000 BC shows that the first residents of the cave were Paleolithic hunters of wild goats, asses, deer, and bison. No longer totally at the mercy of geologic and climatic change, the adaptable newcomers took the first steps on the road to classical, Byzantine, and modern Greek civilization, perhaps spinning tales along the way about the strange giant creatures of old, whose bones could then and now be discovered in the soil of Greece.

Hunting Griffins

AN IMAGINARY LETTER TO A PALEONTOLOGIST

Jack Horner   January 1989
Curator, Museum of the Rockies
Bozeman, Montana

Dear Dr. Horner,

My friend Kris Ellingsen, the artist who draws your fossil bones, once told me that, in the long winter months waiting for the dig season to begin, you cast about for paleontological "diversions" until you can resume the search for dinosaurs and their nests at Egg Mountain in the Montana badlands. I'm taking the liberty of writing this story for you, hoping that it might be that sort of diversion, and asking for your comments, even if—especially if—you decide that I'm chasing phantoms. On the other hand, if you think I might be on a worthwhile track, and you're interested in it, I'd really like to have your opinions about the specific materials that are at the heart of my search.

For a dozen years now I've been pursuing Griffins, those legendary animals of Central Asia described by ancient Greek travelers and natural historians, and depicted in art from Asia

Griffins, from an ancient Greek vase painting. Drawing by Adrienne Mayor.

Minor and the Mediterranean. At first I sought them as an artist—I made etchings of Griffins fighting over gold treasure with Amazons and Scythians.

In the summer of 1978, in a small harbor-front museum on Samos, a Greek island off the coast of Turkey, I happened onto a superb collection of Griffins. Every Aegean island has a little "archaeological" museum to house the bits of marble columns and pottery and statue fragments excavated there, objects that foreign archaeologists deemed too trifling to cart off to the grand world-class museums. But here, amazingly, were the heads of hundreds of bronze Griffins, all retrieved from the island's temple site, dating from the eighth to seventh centuries BC. I spent hours gazing at this treasure, feverishly sketching rank upon rank of hammered and cast bronze busts of the prototypical Griffin, the mysterious predator of the Scythian steppes.

But wait. The original reason I went to Samos was to visit a different museum, an even smaller, dustier museum, in the mountainous interior of the island. I had read in an obscure footnote that a collection of giant bones dug out of the hard red cliffs of a dry streambed had been stored there since the last century, and one of the fossils was nicknamed the "Samotherium"—the Monster of Samos. See, I also knew (more obscure footnotes) that in antiquity Samos had possessed a famous tourist attraction. Huge skulls and thigh bones were unearthed from an area called the "blood-red fields" in the middle of the island. Plutarch (ca. AD 100) wrote that at first those colossal bones were identified as the remains of giant Samian monsters known as Neïdes whose roars caused earthquakes (or whose demise was caused by an earthquake; the text is unclear), so common in the Aegean. Later, the bones were associated with the elephants that the god Dionysos had brought to Greece from India—some texts claimed that many had died in Samos. Dionysos had also slaughtered an army of Amazons in a battle on Samos—some sources believed the impressive bones might be Amazon skeletons. The earth of the battlefield was dyed red, of course, from the awful carnage that resulted in so many corpses.

Back in Athens, under the slow fans of the Library of the American School of Classical Studies, doves and cicadas loud and monotonous in the fig trees outside, I had been poring over what I called "unclassified residua," the outtakes of ancient history, apparent dead ends of classical studies. These enigmatic messages were too obscure and too unrelated to other accepted factoids for "objective" classical scholars to pursue. I had a year before me in Greece, and it became my mission to gather as many of these curious signposts as I could ferret out. Some of the academic scholars working in the library kindly passed along any odd nuggets that their highly focused research turned up. Indeed, I believe that they were relieved to have someplace to *put* these infuriating items that resisted categorization.

Anyway, I carefully filed these anomalies, and eventually patterns began to emerge. But back then, I was just collecting kindling for my imagination; I still planned to use these vague, quirky, yet persistent scraps for artistic inspiration. They were so eidetic, these incongruous references in ancient sources, mentioned fleetingly in dry footnotes, and certainly never rating an entry in scholarly indexes: poison honey, ghosts, tame weasels and friendly dolphins, a satyr arrested by some Roman soldiers, a pickled Triton, villages ravaged by a giant fox, mermaids who mourned Alexander's death, the teeth of a Red Sea shark stored on the Athenian Acropolis, the remains of a Miocene lion in the ruins of a Mycenean treasury, the exact dimensions of sea serpents washed ashore in Phoenicia—and bones, giant bones, mythical heroes' bones, skeletons of extinct races, crystallized skulls, impossible vertebrae, prodigious thighbones, teeth, horns, great claws, stone bones. My file on remarkable bones grew fat, fleshed out with ancient Greek and Roman accounts of fossil-hunting expeditions and scattered hints of an ancient interest in identifying those giant bones that people knew could be found in specific places.

The American School Library in Athens is one of the best classical libraries in the world. Eagerly I turned to scholarly books about Greek and Roman natural history. But if the ancient interest in prehistoric fossils was mentioned at all, it was only to dismiss that interest as primitive, oracle-inspired, cult-oriented, superstitious. It was, I was told, simply a case of mistaken identification. The occasional fossil was casually linked with a mythical hero of the dim past, the favorite son of the town where the impressive bone came to light. Sometimes an offhand footnote remarked on "what a coincidence it turned out to be" that certain locales where big bones had been exhumed according to Herodotus or Pausanias (characterized as "reliable but gullible" by today's scholars) were confirmed in modern times as "actually yielding significant fossiliferous remains."

Taking seriously what most scholars dismissed, I compiled a list of ancient accounts of "giant bones" and set about reading the reports of modern fossil excavations in the Mediterranean. Would the geography match? You know it did. I wanted to rescue the ancient Greeks who found, even searched out, those big bones from the modern scholar's condescending charge that the Greeks' interpretation of the prehistoric remains was "primitive, ignorant, unenlightened, unscientific." I was sure that what was now dismissed as "legend" and "coincidence" might once have been rational, historical. Gradually, I became aware that my sort of mission had been long ago rejected as misguided euhemerism of the past. But it just didn't seem fair that scholars willing to give so much credit to the Greeks for inventing democracy, philosophy, and catapults could give the same people a D– in paleontology.

Since the turn of the century, I found, it had been generally accepted (by zoologists and folklorists mainly, but rarely discussed by classicists) that the idea of the mythical one-eyed ogre Cyclops slain by Odysseus in a cave in Sicily could have been inspired by the discovery in antiquity of prehistoric elephant or mammoth skulls. I was surprised to read how common such skulls were in coastal caves of Italy and the Aegean. The large nasal opening and relative insignificance of the eye sockets make the Cyclopean hypothesis hard to deny: a large one-eyed creature was a reasonable reconstruction.

In my "fossil files" I amassed evidence to suggest that the ancient Greeks and Romans had purposefully collected, identified, preserved, and sometimes even restored or reconstructed the extinct remains they gathered. Slowly I dug out ancient accounts of fossils throughout the Greek world in Herodotus, Pausanias, Aelian, Philostratus, Empedocles, Theophrastus, Plutarch, Pliny, Aristotle. And nineteenth-century field reports demonstrated that modern fossil hunters were lucky in the same places: paleontologists came in droves to the bone beds mentioned in the ancient texts. The *nekrotafion zoön* (animal graveyard) of the island of Samos was at the head of my list of places to visit. The island had all the features: huge bones identified in antiquity according to the best historical, scientific, geographical, and biological knowledge of the day; modern paleontological findings in the same red gullies; etiological ancient theories to account for the remains: the extinct Neïdes, associated with local cataclysmic geophysical events; Dionysos's Indian elephants; and a battlefield littered with the bones of an army of larger-than-life warriors of prehistory.

Before we headed to Piraeus to board a ferryboat to Samos, the elderly professor of archaeology at the American School of Classical Studies invited us to walk the ancient road from Athens to Marathon with him, a road he had discovered. E.V. (Eugene Vanderpool) had arrived in Greece on foot by way of Albania in 1928 and stayed to excavate the Athenian Agora and other sites until his death in 1989. Over the years he had located many ancient roads and deciphered many inscriptions. He possessed an uncanny sense for distinguishing aimless goat paths from the traces of true ancient roadways, and for reading faint letters on stone in the raking light of sunset.

Along the way to Marathon, E.V. pointed out the reddish gullies of Pikermi, where he had a country house, and where the bones of the famous Helladotherium and the prehistoric Pikermi Ape had been dug up in the 1800s. We talked about how the "Pikermi" fauna and the fauna of Samos were the link interconnecting the species of Asia, Europe, and Africa. Greece and the Aegean islands had once been a single land mass connecting the continents. And, besides the Samotherium (a giant prehistoric giraffe), a great variety of remains had emerged from the red earth of Pikermi and Samos: the behemoths Dinothere, Chalicothere, Ancylothere; giant ostriches and rodents; the ancestors of rhinos, hippos, bears, lions, mastodons, swamp elephants, saber-toothed tigers (see chapter 13).

Only after we disembarked in Samos did I discover that the island also possessed a trove of artifacts depicting another fabulous animal, the Griffin of Scythian fame. I was torn between sketching every bronze Griffin that stared out of the glass cases in the harbor museum and rushing to the high mountain village of Mytilini, where I'd heard that the actual bones of the Monster of Samos were stored in a room over the post office. I was convinced that the skull of the great Monster of Samos— one of the earthshaking Neïdes—would resemble an elephant (brought to Greece by Dionysos) or—I dared hope—a Griffin.

It particularly galled me that the classical scholars poohpoohed the idea that the ancient Greeks might have made models based on the huge bones, which the ancient sources themselves tell us were immediately recognized as the remains of prehistoric, extinct species. Wouldn't it be natural to use the remains to reconstruct models or composites of the creatures that had once lived where the bones now lay? Looking at the stony remains, and using the imagination rationally, as Aristotle did, wouldn't anyone speculate about the appearance of an unknown animal? To be sure, some mythical beings appear to be obviously symbolic, imaginary hybrids (Pegasus, Centaurs, the Minotaur, the Sphinx, and their ilk) and no ancient writers ever claimed that they really existed outside of the golden age of myth. But it seemed to me that some other "unknown" creatures like the Griffin as described in historical sources or portrayed in artifacts had a compelling presence, an anatomical accuracy, a stubborn reality about them. I was sure that the modern scholars were underestimating the significance of the (admittedly scattered) statements in ancient sources that unusual remains were collected and sometimes restored. Even when scholars acknowledged that some "strange creatures" described in antiquity were apparently based on real animals, such as the rhinoceros, the connection was brought up only as an interesting exception, an isolated fluke.

But what about the theories of evolution and extinction developed as early as the sixth century BC? What about Theophrastus's rational treatises to explain fossil shells deposited on inland mountaintops? What about the careful excavation in antiquity of tombs of past cultures and the reasonable theories of human development based on those skeletons and relics described by Pausanias and Thucydides? What about the museum that Suetonius tells us Emperor Augustus built to house "the huge skeletons of extinct sea and land monsters popularly known as Giants' Bones, along with the weapons of ancient heroes"? What about the strange skeletons "of all sizes and shapes in incalculable numbers and piled in heaps" that Herodotus was shown by his guides along the walls of a mountain defile in Arabia? The life-size models of stranded "sea monsters" constructed for display in ancient Corinth and Rome? The giant eggs, teeth, bones, and even skins of "unknown" creatures of Asia and Africa exhibited in Rome and Greece? What about the modern excavation in archaeological sites of the bones of extinct animals, pygmy hippos, "unexpectedly large" cattle and horse bones, the teeth of non-Mediterranean sharks, Pliocene deer horns, mammoth tusks, and Miocene lion bones, all purposefully collected in antiquity and stored with other valuables? The scattered evidence from excavations of "exotic remains" was neglected, relegated to appendixes, footnotes, obscure nonclassical journals. Over and over I read the words "unparalleled example," "unique case," "anomalous coincidence." Yet here in Samos was physical proof of ancient interest in fossils, eloquent in its dirt-encrusted state. I was shocked to discover that zooarchaeology, as a discipline, had not even been born until the late 1970s. At the American School I heard archaeologists admit that it "might be a good idea to have paleobiologists study the zoological remains" that turned up in their sites, but meanwhile they would ignore any incongruous findings and concentrate on whatever they could relate to already-existing categories.

Historians of art and literature prefer to categorize depictions of "unknown" creatures as "imaginary/symbolic," or as evidence for a "zoomorphizing impulse." They trace the spread of "a theme" and concoct a psychological or folkloric explanation: the Hydra of Lerna slain by Hercules was a symbol of the malarial mosquitoes that once plagued that swampy region. The monstrous Stymphalean Birds were merely large crested grebes. Sea monsters represent the unknown dangers of the sea. The Griffin was simply a symbol of vigilance, or a representation of "the difficulty of mining gold," or a garbled description of a bird of prey, or a large, vicious dog of Tibet. The important thing about Griffins for art historians is that the imaginary artistic design "can be traced to a Middle Eastern origin." But even as art historians note the striking similarities between the Scythian Griffin and, say, the sixth-century BC *sirrush* carved on the Ishtar Gate at Babylon or the sixth–fifth century BC Monster of Persepolis, to them it's all just a matter of aesthetic influence.

As I drew individual Griffins in the Samos museum, all the while itching to get to that room over the village post office, I found myself hurrying past the elegant, imperious, stream-lined Griffins with long graceful necks. I lingered transfixed before the more ancient, bulky, brutish, leathery beasts. Well, these earlier bronzes were Griffins all right: their features were raptorial-reptilian, with scaly, scored necks and peculiar folds or ruffs; strong, hooked, open beaks; enormous, staring eye sockets. They sported the two distinctive long "ears" or "horns" and a knobbed forehead. All of the bronzes evoked a menacing creature of predatory intent. But the earlier ones looked more vital, more realistic, more "there." Next to those heavier, short-necked, obviously earthbound brutes, the others seemed to be too sublime, supercilious—look, they even had decorations on their necks! These classical, stylized Griffins looked like idealized versions of the older, uglier beasts, the likes of which certainly never appeared in the illustrations of "Artistic Griffin Forms," in learned German and Italian dissertations tracing the dissemination of the "motif of imaginary animals in the ancient world." It seemed like a matter of noble portraits versus homely taxidermy. Those stylish Griffins, beloved by the art historians, emphasized the proud avian features, while the other brutes looked more lizard-like. What was it? Something about them was so dogged, so ponderous, so . . . reptilian, so antediluvian, yes, so prehistoric—

I rushed outside. We had to rent a motorbike at the quay immediately, get to the village in the mountains, find someone with the key to the bone room of Mytilini.

It was a hot drowsy island afternoon. We passed no traffic going up the steep dirt road out of town, except for some still goats in the dust and a low-slung maroon Dodge of the long-finned era, fitted with right-hand drive.

We stopped for the night in Pythagorion, the birthplace of Pythagoras, and the ancient capital of Samos. We climbed to the magnificent stone walls of the ruined city, high above the sea, facing Turkey. There were foot-long black-and-white beaded lizards sunning on the great stone blocks. We were the only visitors at the overgrown temple where all the bronze Griffins in the museum had been buried. We ventured a few yards into the frighteningly black tunnel hewn through the mountain down to the sea, an awesome engineering feat of the sixth century BC. That evening, down in the modern village, I wandered through the small cemetery, and into an old building. It was an *osteotheke*, a bone room, on the seashore. There was not enough soil on the desiccated, rocky island: when Samian villagers died, they were buried for a only few years. Then their bones were reverently disinterred, washed, and stored in open crates on shelves in the bone room. By candlelight I saw that each box was painstakingly labeled with the names and dates and even curling old photographs of the villagers whose skulls and tibiae now poked out of the crumbling wooden and cardboard cartons. The room was cool, peaceful, fragrant with frankincense.

The next day we set off on the motorbike, climbing the twisting rutted switchbacks to Mytilini. I reviewed what I knew about Griffins. From about 800–700 BC to AD 300 (forget the medievally corrupted heraldic Griffins—too domesticated), historians and travelers (Aristeas, Ctesias, Herodotus, Aelian, Pliny) and anonymous artists had described a fierce predatory quadruped, with a head and beak that recalled a raptor. The Griffin (*gryps* in ancient Greek) had two upright, pointed "ears" or horns, a central horny knob or crest, and a sort of ruff, roll, or fold extending from the base of the ears under the throat. Both literature and art suggested that there were different varieties of Griffins, some more like lions, others more like giant birds, yet others like reptiles. Some had wings—though Griffins did not fly—a dorsal crest or mane, scales or feathers; there was a tongue at the base of the jaw or beak, sometimes teeth or bony ridges, a humped brow, prominent eyes or large empty sockets. About the size of a wolf, the Griffin was said to build a nest or burrow of gold in a desert wilderness at the foot of the mountains of Central Asia, where primitive tribes (some said those tribes were hairy and one-eyed; some said they were Amazons; some said they were bald and dressed in skins) found gold deposits. The Griffin laid eggs like agates; some claimed its talons were large enough to use as drinking cups. Renowned for vigilance, ferocity, and speed, the *gryps* preyed on horses, stags, goats, humans.

Artistic representations on vases, sculpture, and jewelry usually showed Griffins alert and alone or seizing their prey; a few had two Griffins fighting, or a lion attacking a Griffin; one unique Scythian artifact depicted two shaggy men fighting a Griffin. Literary sources said that nomads seeking gold in the desert wastes battled these beasts; they never captured the full-grown ones, though the "chicks" were sometimes taken. Griffins were solitary, or in pairs, or with their young, never in herds or packs. A pair of "gruesome, silent, sharp-beaked Griffins" threatened Prometheus chained to his rock in the Caucasus (in Aeschylus's tragedy of the fifth century BC).

Along a corridor of a villa near Piazza Armerina, in Sicily, is a mosaic, seventy yards long, called the "Great Hunt." Created in about AD 300, it illustrates the capture of exotic animals to be transported from the fringes of the empire to Rome. The scene narrates in meticulous natural detail the methods of capturing gazelle, antelope, lion, tiger, wild ass, boar, ostrich, leopard, bear, elephant, camel, tiger, hippopotamus, rhinoceros—all real animals that were displayed in Rome. The capture techniques involve nets, cages, horsemen, hounds, and traps baited with appropriate prey and decoys. If you "read" the long mosaic from left to right, like a comic strip, you come to the very last exotic animal at the end of the pavement. There a large crate is baited with a man, nervously peeping between the slats at the prodigious claws of—a powerful Griffin. The beast is preoccupied with getting at the man inside. I couldn't shake that image, with its echo of men of the steppes capturing young Griffins, and those gruesome Griffins drawing near the man chained to the rock in the Caucasus.

In the high mountain village of Mytilini there are deep pools of shade under the plane trees. The postmaster goes to get the key from the mayor and unlocks the room upstairs, and we enter the paleontological "museum" of Samos. Light slanting through the dusty glass reveals a jumble of great fossil skulls and vertebrae. The postmaster points out the Samotherium skull and thighbone, awesome and stony. He shows us yellowing clippings of workers and men in suits posing next to the bones half-buried in the gorge, the *nekrotafion zoön.*

Years later, one Sunday in the fall of 1983, a member of our five-person archaeological survey team (we were searching for ancient roads connecting Attica's network of watchtowers and fortresses) presented me with an old silver chess piece in the shape of a Griffin. He had traded a Montana tractor cap for it in the flea market below the Athenian Acropolis. It was ouzo-hour, after another long day in the American School Library. I showed the chess piece to an expert on temples, Dr. Judith Binder, and recounted my excitement about the bronze Griffins of Samos. She insisted I must go to the ruins of Olympia to see the mother Griffin with her "pup."

November begins the season of the wildflowers in Greece. First come the grape hyacinths, cyclamen, and tiny irises and rare orchids, then the purple oregano and thyme blossoms, and the anemone "windflowers." The last petals to fade are the blood-red poppies. We drive south to Olympia. Where the first Olympic Games were once held, Greek families are flying kites in the ruins of the stadium; it's a warm, windy, bright blue day. I'm anxious to find that worked sheet of bronze, made in about 620 BC, with a unique image: the only known depiction of a mother Griffin with her young. The label reads: "Female Griffin nursing her young. The fruitful imagination, the profoundly human sensitiveness of the artist transformed the *ferocious imaginary bird, borrowed* from Oriental art, into a peaceful and loving creature" (my italics). The muscular, stocky mother is shown crouching, with one paw raised, tail curled around her haunches. Nestled alongside her belly is the newly hatched Griffin, a small version of its mother. The scene is so familiar, yet so incongruous.

In the searing August of 1985 (119 degrees Fahrenheit) at the desolate border between Macedonia and Serbia; a Romani youth fixes our radiator. We fill five canteens with spring-water, buy some tiny, dusty wild strawberries from roadside kids, and set off through Yugoslavia. Four days later we cross into Austria, arriving in Klagenfurt, a town I'd waited seven years to visit. In the center of the town square would be a statue sculpted in about 1605. I was keen to see this Dragon of Klagenfurt because an old book on "dragon lore" mentioned that the sculptor used as his model a fossil skull that had been unearthed nearby. The skull was that of an Ice Age woolly rhinoceros. I was jubilant. Here was the paradigm of the very process that I believed the ancient Greeks should have been credited with. If only I could find the model for the Griffin . . .

Back home in Montana on a snowy day I stared at the post-cards and the mugshots I had taken of every angle of the Kla-genfurt dragon. I got out my notes and sketches from the mu-seum at Nauplion, in southern Greece. In 1979, I'd sketched a few vase paintings of stylized Griffins, but then used up my drawing pad in front of a case of huge, bizarre terra-cotta heads. Ridged, crested necks, bulbous snouts, bulging eyes, a grin full of tusks. The label said only that the eighth-century BC "masks" came from Tiryns and Asine. Some years later, at the Library of the Center for Hellenic Studies in Washing-ton, DC, I tried to find out more. In vain, for every reference said the same thing: "These grotesque terra-cotta heads are unique . . . most likely cult objects . . . larger than life, no known parallels . . . without comparanda . . . use and origin unknown . . ." The German scholar who discovered the heads in 1926 promised to publish an article about them in 1934, but it never appeared. The director of the Hellenic Center, Zeph Stewart, who knew everyone, thought maybe the scholar had died in the war. I immersed myself in archaeological field reports of Tiryns and nearby sites. Were there any "unexpected" fossil remains in the strata of fire scars, obsidian blades, broken pots? If there were, they were not recorded in the archaeological journals.

Years passed; I added more Griffin lore to my files. My friends were amused by my magpie "hobby" of squirreling away odd, antiquarian detritus. Every now and then when one of my files reached a certain girth, I would publish an article on some obscure topic of ancient natural history. The Griffins languished, but I couldn't let them go. I began to flag before the immensity of the puzzle I wanted to solve. It was too daunting. It would mean not only digging out more deeply buried information but trying to assimilate and then refute those lovingly crafted theories from a whole raft of well-established scholarly disciplines whose adepts wanted to deal only with well-known attractions, inscriptions, and signs along their network of roads through their own territory. I was a trespasser, with a scribbled map, ignoring "Posted" signs.

It began to sink in: each discipline that claims the Griffin and its lore as an object of study cossets its own accepted—and circumscribed—interpretation. My project seemed sprawling, anomalous, without analogy, inexcusably flaky, bootless. Why couldn't I be satisfied just drawing and etching imaginary Griffin vignettes? Why did I need to capture the animal and pin down its identity? I dreamed about Griffins, but on my etching plates I could summon up only Amazons and Scythians, the old familiar enemies of the Griffin.

I tried to tempt friends who were classical scholars to reexamine the "Griffin problem." No dice. Maybe I could interest the cryptozoologists. Here was an emerging field eager to establish scientific credentials, but temperamentally drawn to fringe, marginal topics like mine, which I now called "paleocryptozoology"—the "study of unknown ancient animals." Were they my fellow "scholars of academic outtakes"? I joined the International Society of Cryptozoology and came to understand that they would be most pleased if I could prove that the Griffin was a relict animal that actually—perhaps even recently—preyed on Scythian horses. Arindam C, a philosopher visiting Bozeman from India, expressed interest in my project, but he was really only fascinated with the epistemological problems involved in the effort to describe imaginary things. I subscribed to the journal of the Society for the Investigation of the Unexplained, and avidly read of their anomalies, but winced over undocumented pseudo-scholarship and the ubiquitous UFO connection. Maybe I was really laboring in the field of antique folklore, of "ancient popular culture." I subscribed to a folklore journal, and fretted about the hopelessly extinct, invisible Griffins that I imagined restlessly pacing in my file cabinet.

In 1988, a brief science abstract about "pygmy pachyderms" in Cyprus caught my eye. These Pleistocene animals were believed to have become extinct long before the appearance of humans in the Mediterranean. I remembered an article in a folklore journal of the mid-1970s about the great numbers of pygmy hippo bones found in hillsides and caves of Cyprus. The author, David Reese, explained how the islanders had identified the bones as those of (A) antediluvian beasts or (B) early Christian saints hiding from Muslims in Cypriot caves. I wrote to the author and learned that hippopotamus remains had also been found at sites near Tiryns. The previous summer in Athens, a specialist on Neolithic occupation of caves in the Mediterranean, Don Kelly, had given me his list of faunal remains found in caves throughout Greece—the bones of extinct pygmy hippos were notable. And now, said this abstract, evidence revealed that humans and pygmy hippos and dwarf elephants had lived at the same time on Cyprus. The cryptozoologists would love it. Not only were the bones radiocarbon-dated to about 8200 BC, but they showed the distinctive marks of butchering and burning. The early Greeks may have hunted the hippos to extinction.

I hunted up a drawing of a prehistoric hippopotamus skull. As I stared at it, I found myself back in Nauplion, 1979. Those hideous grinning terra-cotta masks . . . The tusks, the snout, the protuberant eyes: it had to be true. Placed side by side, the profiles were a matched before-and-after set, grotesque fleshy mask and bare skull.

A decade after I'd first visited Samos, I was back in the American School Library in Athens. I pulled down from the shelf the translation of an obscure Russian book about the frozen tombs of Scythia and learned of an astounding discovery that would have made Herodotus grin. I had just returned from southern Turkey, where the temperatures had climbed to unspeakable levels; indeed the heat was, I must say, "without parallel," "with no known analogue." We had made our way from ancient Halicarnasus to Athens by way of Samos, following the same route Herodotus had taken as he completed his travels two millennia ago. In Samos I visited again the archaeological museum, now in a brand-new building. I spent hours among my Griffins; again we rented a motorbike, headed for the interior. It was breathlessly hot and still. There was more traffic now on the steep dirt road. The bone room in Mytilini that we had visited ten years before was now a real museum with a gift shop—I bought a souvenir Samotherium key chain and postcards. But the fossil skulls of the Monster of Samos had been taken away to museums in Vienna and Stuttgart. On a new map I saw that Plutarch's "blood-red fields" were in a gorge just west of Mytilini; we had passed it on the bike. And there was a new mystery—a very large, very long-jawed fossil skull encrusted with red dirt, carelessly left on the tile floor in an unswept corner. Why was it not labeled in a glass case? The curator explained it had just been dug up on a nearby island, Ikaros. It was so hot in the museum, so dry. The glass cases contained a few impressive but unrelated enormous bones, teeth, horns, the ghosts of Neïdes from the red cliffs.

Now I carried the thick Russian book to a library table. During the Stalinist era, Soviet archaeologist Sergei Rudenko had exhumed a remarkable set of "drawings" tattooed on mummified Scythians, a biographic medium that gave eloquent testimony to the "reality" (on some level) of the Griffin for the nomads. But it was the other artifacts, jewelry, and cups worked in gold, hunting scenes with obvious parallels to Greek art, that became famous, while the tattooed messages about Griffins inscribed in a unique text that summoned up the flesh-and-blood presence of that animal fell into obscurity. This pattern of the canon rejecting the anomaly was by now all too familiar to me. It was no longer surprising that the most provocative traces are the unique ones, too unusual to demand attention. Again and again, if I found any official mention of one of my "classical residua," it was merely a deadpan note of its utter unrelatedness. The adjectives became a frustrating litany of useless signs: "unique," "no comparanda," "untypical," "an isolated case," even "grotesque." No analogies? No meaning for scholars.

In the Russian's book, one must wade through Marxist-Leninist theory applied to the ancient Scythians, before finally learning that in the late 1940s, in tombs excavated in the frozen valley of Pazyryk, in the Altai Mountains of Central Asia, Rudenko found Scythian people who had been buried with valuable objects in the fifth century BC, the same century in which Herodotus wrote his travel books about the same lands. By pouring boiling water on the permafrost, Rudenko was able to extricate jewelry and horse equipage of wood, leather, cloth, and gold decorated with varieties of fabulous Griffins seizing rams, stags, horses. In the tombs, men and women were buried together, apparently with equal ceremony. There were gilded human skulls. Censers containing cannabis seeds.

Right, right, Herodotus had reported all these things in the fifth century BC, but it had all been taken as folklore by modern commentators. Herodotus had said that the Scythians, "though they seemed reasonable in all other aspects," gave women equal political and social status; both men and women were fantastic horse riders; they worshipped their ancestors and gold-plated their skulls for drinking vessels; they loved to take saunas and seemed to really enjoy themselves when they burned the seeds of hemp plants "like incense." They battled animals called Griffins to reach gold deposits in the mountains.

But Herodotus (and later Hippocrates and others), also mentioned that the Scythian warriors marked themselves indelibly, with tattoos. When Sergei Rudenko opened the frozen barrows, he found not skeletons but mummies. And the arms, legs, and torsos of the men and women were still covered with blue-black tattoos, a panorama of animals, real and unknown. This zoographic welter of realistically detailed, nearly overlapping images showed familiar rams, onagers, stags, horses, eagles, and many fantastic animals, mostly Griffins, some winged, some apterous, some beaked, some fanged, some horned, some crested or maned, some equipped with murderous talons. Why were the recognizable animals sprawled in death poses, while every one of the unknown animals was shown very much alive?

Twenty years before Rudenko's expedition, the pioneer paleontologist Roy Chapman Andrews set out in 1923 to find dinosaurs at the foot of the Altai Mountains, Mongolia. He had heard the folklore about the "Flaming Cliffs" and the "Red Beds." He heard that the basin was "paved with bones" and that one could find countless "dragon's" skulls, teeth, claws, horns, eggs. His team was quite giddy with their success: they found extensive remains of many dinosaurs, including the gigantic Baluchitherium—a Miocene ancestor of the rhinoceros that stood thirteen feet at the shoulder. Among their finds was also the Protoceratops—a creature of many million years ago with "great round eyes and a thin, hatchet face, ending in a hooked beak," and between the head and neck a "circular bony frill." This creature, about nine feet long, was the ancestor of the huge Triceratops, which appeared about two million years later years later in Montana, and whose skull alone attained a length of eight feet. I'd seen those colossal Triceratops bones in your Museum of the Rockies in Bozeman.

I located Andrews's book describing his expeditions during a sweltering heat wave in Ithaca, New York, in 1988. I had just

one day in the Cornell Library before we left for an archaeological survey in Turkey. I quickly turned to the chapter on
dinosaur eggs, the most exciting of Andrews's finds. The discovery of a great many eggs, with embryonic fragments and
newly hatched babies of the Protoceratops and other species,
had been a bombshell in the paleontological world, without
parallel until you yourself found the eggs of the Maiasaura
at Egg Mountain on ranch land in Montana half a century
later. I'd seen your amazing display of that clutch of eggs and
a petrified hatchling in the Museum of the Rockies. Everyone
was excited by your radical theories about dinosaurs caring
for their young, a real-life detail that made those ancient reptiles seem so vital. (That mother Griffin protecting her baby
at Olympia. Her nest would have been flecked with gold . . .)

Andrews and his team had found a vast nesting ground
with all manner of stone eggs in the 1920s. When they excavated a Late Paleolithic–Early Neolithic "Dune Dwellers"
site a few miles away, they found jewelry made from those
dinosaur eggs and the eggs of now-extinct giant ostriches. I
recalled that decorated eggshells of giant ostriches had been
excavated in the ruins of ancient Greek cities too. Andrews's
team joked about how they had been beaten to the discovery by millennia, by the people who had first collected those
strange stone eggs, some smooth and others "beautifully stri-
ated, with a variety of patterns" and textured surfaces. Egg-
shaped stones, with bands, swirls, and patterns . . . like agates.
(The Griffins had laid eggs of agate . . .)

I paged through the illustrations, the first-ever photos of
clutches of dinosaur eggs, the members of the team at their
tents, a camel caravan, and a photo of a "fierce Mongolian dog
which eats the dead and attacks the living." I remembered

one art historian's theory that the Griffin was "an imaginative personification" of that very mastiff. I paused at a drawing of the Triceratops, and then flipped to the underexposed photograph of its smaller, earlier relative of Central Asia, the Protoceratops, a profile shown in situ, still embedded in the friable sandstone of the Flaming Cliffs. I drew in my breath.

That hatchet face, the powerful open beak, the large staring, empty eyes, the ridge at the neck, that primitive, almost leathern look about it . . . I knew that profile. It was my Griffin, the *real* Griffin—it was that hammered bronze Griffin trapped in the glass case of the Samos Museum.

Later, on the way to Turkey, under the summer stars on the deck of the ferryboat from Venice to Izmir, I thought about the Greek hero Perseus, on his way to find the nightmarish Gorgon. On the journey through the land of the Scythians and the one-eyed Hyperboreans, he traverses an eerie landscape populated by rain-eroded "statues"—the remains of petrified animals and men, frozen to stone by the stare of the hideous Gorgon. He finds a magic tooth, a single eye, shared by three terrible creatures. His mission is to slay the unimaginable monster that turns living beings into stone, traps them in a limbo of extinction, and their remains, in their *utter unrelatedness*, become enigmatic rock markers along the road . . .

Yours truly,
Adrienne Mayor

CHAPTER 15

Siegfried and the Dragon

A FEARSOME DRAGON CALLED FAFNIR was featured in Germanic/Norse legends of the Middle Ages about the hero Siegfried. The story is the centerpiece in the epic saga the *Nibelungenlied*, in which Siegfried tracks and slays Fafnir. Richard Wagner's famous opera cycle *The Ring of the Nibelung* (1857) captured the Romantic Sturm und Drang of the medieval fantasy.

In the legend, Fafnir, who had been transformed into a hideous dragon by a powerful curse, guarded a hoard of golden treasure. The dragon was so huge that the very ground shook when it walked. A distinctive rocky prominence, called Drachenfels (Dragon's Rock), at Konigswinter on the Rhine in Germany, was identified as Fafnir's dwelling place. The ruins of a medieval castle, Burg Drachenfels, built on the summit in about 1150, give the craggy hill a fairy-tale aura. After Lord Byron visited and wrote verses about Dragon's Rock in about 1815, the place became a must-see tourist site.

A cave below the castle was believed to be Fafnir's lair. It was here that Siegfried killed the dragon and became invincible by bathing in its blood. In 1913, a stone temple with columns, the Nibelungenhalle, was constructed as a shrine to the Wagnerian spirit of the legend. Inside the art nouveau "ancient" temple, paintings, sculptural reliefs, and mosaics depict scenes from the opera. And in a mossy grotto lurks a huge stone dragon, forty-two feet long: Fafnir defending his cave.

According to the legend, the hero Siegfried tracked Fafnir to his lair by following a trail of the dragon's enormous footprints sunk deep in the earth. What might account for this vivid detail in the story?

Notably, conspicuous fossil trackways are found in bedrock in Germany, made by two types of massive dinosaurs. In 1941, the German paleontologist H. Kirchner speculated that observations of Triassic dinosaur tracks in sandstone near Siegfriedsburg in the Rhine Valley of western Germany might have been the inspiration for the legend of the dragon Fafnir's footprints.

Since then, more dinosaur tracks have been analyzed by paleontologists in northern Europe. Immense three-toed footprints of a Theropod dinosaur were recently found near Münchehagen, Germany. Another long trackway left by a massive thirty-ton Sauropod dinosaur from 140 million years ago can be seen embedded in a quarry at Rehburg-Loccum, near Hannover, Germany. The footprint's magnitude—four feet wide and seventeen inches deep—would certainly lead anyone in antiquity or the Middle Ages to visualize a legendary dragon of dreadful size and shape. Notably, Sauropod tracks were also associated with a fabled great beast in China (chapter 16). It is plausible that the story of another medieval dragon-fighting hero of Old English epic, Beowulf, may have been influenced by observations of the remarkable fossil remains of woolly mammoths. (For another dragon-slaying hero in Greece, see chapter 2; for the impressive fossils of long extinct animals, chapter 13). In the Americas, indigenous peoples interpreted Theropod and Sauropod trackways in rock as the footprints of fantastic birds and monsters.

The dragon Fafnir as a fossil monster, Wagner's *Siegfried*, Chicago Lyric Opera, photo Dan Rest.

Since it premiered in 1876, Wagner's famous opera *Siegfried* in the *Ring* cycle features the hero fighting a medieval-style dragon, portrayed in various imaginative ways onstage. In 1996, for the first time in opera history, the Lyric Opera of Chicago portrayed Fafnir as a huge, frightening "fossil monster," a kind of fantasy dinosaur skeleton. The reviewer for the *New York Times* declared that this marvelous Fafnir exceeded the "wildest expectations" and stole the show. The dragon was conceived by John Conklin, the set designer. The theatrical puppeteer Lisa Aimee Sturz created the huge skull, the skeletal segmented tail, and giant talons, expertly manipulated in time to Wagner's music by sixteen people hidden underneath. I regret not having seen the actual performance but have studied the photographs and corresponded with Lisa about the project. The radical decision to cast the dragon in this fashion was thrilling for me, as it parallels my notion that discoveries of remarkable fossil skeletons may have influenced some images and tales of dragons.

Tracking the Lucky Rhino in China

IN THE JURASSIC ERA, massive seventy-ton Sauropod dinosaurs tromped around what is now China, leaving deep tracks in mud that over time became stone. About 150 million years later, a conspicuous Sauropod trackway was well known to villagers in Tongsi, China. The townspeople believed that the fossil footprints had been made by a legendary beast in Chinese folklore.

The striking set of eighteen Sauropod dinosaur footprints are embedded in rock at Luoguan Mountain (near Zigong City, Sichuan Province, China). They were "discovered" by Chinese paleontologists in 2009, but it turns out that the impressive Jurassic tracksite had been revered by local people for centuries. Following the ancient trail up the mountain was thought to bring good fortune.

According to the local oral traditions, the huge oval tracks, about 8 inches across and 12.5 inches long, were made by Divine Lucky Rhinoceros. In the age-old story, the venerable Rhinoceros trudged up Luoguan Mountain to gather Lingzhi—"mushrooms of immortality." These special mushrooms are a rare red bracket fungus that grows on very old maple tree stumps. Also known as Reishi mushrooms, the

Sauropod dinosaur tracks, Luoguan Mountain, Tongsi, China, photo Guangzhao Peng.

red-varnished kidney-shaped *Ganoderma lingzhi* are still believed in China to have miraculous medicinal powers. As the Divine Lucky Rhinoceros trekked up the slope seeking the red mushrooms, his footprints sank deep into the stone.

What is so interesting about this tale is that there are no wild rhinoceroses in China. In antiquity, however, people would have known of three different types of Asian rhinoceroses that did roam China (along with elephants). Two-horned Sumatran and one-horned Javan rhinoceros species flourished during Neolithic and Bronze Age China, even in the north when the climate was warmer than today. Some ancient texts mentioned a rhino with two small forehead horns and one larger horn on the nose. Bronze Age vessels from the late Shang dynasty (1600 to 1046 BC) are decorated with anatomically realistic rhinoceroses.

But rhinoceroses were hunted extensively. Oracle bones have characters signifying one-horned rhinos, and other characters indicating that hunters trapped them in pits. The record of a massive hunting expedition of the first ruler of the Zhou dynasty, King Wu, states that in about 1045 BC he killed 22 tigers, more than 5,000 stags, 353 boars, and 12 rhinoceroses. Some rhinos were taken into captivity for imperial court zoos as early as 500 BC. Rhino hides and horns were boiled to render glue, and the fibrous horns were used to make composite bows. The tough rhino hide became very hard when dried, and could be pieced into armor, helmets, and shields that protected against bronze weapons. Rhino-hide armor was widely used during the Shang dynasty, through the Warring States period of the fourth century BC, until about 200 BC and the invention of a powerful crossbow that could pierce rhino hide.

Killing a rhinoceros was believed to ensure rain. Not only were their hides used for armor; rhinoceroses were also slaughtered for their horns. The horns were prized for medicine and for drinking cups, which were believed to cause the contents to fizz when they detected poison (see chapter 4).

古今圖書集成

鼻角獸圖

博物彙編禽蟲典第一百二十五卷異獸部彙考三之六

Lucky Rhino, Chinese woodblock print, from Gujin Tushu Jicheng, Imperial Encyclopedia, 1700–1725. Library Book Collection, Alamy Stock Photo.

Rhinoceros-horn drinking cups were often carved in the distinctive shape of Reishi mushrooms, recalling the Divine Lucky Rhino's search for mushrooms in the Tongsi local tale.

But the *unlucky* rhinoceros of China had vanished, hunted to extinction by the time of the Song dynasty, AD 960 to 1279. With the massive slaughter and disappearance of the Chinese rhino, what was once a real, magnificent animal became a legendary creature. The sad fate of the Chinese rhinoceros gives us an idea of the great antiquity of the local oral tradition about the Divine Lucky Rhinoceros tracks in stone. Venerated yet hunted into extinction by the thirteenth century, the Chinese rhinoceros survives today only in age-old folk memories of a massive wild beast that disappeared eight hundred years ago.

Fake Fossils

PALEONTOLOGICAL HOAXES and fraudulent fossils are assumed to be modern phenomena. The earliest case is generally thought to have occurred in 1725. More than a thousand phony fossils, later dubbed "lying stones," ruined the reputation of the arrogant but gullible professor Johann Beringer of Wurzburg, Germany. The fakes were bizarre little organisms, such as frogs, lizards, and spiders in webs, carved on soft limestone and planted by his rivals. It was a serious enterprise. Some of the figures even had inscriptions, which one would think might've given a scientist pause. But in 1725, Beringer believed that the creatures in stone were victims of Noah's Flood (see chapter 20) or even divine creations. After the hoax was revealed, Beringer tried to hunt down and destroy all the copies of his book about the stones, but some survived. Some of the prank specimens survived, too, and can be viewed today at the Teylers Museum in the Netherlands and at the Oxford University Museum.

Other fossil fakeries have been motivated by a desire to fool experts. The notorious Piltdown Man fraud was a clever construction of human and orangutan skull and jaw fragments that were artificially weathered. The hoax was perpetrated by the eccentric Charles Dawson in 1912. Dawson presented the skull as the "missing link" between humans and apes, claiming he'd discovered it in a quarry in England. His fakery was revealed with Carbon-14 dating about forty years later.

Fossil forgery for profit is another age-old practice. For example, fossil collecting became fashionable in Europe in the 1700s. Small specimens of fossil fish, shells, and leaves impressed in limestone were highly prized Grand Tour souvenirs (chapter 42). Many of these objects were placed in cabinets of curiosities. It was worth the time for quarrymen and stoneworkers to carve counterfeits or enhance real fossils in limestone to meet collectors' demands.

Insects and reptiles trapped in prehistoric amber (pine tree resin) are small, portable fossils with great appeal to collectors and therefore to counterfeiters. One of the earliest fakes was a fly encased in Baltic amber acquired by H. F. Loew, a German entomologist, in about 1850. The Natural History Museum in London purchased his entire collection in 1922. The fly in amber was one of the scientific stars among more than two thousand specimens. A prominent entomologist studied the specimen in 1966 and pronounced the perfectly preserved red-eyed fly to be thirty-eight million years old. The insect was hailed as the oldest known member of the Muscidae family, demonstrating that houseflies had not changed over eons. But in 1993, fossil insect specialist Andrew Ross discovered the Victorian ruse. It turned out that the insect was a modern "latrine fly," painstakingly embedded in a real piece of Baltic amber.

Fossil forgery has a long history in China. For example, well-preserved fossil fish impressions in slabs of limestone were so popular in twelfth-century China that numerous counterfeits were produced. Today, counterfeit fossils of dinosaur and other skeletons, and dinosaur claws and eggs, are still being fabricated in China, often by impoverished farmers and villagers. At the grand international bazaar that is the annual Tucson Fossil and Mineral Show, I have seen crates filled with dinosaur eggs from China, each one composed of tiny fragments of various fossilized eggshells, meticulously pieced together. There were also small composite bat-winged skeletons that resembled miniature pterosaurs, sold as "dragon fossils."

Since the startling discovery of the first feathered dinosaur remains in China in the late twentieth century, very sophisticated faked dinosaurian fossils have fooled amateurs and scientists alike. A scandalous incident occurred in 1999 when the cover of *National Geographic* featured what was claimed to be the "missing link" between birds and dinosaurs. Some paleontologists were suspicious. And in fact, the "Archaeoraptor" was later exposed as a convincing composite of real fossils. The body of a primitive bird (*Yanornis martini*) was attached to the tail of a real feathered dinosaur, *Microraptor zhaoianus* (see chapter 2 for clever composite mer-people in classical antiquity).

Some experts estimate that a high percentage of fossil skeletons and eggs in local and even some larger Chinese museums are composite chimeras and faked specimens. As interest in paleontology grows, and as more and more fossil museums pop up in China, doctored and phony specimens are proving lucrative. Besides dinosaurs, Chinese-made fakes include birds, turtles, crocodiles, frogs, pterosaurs, saber-toothed tigers, and insects.

Bogus fossils have become widespread as dinosaur and other fossils entered popular culture, and command outrageous prices in auctions. Early scientific discovery of trilobites (Paleozoic marine arthropods with segmented bodies and a dazzling variety of shapes, spines, and odd protuberances)

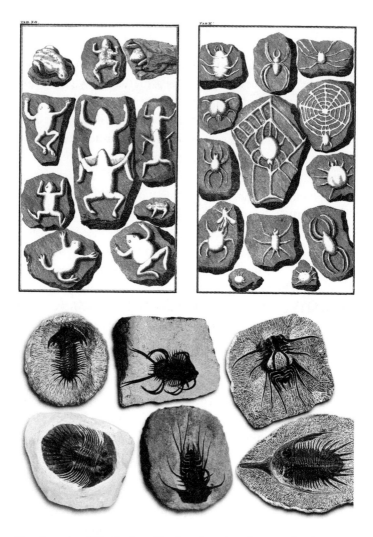

Top: Examples of fake fossils, spiders in webs and reptiles, carved on limestone to discredit Johann Beringer in 1725. Engravings from Beringer, *Lithographiae Wirceburgensis* (1726). Bottom: Examples of false trilobite fossils from Morocco.

occurred in the nineteenth century in Czechoslovakia. Paleontologists hired "rock men" to collect specimens around Prague. Scientific interest was followed by popular interest, and "rock men" began making false trilobite chimeras from fragments. New discoveries of abundant trilobites in the deserts of Morocco in the 1970s generated a lively fad for owning the primordial fossils. Trilobites are portable, intriguing, bug-like fossils, and their many bizarre shapes delight collectors. In turn, this inspired dealers to request counterfeits and "enhanced" specimens, to be sold for extravagant sums to the unwary. Moroccan fakes began flooding the market on an industrial scale in the early 2000s. Most trilobite forgeries are made by poor but extremely skilled artisans in the Atlas Mountain region, but others come from Russia, Canada, and Bolivia.

Some trilobite fossils are found intact, inside split geodes. But those from Morocco are mostly embedded in hard rock that must be smashed and split, thus breaking the creatures' delicate spines, quills, and eyestalks. Such specimens are invariably damaged and require some repair and/or restoration. It is easy to see how this natural situation encourages overrestoration and the piecing together of broken fossils, sometimes from different species and eras. Rising popular demand has resulted in multitudes of counterfeits. Some are primitive, but increasingly the fakes are artistically fabricated by specialists. Some paleontologists refer to round slabs of rock sprinkled with an unnatural assemblage of fake arthropods as "trilobite pizzas."

Counterfeiters can create forgeries modifying real fossils to make them larger or to give them a more arresting appearance. Others are composites like the Piltdown skull, the Archaeoraptor, and trilobites. Some forged fossils are carved out of stone or clay or cast in resin. Invertebrate fossils, such as sea lilies and other marine creatures, are easily faked with molds and casts. Pieces of fake "amber" enclosing real but modern insects and even snakes and lizards are very popular and easy to make. Certain forgers make a living from selling "fossils" of dragonflies, butterflies, and fish expertly painted on slabs of limestone. Some false "fossils" for sale online and at fossil shows are simply conglomerates and other oddly shaped rocks. Objects passed off as coprolites (fossilized dinosaur poop) are amusing for their crudity, while carefully forged fossils from China and Morocco are admired for their cunning beauty and stunning craft. More than one paleontologist has exclaimed, "Faking is a grand art in itself."

Fossil replicas were not always intended to defraud, however. Fossils gathered in antiquity, from large vertebrate bones to small shells, emerge from archaeological sites around the world. These discoveries are mute testimony to ancient people's interest in living organisms somehow transformed to stone. Such marvels were worked into decorations, placed in graves, or dedicated in temples—and they were sometimes duplicated for reasons not yet understood.

In Malta, islands south of Sicily, fossils attracted attention at a very early date. In the sixth century BC, the Greek philosopher Xenophanes observed marine shells embedded in Malta's bedrock and concluded that the islands had once been under the sea. As early as 3000 BC, heaps of teeth from the gigantic Miocene shark *Carcharodon megalodon* were dedicated in sacred sites. By 2500–1500 BC, Maltese potters were using the serrated shark teeth to decorate clay bowls with parallel grooves. Much later, in the Middle Ages, Maltese shark teeth (*glossopetrae*, tongue stones) became such a sought-after miracle remedy in Europe that laws forbade faking them.

The Maltese had been manufacturing "fossils" for their own uses since the Neolithic period. As Xenophanes had noticed, helicoid gastropod fossils (screw-shaped shells) are common. These small Miocene fossils turn up in vast numbers in the most archaic stone temples in Malta. But what really surprised the archaeologists were the oversized man-made replicas among the real fossils, some carved from limestone and others modeled in baked clay. The only other similar artifacts known from this era are gold and marble shark vertebrae discovered in Minoan sanctuaries on Crete.

These artifacts are the earliest datable replicas of fossils. Do they represent ancient efforts to figure out how the mysterious spirals had been formed? Were the fossils so valuable that forgeries were worthwhile? Were they objects of veneration? All we can say for sure is that from earliest antiquity, fossils were not only highly prized but artfully imitated.

CHAPTER 18

Cuvier and the Mammoth Foot

GEORGES CUVIER (1769–1832), the father of modern pale-ontology, was the first European naturalist to articulate a scientific theory of extinction, based on his studies showing that mastodons and mammoths, which became extinct between six thousand and ten thousand years ago, were the prehistoric ancestors of living elephants. This crucial advance in understanding the fossils of long-extinct creatures came about in part because of Cuvier's deep knowledge of ancient cultures' discoveries of mammoth and mastodon fossils in Mediterranean lands and in the Americas.

Cuvier gathered every known account of "giant bones" in classical literature, and he also maintained an extensive archive of Native American discoveries and legends, sent to him by various Euro-American colonists and explorers. Yet the influence on Cuvier's thinking of ancient accounts of "the stone bones of giants and monsters," and Native American observations of remarkable tusks, molars, and bones, is un-appreciated today. One reason is that the leading historian of paleontology, Martin Rudwick, in his translations of Cuvier's essential works into English (1997), inexplicably decided to omit Cuvier's French essays describing his avid curiosity about Native American fossil traditions and their role in his thinking. This omission leads other commentators on Cuvier's theories, such as Elizabeth Kolbert ("Annals of Extinction," *New Yorker,* December 16, 2013), to overlook a significant body of evidence, one that Cuvier himself acknowledged.

Cuvier relied on friends and travelers in the Americas to send him every scrap of evidence they heard from Native Americans about petrified teeth, bones, and tusks found in the ground, including many actual specimens of fossils, which he eagerly examined in Paris. The first mastodon molars to be studied in Europe had been discovered by Abenaki Indian guides on the Ohio River in 1739, another little-known fact. These finds were crucial to Cuvier's theories, as was the accurate identification of mammoth molars as elephant teeth by enslaved Africans at Stono Plantation, South Carolina, in about 1725 (see chapter 20).

But one zoological object said to have been shipped across the Atlantic seemed just too good to be true.

Cuvier described the startling specimens from America in 1812 (*Recherches sur les ossemens fossils,* vol. 2, "Grand Mastodonte," and in the 1821 edition). These were an elephantine molar and the forefoot of a proboscidean, complete with five toenails (the front feet of mammoths, mastodons, and today's elephants have five toes, the back feet four). Cuvier examined the relics and made sketches of the foot. He wrote, "On display now in Paris is a specimen, which, if authentic, confirms without doubt that the species [mammoths] once existed. This is a foreleg with five toenails. The owner asserts that he obtained it from a *comanchero* [Mexican trader] who bought it from *les sauvages* west of the Missouri River, who found it in a cave along with a molar." "But this limb is so fresh," marveled

Cuvier, "it appears to have been hacked from an elephant carcass." If authentic, Cuvier continued, it "is almost enough to make one doubt that mammoths are extinct!" Ever the scientist, however, Cuvier noted that "it so perfectly resembles the foot of an elephant I could not refrain from suspecting fraud, at least in the story of the Mexican."

From Cuvier's biographer, the paleontologist Philippe Taquet, I learned that the four ink drawings of the foot and handwritten notes were among Cuvier's unpublished papers in the National Museum of Natural History, Paris.

Cuvier's longhand notes on the sketches add more details to his published accounts: "Foot said to be that of a 'Mammouth,' found by Pawnee Indians beyond the Missouri, in a cave along with a very worn tooth, of which even the roots

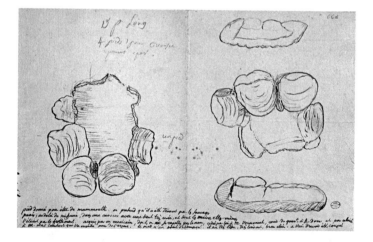

Cuvier's original 1812 drawings of the "mammoth foot" said to have been discovered in a cave, with a much-worn molar, by Pawnees west of the Missouri River and sold to a Mexican trader. Georges Cuvier, Ms 630-2, folio 668, 1812 © Muséum national d'histoire naturelle, Paris.

showed much wear. Acquired by a Mexican, name unknown, who delivered it to M. Vermonnel comi. du gouvt. when he was at St. Dom., who then gave it to M. René Lambert, who exhibited it for money. The foot is not decomposed; it is smooth, glossy, light brown, and looks like it was cut off." M. Vermonnel appears to have been a French government commissioner; St. Dom. could be St Domingue, now Haiti, a French colony until 1804. Cuvier does not indicate the name of the person who showed the specimens in Paris. Was it Lambert, who presumably recorded the chain-of-custody story? No dates are given for the events in the account.

I eagerly awaited the arrival of the drawings that Cuvier made of the specimen. Was the foot hairy? I was hoping that it might resemble the foot of a woolly mammoth discovered in 1901 preserved in permafrost in Siberia, displayed since 1912 in Cuvier's old museum.

Unfortunately, however, Cuvier's sketches indicate that only the pad of the foot and the five toes were preserved, with no portion of the beast's leg. I imagine that Cuvier was also disappointed that more of the leg was not included. From early discoveries of frozen specimens in Siberia, he knew that mammoths and mastodons were covered in thick hair.

Fossil ivory tusks taken from mammoth and mastodon exposures in the ice of Siberia had been a precious commodity since antiquity, traded to Russia, Mongolia, and China, and arriving in Europe by the early seventeenth century. At least four discoveries of woolly mammoth carcasses, with hair, blood, flesh, and bones, preserved in Arctic ice were reported by European explorers in Siberia between 1686 and 1806. Ysbrand Ides, an envoy of Peter the Great, reported that he had discovered a frozen mammoth and carried off one of the feet in 1696.

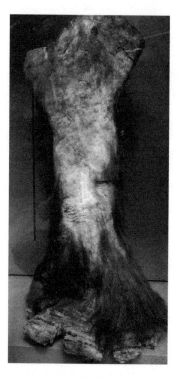

Woolly mammoth foot, found frozen in Siberia, 1901, photo Matt Mechtley, Muséum national d'histoire naturelle, Paris.

Removal of the tusks and a foot was a common practice to validate one's discovery. Other discoveries of frozen mammoths appeared in accounts by Swedish (1720), German (1724), and Russian (1739, 1787) explorers.

Cuvier was familiar with these discoveries: in 1796 he was the first to identify the woolly mammoth of Arctic regions as an extinct relative of modern elephants. This means that the foreleg with the molar from America would chime with "fresh" mammoth finds already known to Cuvier. The first documented account of the removal of an entire frozen mammoth carcass to a museum was in 1806, by Scottish botanist Michael Friedrich Adams, who had laboriously recovered the exposed remains of a mammoth preserved in ice in Siberia. It had been discovered by Ossip Shoumachoff, a nomadic Tungus hunter in Siberia in 1799, who was looking for valuable tusks to sell to international merchants. The mammoth in the Lena riverbank slowly emerged from the ice over five years, the tusks and feet first. By the time Adams arrived, the carcass was missing both tusks, one ear, most of the hide—

and notably—one foreleg. Shoumachoff had already sold the tusks, hide, and presumably the front foot. Cuvier wrote (1821) about this "Adams" mammoth skeleton, which was reconstructed and mounted, apparently with a substitute foreleg, in 1807–15, in the Russian Academy of Science, St. Petersburg.

The foot and tooth from America seen by Cuvier no longer exist. If this *was* a ruse, it is a complex one. (See chapter 17 for other fossil frauds.) The showman was clever to include a well-worn pachyderm tooth with the apparently fresh foot. The provenience and chain of custody are remarkably detailed. The details of names and places give the account credibility. On the other hand, those who seek to deceive often provide a plethora of details to lend an air of truth.

The incident raises intriguing questions. Where did the foot come from? Could it have been removed from a preserved mammoth carcass or parts of one that was naturally preserved in anaerobic conditions of a bog, or mummified in an extremely dry desert cave in America? Mummified Pleistocene sloths, condors, and mammoth hair and dung have been recovered from arid desert caves in Utah, New Mexico, and other southwestern locales. Native Americans had an interest in extraordinary fossils and other relics, and carried out far-reaching trade of such items among themselves and with Mexican *comancheros*. So it is not impossible that a mammoth tooth and mummified foot were obtained by Pawnee traders and made their way via a Mexican trader and Frenchmen to Paris.

But as we have seen, preserved mammoth remains from Arctic ice were known in Europe by this time. Possibly the foot displayed in Paris came from one of these carcasses. But if so, surely more of the woolly mammoth leg would have been displayed for maximum impact.

There is another possible explanation. Cuvier compared the foot to that of a living elephant. Were there any living elephants in America at the time? Could the foot have come from a recently deceased captive elephant in a traveling menagerie? Delving into the history of circus elephants, I learned that the first live elephant in America was a two-year-old calf from Calcutta, India. It arrived in Salem, Massachusetts, in 1796 and was first displayed in New York and Philadelphia. President George Washington paid to see this elephant in Philadelphia in November 1796. This elephant continued to travel around New England, Pennsylvania, and the Carolinas until 1818, when advertisements about it ceased. Its fate is unknown and nothing is written about the disposition of its remains. If the elephant had died before 1812 and only its remains were displayed until 1818, might one of its front feet have been acquired by Lambert?

The second elephant, Old Bet, arrived in Boston in 1804 and was exhibited around New England until she was killed by an irate farmer in 1816 in Maine. Old Bet's owner continued to show the elephant's remains for five years after her death, until 1821. That year he sold Old Bet's remains to the American Museum in New York. Bet's remains were described in one source as "the hide and bones." Another source indicates that the skeleton and hide were stuffed and mounted for permanent display. But the timing of Old Bet's death in 1816 makes it impossible that her forefoot ended up in Paris.

By 1818 four live elephants were being exhibited on the road, in Boston, Philadelphia, and other cities, but they are also too late to account for Cuvier's specimen seen in 1812. This narrows down the possibilities considerably. If the preserved foot seen by Cuvier was removed from a deceased captive elephant in America, it could only have come from the sole elephant in America at that time, the Indian elephant seen by George Washington in 1796—but only if that elephant had expired before 1812. The curious story of the mammoth foot from America remains mysterious: where did the well-worn tooth come from? Who concocted the highly detailed chain-of-custody narrative? And why?

Of course, living elephants were also displayed in Europe in Cuvier's time. The Jardin des Plantes, for example, where Cuvier carried out his work, opened a menagerie in 1794 and acquired two elephants from Ceylon (Sri Lanka) in 1797. Earlier, in 1771, Parisians were entertained by an elephant doing tricks in the rue Dauphine. The foot could have been taken from a deceased elephant in Europe; it could then have been passed off as a mammoth relic with an exciting discovery story involving "les sauvages" in America. A mammoth tooth would serve to verify the claim.

So we are left with four possibilities: the foot belonged to a deceased living elephant acquired in Europe or America, or the foot was from a preserved Pleistocene mammoth acquired in Siberia or America. The explanation given by the owner—that the foot and molar and accompanying story record the authentic discovery of the forefoot of a long-extinct mammoth naturally mummified by extremely dry conditions in a cave of the Southwest—would be an amazing revelation. And Cuvier's account would contain a heretofore unrecognized milestone in paleontological history.

CHAPTER 19

Geronimo's Dragon

SINCE WRITING *Fossil Legends of the First Americans* in 2005, I sometimes receive letters from schoolchildren about remarkable remains described by Native Americans. A few years ago, a third-grader wrote to say that his dad had read parts of my book to him. Next, they read Geronimo's autobiography together. The boy was excited to recognize an Apache fossil legend in Geronimo's life story. This was new to me, and I was delighted to learn about it from his letter.

Geronimo (1829–1909) was a spiritual leader and fearless warrior who defended Apache territory against incursions by Mexico and United States. During the Apache Wars in 1858, his mother, wife, and three children were killed, and he sought revenge in relentless raids on the invaders. Eluding capture numerous times, Geronimo was called "the worst Indian who ever lived" by the local white settlers.

Not until 1886, after many escapes, was Geronimo finally taken prisoner. He was fifty-five years old. After a long-drawn-out pursuit, he surrendered in Skeleton Canyon, Arizona (so named for the bones of cows and cowboys who had died on cattle drives up from Mexico). In 1894, Geronimo and 341 other Chiricahua Apache captives were transferred to Fort Sill, Lawton, Oklahoma.

Twenty years after his capture, and until his death, Geronimo was still a prisoner of war at Fort Sill. The old Apache never saw his homeland again. Capitalizing on his notoriety, Wild West shows exhibited Geronimo in staged events, always under army guard. On his deathbed in 1909, Geronimo confided to a relative that he regretted surrendering: "I should have fought until I was the last man alive."

Geronimo, engraving based on photograph by A. Frank Randall, 1886.

Five years earlier, in 1904, Geronimo and Stephen Melvil Barrett had become friends, after they shared watermelon *à l'Apache* (cut in large chunks) at the Apache's tipi. Barrett was the superintendent of education of Lawton, Oklahoma, and an Indian translator. Geronimo recounted his life story to Barrett, who sought permission to publish it. But the army officers in charge of prisoners at Fort Sill angrily rejected the idea of transcribing Geronimo's life story. They declared that he should be hanged instead of spoiled with attention.

So Barrett wrote to President Theodore Roosevelt for permission to publish the autobiography. The president readily directed the War Department to give official approval. Geronimo spoke in Apache and Spanish. Barrett asked Geronimo's close Apache friend, Asa Deklugie, to translate Geronimo's Apache words into English, to ensure authenticity. Barrett strove to tell the Apaches' side of the conflict. He thought it was important to "extend to Geronimo . . . the courtesy due any captive, the right to state the causes which impelled him in his opposition to our civilization and laws."

The autobiography was published in 1906. Geronimo begins by recounting his tribe's traditional creation story.

In the beginning the world was dark, and there were many hideous, nameless monsters. These terrible, enormous beasts were lizard-like. In Barrett's and Deklugie's translation, Geronimo calls them "serpents" or "dragons." These creatures of land made war on the great creatures of the sky. Some of the serpents were too wise to be killed in these cosmic battles, however. These monsters took refuge in perpendicular cliffs in the mountains and deserts of Arizona. Their eyes turned into brilliant stones that you can see embedded in the rocks of the desert.

One huge dragon, covered with a coat of layered horny scales, was invincible. Arrows could not penetrate its hide. This monster lived on top of a steep cliff in the desert. The powerful dragon was finally slain by a young Apache hero. With a tremendous roar, the dragon rolled down the precipice into the canyon below. Then a terrific thunderstorm swept over the mountain with flashing lightning and driving rain. After the storm passed, the people could see, far down in the canyon below, the immense body of the dragon in the rocks. Geronimo says that the bones of that dragon could still be seen at the bottom of the cliff.

This Apache scenario, narrated by Geronimo in 1906, ends with what sounds like personal knowledge or even firsthand observation of impressive bones at the base of a cliff. This is exactly where paleontologists look for dinosaur fossils today.

Enormous skulls and bones of massive reptiles—dinosaurs of the Jurassic and Cretaceous epochs—continually weather out of eroding cliff faces and gullies in the deserts of Arizona and New Mexico. And the skeletons of dinosaurs are often revealed by fierce thunderstorms, just as in the Apache tradition. Geronimo's story suggests how fearsome-looking fossil skeletons discovered by Native Americans might have inspired exciting stories of monsters and their deaths in the remote past.

Enslaved Africans Were First to Identify Mammoth Fossils in America

LABORING IN A SWAMPY FIELD on Stono Plantation (South Carolina), a crew of enslaved Africans dug up some colossal teeth in about 1725 (some years before the great Stono Rebellion of 1739, the largest slave revolt in the Southern Colonies). The English botanist Mark Catesby had been traveling around the American colonies collecting specimens, describing and illustrating the wildlife of the New World (his two-volume work was published in 1732–43). Catesby eagerly visited Stono to view the amazing discovery. His hosts, the plantation owners, assured him that the great molars were all that was left of a giant victim of Noah's Flood from the Bible. At that time, this was the common explanation for all oversized fossils in Europe and the American colonies.

But Catesby decided to question the men who discovered the immense teeth on the plantation. He reported that the "Opinion of all the *Negroes*, native *Africans*, who saw the teeth" was unanimous. These were the molars of a familiar animal from their homeland. The Africans insisted that the big teeth belonged to an elephant. Catesby agreed with the

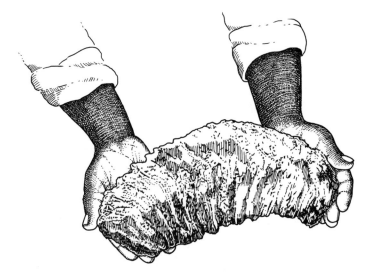

African holding mammoth tooth. Drawing by Michele Angel.

slaves. Unlike the white plantation owners in the Carolinas, Catesby had himself examined some enormous molars of an African elephant in a museum in London. Like the African workers, he immediately saw the similarities.

In Paris, Catesby's account intrigued the famous naturalist Georges Cuvier (see chapter 18). At the time, Cuvier was developing his new theory that massive fossils around the world belonged to prehistoric creatures, mammoths and mastodons. He was gathering evidence from indigenous oral traditions in the Americas to show that these animals, known only by their petrified remains, were the ancient ancestors of today's elephants, and that they had all perished in a catastrophe eons ago. Impressed with Catesby's report, Cuvier translated it into French. Cuvier held some deplorable "scientific racist" notions of white superiority common in his era. Yet he honestly declared in 1806 that it was "les nègres" in America who had correctly recognized a fossil elephant species before any European naturalist had even realized that extinct mammoths were related to living elephants.

The enslaved people working at Stono Plantation were originally from the Kingdom of Kongo (Angola and Congo) in Central Africa. Some of the men may have only recently arrived in the Carolinas. Their homeland was the habitat of the living *Loxodonta* elephant species of Africa. The teeth the men found at Stono belonged to a great Columbian mammoth of the Pleistocene era, which had died thousands of years ago and became buried in the swamp. Mammoth teeth are flat with ridges, unlike the sharp, pointed teeth of mastodons found along the Ohio River. Mammoth molars closely resemble the "grinders" of living African elephants. The Africans had routinely observed the skeletons, skulls, and teeth of elephants in Africa, and that experience allowed them to correctly identify the mammoth teeth in America. They must have been excited to find the remains of a familiar animal so far from home.

Meanwhile in Virginia, enslaved Africans (owned by George Washington and others) loaded plantation crops on barges on the Potomac. These workers often pointed out strange Miocene fossils of whales and shark teeth that eroded out of the cliffsides above the river. In 1782, for example, workmen digging in salt marshes in Virginia unearthed teeth and "Bones of uncommon size." Major Arthur Campbell sent some of these bones and molars to Thomas Jefferson at Monticello. Campbell included a letter saying that "Several sensible Africans have seen the tooth, particularly a fellow" owned by Jefferson's neighbor. "All [the Africans] pronounced it an Elephant," wrote Campbell. This means that the teeth belonged to a mammoth like those unearthed at Stono, rather than to a mastodon. Once again, the Africans correctly identified the fossils that bewildered their white masters.

Jefferson had a hard time accepting Cuvier's idea that all these behemoths were extinct. He wanted to believe that these magnificent beasts—then known as "Ohio Monsters"—still flourished somewhere in the New World. The discoveries of enormous teeth and bones on plantations and along the Ohio River encouraged his dream. He hoped that on their expedition of 1803–6 Meriwether Lewis and William Clark would find living Ohio Monsters in the Northwest Territories. Instead, Lewis and Clark found vast herds of massive bison that had inherited the plains of North America after the demise of Pleistocene megafauna. Unfortunately, we have no record of the thoughts of York, an enslaved black man who accompanied Lewis and Clark across the continent to the Pacific and back. York was born in Virginia in 1770 and may have observed discoveries and identifications of mammoth fossils by Africans. It would be fascinating to know his reactions to the great beasts of the American savannas.

FORMIDABLE WOMEN

Beauty Secrets of the Ancient Amazons

CABBAGE, CANNABIS, AND FRANKINCENSE

GALLOPING FOR MILES ON FAST HORSES, hunting, making war, marauding, and plundering, hot and dry in the summer and bitterly cold in the winter—life on the steppes was dirty, dusty work for the Scythians of antiquity. The Scythians were nomadic tribes whose lives centered on horses, archery, and warfare. They crisscrossed the vast steppes from the Ukraine to Mongolia. These tribes flourished from about 800 BC to AD 500. The men and women of Scythia were famed for their endurance and ability to withstand wintry temperatures and snow.

The rugged lifestyle of the Scythian women influenced countless ancient Greek myths and legends about fierce Amazons, whose thrilling exploits were illustrated in Greek art. Many ancient vase paintings depict Amazons wearing distinctive woolen leggings and tunics, leather boots, felt hats with earflaps, and animal skins—accurately reflecting the clothing worn by Scythian mounted archers of both sexes. Articles of clothing designed for cold weather, along with quivers full of arrows and horse gear, have been found in the graves of real women warriors of Scythia, who roamed across Russia, Ukraine, Siberia, and Central Asia twenty-five hundred years ago. The women's skeletons reveal the effects of a harsh outdoor life of riding and warfare. Many of the horsewomen's bones bore signs of injuries, such as broken limbs from falls, bowed legs, arthritis, combat wounds, and embedded arrowheads.

How did saddle-sore, battle-scarred Amazons relax and tend to their bodies?

The Scythian heartland was the territory north of the Black Sea around the Don River (the ancient Tanais) in southern Russia. In antiquity, the Greeks called the Don the "Amazon" River because it was said that the Amazons liked to bathe there. The Don freezes over from November to April. But the real-life Amazons had a secret weapon against icy temperatures. In an obscure treatise, *On Rivers* by Pseudo-Plutarch (probably third century AD), the author reported that along the Amazon (Don) River where the Amazons used to bathe, "there is a plant called *halinda*, like a colewort. Bruising this plant and anointing their bodies with the juice made the Amazons better able to endure the extreme cold."

What was this mysterious folk remedy for warming the body in ancient Scythia?

Pseudo-Plutarch gives a clue for identifying the ancient Scythian word *halinda* by comparing it to colewort, a primitive headless cabbage. Some botanical detective work reveals that *halinda* was a plant in the Brassicaceae mustard family. The mustard family includes *Brassica oleracea* or *Brassica napus*, a hardy wild winter cabbage of Russia and Siberia, related to the bright yellow flowering rapeseed now cultivated for industrial and edible canola oils. The leafy coleworts are the ancestors of today's edible cabbages, kale, collards, brussels sprouts, broccoli, cauliflower, mustard, and rapeseed/canola oil.

These cruciferous plants were first cultivated between twenty-five hundred and four thousand years ago. To make them more pleasant tasting, farmers bred them over the centuries to reduce the amount of mustard oils, the sulfur-containing glucosinolates, which give the wild species their pungent, bitter taste. The Scythian nomads of antiquity would have used the plants growing wild on the steppes north of the Caucasus, around the Don River.

Crushed wild cabbage yields mustard oil, a skin irritant. The oil activates thermo-sensitive transient receptor potential (thermoTRPV1) in cellular and nerve channels to create a sensation of warmth. In the chemical process, discovered in 2021, mustard oil switches on the same receptor responsible for sensing heat. Rubbed on the body, Brassica oil is a strong stimulant of circulation, sending blood to the skin surface, causing a warm sensation and alleviating and masking pain signals from inflammatory injuries and arthritis, common among the Scythians, as skeletal studies show. The analgesic action of the wild cabbage is similar to that of capsaicin, the irritant oil from hot chili peppers from the Americas, which today is applied as a topical ointment to relieve arthritis and other pains. The real-life Amazons of ancient Scythia could also have benefited from cabbage oil's antibacterial properties, perhaps using it as a poultice for wounds. And in the summertime, *halinda* oil would be useful as an insect repellent.

For Scythians out on the wide steppes, bathing in rivers was not always convenient. A cleansing vapor bath was a special occasion usually undertaken as a purification before funerals in the spring. In the fifth century BC, the inquisitive Greek historian Herodotus visited the Black Sea region and brought back detailed descriptions of this Scythian-style toilette (1.202; 4.73–75). Their unusually refreshing sauna sounds like a New Age spa treatment.

The Scythians, remarks Herodotus, scrub their heads with soap (tallow and oil) and water, but they never wash their bodies with soap. Instead they prepare a little tent for a vapor bath with a special ingredient: cannabis (hemp, marijuana). "A plant called *kannabis* grows in Scythia," writes Herodotus, "similar to flax but much thicker and taller. This plant is wild in Scythia. But the Thracians cultivate *kannabis* and weave garments from it that are just like linen. Unless you are quite familiar with hemp you would think this cloth is linen." Herodotus speaks with authority, apparently having seen and touched hemp clothing.

Hemp pollen, fiber, and textiles are found in ancient sites from the Black Sea to China. Hemp was also prized for the flax-like fiber that can be plaited into twine or rope and woven into textiles for clothing. Hemp clothing has been recovered from Scythian graves. Scythian women probably used hemp to make lariats, which were useful for herding their horses. The hemp lariats were also weapons. Scythian horsewomen were notorious for their skill with the lasso in battle.

Herodotus tells how the Scythians would construct a small tent for a vapor bath by fixing in the ground three or four long sticks to make a tipi-like enclosure. Pieces of woolen felt or hides are stretched over the poles, overlapping to fit as close as possible. Inside the tipi they place a large stone bowl or brazier and fill it with red-hot stones. The procedure is remarkably

similar to preparations for Native American sweat-lodge ceremonies. As the Scythian men and women enter the felt tipi,
wrote Herodotus, "they toss handfuls of *kannabis* seeds onto
the heated stones. These seeds smoulder and smoke and create great clouds of steam." In fact, of course, they would have
tossed more potent marijuana flower *buds*, not seeds, on the
stones, in this ancient version of "hot-boxing."

Herodotus declared that the cannabis smoke "produces
such a delightful vapor that no Greek vapor-bath can exceed
it!" Emerging from their little tents, "the Scythians howl with
joy, elated by this intoxicating steam-bath that serves them
instead of a water-bath." One has the impression that Herodotus was speaking from experience or at least observation.

In another passage about the land between the Black Sea
and the Caspian (now Turkey, Armenia, Azerbaijan, Iran),
Herodotus describes the custom of gathering an intoxicating
"fruit" to use when they assemble in large groups. The nomads sit in a circle around a fire and throw this "fruit" onto
the embers. The "fruit" would have been cannabis buds, as
in the previous passage. "As it burns, the people inhale the
fumes and become intoxicated, just as Greeks become inebriated with wine." Herodotus continues, "They keep adding
more to the flames and become even more intoxicated and
dance and sing around the fire. Herodotus's language indicates
that women and men participated together. And we now can
confirm his account, because archaeologists have discovered
equipment for making the tipis and personal hemp-burning
kits in ancient nomads' burials in Kazakhstan and other sites
across ancient Scythia.

Both men and women were buried with their own personal hemp-smoking equipment—poles for making the little

tipis, braziers for heated rocks, and golden vessels for smoking that still contain burnt hemp seeds and residue. It is worth noting that cannabis would also have served to ease the aches and pains from the rigors of daily life, arthritis, and constant battle. There is no evidence that cannabis was a drug taken before battle. It seems that cannabis was used for recreation and relaxation, funerals, and pain management. Some art historians have speculated that psychotropic cannabis hallucinations may have played a role in the famous Scythian "animal style" art form in artifacts and tattoos, depicting real animals and fantastic creatures in surrealistic ways.

Herodotus next divulges a recipe for an Amazon beauty mask (4.8 and 23–31). Scythian women, reports Herodotus, concoct a mixture of cypress, cedar, and frankincense. They pound these ingredients into a paste on a rough stone, adding a little water. When the substance takes on a smooth, thick consistency, they cover their faces, and indeed their whole bodies, with the paste.

Today, all three of these ingredients are used in perfumes, cosmetics, and pharmaceuticals. Russian cedar (*Pinus sibirica*) and cypress (*Microbiota decussata*) grow at high altitudes, as easily available to the Scythian nomads as local cannabis. Fragrant cedar and cypress oils have antiseptic qualities, helpful in fighting infection. Both are astringents, improving oily, flaky skin, employed today against acne and dermatitis. Frankincense also appears in ancient Egyptian recipes for beauty masks, used for toning skin and smoothing scars, and today it is found in products reputed to rejuvenate skin. Frankincense has antiseptic, anti-inflammatory properties. But even more interesting is the recent finding that the aromatics in frankincense alleviate anxiety and depression.

Small lumps of frankincense, the aromatic resin of *Boswellia* trees of the Arabian Desert (also found in India), would have been a precious trade commodity (see chapters 1 and 50). From the grave goods recovered from their burials, we know that the Scythians engaged in far-reaching trade, across the Incense and Silk Routes from the Mediterranean and Middle East to Asia.

According to Herodotus, after applying the special paste to their faces and bodies, the women retire for the night. When they remove the salve the next morning, comments Herodotus, a sweet scent is imparted to them, and their skin is clean and glossy. Once again, the ever-curious historian provides us with vivid "you-are-there" details in these intimate accounts of the Scythian lifestyle.

Arab Warrior Queens

NEO-ASSYRIAN RECORDS of the eighth century BC name several queens who ruled Qedar, a confederation of nomadic Arab and Semitic tribes that ranged from the Syrian desert to the Nile (the area shown in the map in chapter 1). The Qedarites (Kedarites) were also mentioned in the Old Testament and by Greek and Roman writers. These people rode dromedaries—swift Arabian camels—and horses, and were traders of sheep, goats, horses, spices, and aromatic incense and perfumes.

Zabibi (her name means "raisin") was "Sarrat qur Aribi" (queen of the Arabs") from 738 to 733 BC. Some scholars have suggested that she was part of the dynasty of female rulers that included the queen of Sheba who met King Solomon in the Old Testament. Queen Zabibi ruled as a vassal or client who paid tribute to the Assyrian king Tiglath-Pileser III. Queen Zabibi's successor was another woman, Samsi (Arabic, "sun").

Tiglath-Pileser III's inscriptions on stone slabs and clay tablets of 733 BC mention "Samsi, Queen of the Arabs." One says she paid tribute in camels and another says that she violated an oath that she swore by the god Shamash. Samsi had allied with Rakhianu, the ruler of Damascus, Syria, and together they led a rebellion against Tiglath-Pileser III in 732 BC. The

Arab girls and women in Samsi's army rode horses and used bows and spears. The decisive battle took place on the plain below Mount Saquurri (site unknown, south of Damascus). Samsi's army was defeated and her tents were burned. According to Assyrian archives, Queen Samsi was not captured but "fled into the desert like a wild she-ass."

The Assyrian comparison to an ass was apt, not an insult. The Syrian *hemippe*, an extinct species of small (about three feet at the shoulder) ass, was a very strong and swift onager. Herds of onagers were once common, roaming across the nomads' territories of Syria, Israel, Jordan, Saudi Arabia, and Iran. The Syrian onagers were dark and tawny in summer and pale sand-colored in winter. Considered in antiquity to be as beautiful as thoroughbred horses, the wild asses were notoriously elusive and impossible to tame or domesticate. The last two wild Syrian onagers on the planet both died in 1927: one was in the wild, shot by a hunter in Jordan, and the other died a captive in a zoo far from home, in Vienna, Austria.

In 732 BC, Queen Samsi surrendered and negotiated an agreement with Tiglath-Pileser III that allowed her to remain queen of the Qedar until 728 BC. She was succeeded by Queen Yatie.

Queen Yatie joined the coalition of Chaldeans, Elamites, and Aramaeans to fight the Assyrian king Sennacherib in 703 BC for control of Babylon. Her successor was a woman called Te'el-hunu. Unfortunately, nothing is known of her except her name. The Qedarites also disappeared from the historical record by the first century AD.

One of the best-known Arab-Muslim warrior women of later times was Khawlah bint al-Azwar, sister of Dhiraar bin al-Azwar, commander of the Rashidun army in the wave of

Khawlah bint al-Azwar, on Jordanian postage stamp, 1981, photo courtesy of Mahdi Bseiso.

seventh-century Muslim conquests after the death of Muhammad. Khawlah fought alongside her brother in the great Battle of Yarmouk, which ended Byzantine rule in Syria, in AD 636. She was wounded in hand-to-hand combat with a Greek soldier.

In 2019, 134 female cadets graduated from Khawla bint Al Azwar Military School, Abu Dhabi, United Arab Emirates. The "Khawla School," sponsored by the United Nations Entity for Gender Equality, trained women from Bahrain, Saudi Arabia, Jordan, Egypt, Yemen, Sudan, and the United Arab Emirates to serve in security and peacekeeping operations.

Chiomara, Courageous Celtic Woman

EVERYONE'S HEARD OF BOUDICCA, the acclaimed warrior queen of the Celtic Iceni tribe of Britain who led the revolt against the Roman occupiers in AD 60–61. Ancient historians described the women of the Celts and Gauls as robust and brave. Diodorus of Sicily, for example, wrote in the first century BC that the Gallic women were tall like the men and of equal courage. Ammianus Marcellinus, in the fourth century AD, declared that the females of Gaul were as big and as strong as the males. Fearsome with flashing eyes and gnashing teeth, the women were brave fighters in battle.

Mystery surrounds the ancient Celtic woman often referred to as "Chiomaca," the wife of Ortiagon, chief of the Gauls in Asia Minor. Several modern writers claim that Chiomaca was a Celtic woman warrior who "fought and bravely killed a Roman centurion in 186 BC" during the Galatian War. What is the true story?

If we go back to the original ancient accounts, we can set the record straight. First, we learn that this woman's name was not Chiomaca but *Chiomara*. She was captured by the Romans in 189 BC (not 186 BC), after Gnaeus Manlius Vulso's army defeated the Galatians, the Greco-Gauls who had migrated to Asia Minor, now central Turkey. The ancient sources are Plutarch's *Bravery of Women*, Polybius, Livy, Valerius Maximus, and Florus.

According to the ancient accounts, Chiomara did not actually fight in the battle. She was captured along with other Galatian women and slaves. While she was a prisoner, she was raped by a Roman centurion. The centurion then demanded a ransom from Chiomara's husband, the chieftain Ortiagon. Chiomara, who had been captured with her slave, was allowed to dispatch her slave with the demand for ransom.

Ortiagon sent two Galatians to deliver the ransom. The centurion released Chiomara but insisted on embracing her first. While his back was turned, as he was either counting the gold or embracing her, Chiomara gave the Galatian men a signal to kill the centurion. The Galatians beheaded the Roman soldier and presented his head to Chiomara. She then wrapped the Roman's head in her robe and escaped. She delivered the head to her husband, saying, "Only one man should have me."

It is fascinating to trace how the false tales about Chiomara came to be perpetuated. No ancient Greek or Roman historian ever described Chiomara taking part in the battle, yet typical modern accounts state that in 186 BC she participated in the skirmish as the Gaulish soldiers retreated. One modern account says, "Chiomaca stood her ground and killed several Roman soldiers before she was captured [and] raped by a centurion. Later she escaped, found the officer, cut his head off, and presented it to her husband." This account was written by David Jones in *Women Warriors: A History* (1997, rpt. 2005, p. 148). Jones cites his source as Norma Goodrich, *Medieval*

Myths (1977). But the citation is incorrect, for the story of Chiomara does not appear in that book. In fact, Jones found the story in Jessica Amanda Salmonson's popular *Encyclopedia of Amazons* (1991, p. 57). Salmonson's entry reads: "Chiomaca: A martial princess of the Gauls [who was] captured . . . in 186 BC. She refused to leave the battlefield but raged on with her few companions. When captured, she was raped by a centurion. She subsequently killed the centurion and chopped off his head which she delivered to her husband." Salmonson's source

Chiomara presenting Roman centurion's head to Ortiagon, medieval woodcut, Johannes Zainer, 1474.

was Sarah Hale's 1855 book, *Women's Record: Or Sketches of All Distinguished Women, from Creation to A.D. 1854* (1855, p. 30).

In 1855, Sarah Hale spelled Chiomara's name correctly, but Hale said nothing about Chiomara taking part in the battle. Hale gave an embellished account of the delivery of the ransom. She says that the Galatians killed the centurion as he accepted the gold, and she claims it was Chiomara who cut off his head and presented it to her husband. Jones and Salmonson each published garbled accounts derived from Hale's book of 1855.

The truth, according to the evidence in the five ancient sources, is that the historical Chiomara did not participate in combat, nor did she behead the Roman centurion herself. So she was not really a warrior woman or a "martial princess" who took part in battle. However, the accounts by ancient Greek and Roman historians do all agree that Chiomara was a brave and resourceful Celtic woman, worthy of respect.

CHAPTER 24

Camilla

WHY IS THERE AN AMAZON
IN THE *AENEID*?

THE STORY OF CAMILLA, the legendary warrior woman of
Virgil's *Aeneid*, is sometimes overlooked, overshadowed by
more renowned episodes, like the scene with ghosts in Underworld and the tragic love affair of Dido and Aeneas. Camilla's tale raises intriguing questions. Why did Virgil include
an Amazon-like woman in his epic poem about the founding
of Rome? Was Camilla invented by Virgil? Or was her story
based on a lost Italian legend?

Virgil and his Roman readers knew all about Amazons in
Greek mythology, "the equals of men" in courage and battle.
The greatest Greek heroes, from Heracles and Theseus to Achilles, had proved their valor by overcoming the formidable Amazon queens Hippolyte, Antiope, and Penthesilea. One of the
most exciting Greek myths about the Trojan War recounts how
the valiant warrior queen Penthesilea and her twelve Amazons
came to aid the Trojans. Virgil described Penthesilea early in
his epic: "Ferocious Penthesilea, with her gold belt fastened
beneath her exposed breast, leads her band of Amazons with
their crescent light-shields." He calls her a *belletrix*, a warrior-
ess, "who dares to fight with men." The Amazons fought and

187

died fearlessly on the battlefield at Troy. Penthesilea herself was killed in single combat with the Greek hero Achilles.

The Romans also knew that Athenians, in their own foundation legend, celebrated their glorious victory over powerful Amazons, in a great battle that tested the mettle of the young city and its founder Theseus. In Virgil's grand epic poem about Rome's founding, then, it seems fitting that Rome's own heroic founder, Aeneas, would also triumph over Amazons.

The ancient Trojan War legend is key to understanding Virgil's *Aeneid*. In his epic, Aeneas and his followers are survivors of the Trojan War, who sail off to Italy to make a new life. Their conquests consolidated the land and overcame the indigenous Italian peoples who would be absorbed into the new world of Rome. Traditions about Trojans in Italy had arisen several centuries before Virgil started writing the *Aeneid* in about 25–19 BC. The idea that some Trojan refugees sailed to Italy can be traced to a poem by the Greek poet Lycophron, written in about 250 BC. That poem recounts the fates of those who escaped from Troy after the Greeks destroyed the city.

Lycophron also tells how a young Amazon named Klete had been left behind in the Amazons' stronghold on the Black Sea while Penthesilea went to fight for Troy. When Penthesilea did not return, Klete and some other young Amazons set out by sea to search for their lost queen. Swept away by storms, they were shipwrecked on the toe of Italy. These Amazons named the place after their leader, Klete, and she and her descendants ruled the region. The town Caulonia was named after Klete's son Caulon.

Virgil relied on the body of legends about Trojan survivors described by Lycophron for the tale of Aeneas and his Trojans. Virgil's familiarity with the story that Amazons had settled in

Italy around the same time that Aeneas and his Trojans arrived provides another reason for Virgil to include Amazon-like women in the *Aeneid*.

Historical accounts of real female fighters were also well known to Virgil and his audience. Cyrus the Great of Persia had died trying to defeat Tomyris, the warrior queen of the Massagetae, as recounted by Herodotus. Roman historians told how Alexander the Great had dallied with the Amazon queen Thalestris. Romans admired the romance of King Mithradates and the horsewoman-archer Hypsicratea during the Mithradatic Wars, in 89–63 BC. And everyone knew that Pompey had displayed a troop of captive "Amazons" from the Caucasus in his triumph of 61 BC in Rome. A generation later, while Virgil was writing the *Aeneid*, in 27–22 BC, the notorious one-eyed Nubian warrior queen Amanirenas defeated Roman forces in two battles.

All these historical female fighters would have primed the Romans for an exciting Amazon episode in the *Aeneid*. In Virgil's epic, Camilla is a warrior maiden of the Volscian tribe fighting on the side of the indigenous Italians against Aeneas and the Trojans, the forefathers of the Romans. Camilla allies with Turnus, the leader of the Rutuli tribe.

Like Penthesilea, Camilla is described as a *belletrix*. In the epic, she fights with reckless passion and slays many Trojan warriors, "exulting like an Amazon." She accepts the challenge to fight the son of the hero Aunus. Camilla ruthlessly kills the son of Aunus in cold blood. In her magnificent and ferocious beauty, so vital yet doomed, she seems to represent the untamed vigor and nobility of the indigenous Italians, who are fated to be overcome yet incorporated into the new Roman world.

Camilla slaying the son of Aunus, engraving by Wenceslas Hollar, ca. 1650.

Ultimately, like all valiant Amazons of myth, Camilla loses her life. Camilla does not die by the hand of Aeneas but is slain in a sneak attack by a minor figure. The stealthy warrior Arruns stalks Camilla and hurls his spear while she is distracted. This unfair ambush brings up complicated issues. For some scholars her manner of death seems anticlimactic. But one could say that it makes Camilla's death, after such heroic actions, doubly tragic, because she is denied the chance of face-to-face combat with Arruns. It recalls the pathetic death of Achilles, felled by an arrow in the back of his ankle, shot from afar by the unheroic Paris.

Arruns is able to kill Camilla because she is momentarily distracted from her lust for warfare by her lust for spoils. Her fall is sometimes attributed to a feminine weakness for glittering riches. But many mythic male heroes succumb to similar desires for trophies and treasure. The lesson might instead be Virgil's warning against material excess in the new imperial era.

Camilla's dying words are gallant and fierce. Her Amazon companions gather to mourn the loss of their leader. Virgil gives them interesting names: Larina means "protector"; Tulla means "supporter"; Acca means "mother"; and Tarpeia, "funeral urn." To avenge Camilla's death, her patron goddess Diana sends the nymph-archer Opis (the name means "sight" or "vengeance") to kill Arruns.

Was Camilla totally imaginary? Many scholars have wondered whether there were Roman or Italian oral traditions about Camilla or someone like her. Was Virgil drawing on ancient, unwritten Volscian legends? Or did he invent Camilla, modeling her on Penthesilea, the Amazon queen who fought the Greeks at Troy?

No legends about Camilla are known before the *Aeneid*, but it is plausible that there were ancient Etruscan, Volscian, or other Italian folktales about Camilla or women like her. Prominent Romans of Virgil's day (including Virgil's patron, the emperor Augustus) were proud of their Volscian heritage; folklore about their ancestors may have circulated orally in Rome. It is striking that Virgil gives Camilla a charming childhood legend. Her upbringing has a fairy-tale quality that combines familiar folk motifs and themes—but it also contains some unique details. Some details hint that the poet was drawing on lost Italian folktales about a young woman who was raised to be a warrior.

Camilla's father, the Volscian king Metabus, was driven into exile. Escaping from his enemies with his infant daughter, he runs into an obstacle, a raging river, the Amasenus. The name sounds a bit like "Amazon." Metabus comes up with a risky idea and prays that it will work. Metabus lashes the baby girl to his spear and throws it across to the other bank. He swims across and retrieves his precious daughter in the grass. This strange exploit is not a known folklore motif. Was it based on some real event that became legendary?

In his prayer, Camilla's father promises to dedicate his daughter to the goddess of the hunt, Diana. Like many other folk heroes, Camilla was raised in the wilderness, nursed by a wild animal. The Romans would be reminded that a she-wolf had nursed Romulus and Remus, the founders of Rome. Virgil chooses a wild horse to provide Camilla's nourishment. Notably, this detail echoes something that Herodotus and other ancient historians had reported about Amazons—that they fed their babies horse's milk.

As a girl, Camilla outruns the wind and flies over grass so lightly she never bends a blade. She could even dash over the waves of the sea without getting her feet wet. This poetic imagery gives Camilla a mythic nymph-like quality. But it also brings to mind the Greek wild girl Atalanta, a runner and huntress companion of Diana (Artemis), who was exposed as a baby in the forest and nursed by a mother bear. Camilla was raised to be a huntress among the shepherds. Also like Atalanta—and like girls of steppe nomad tribes who were the models for mythic Amazons—Camilla learns to ride, throw a javelin, and shoot a bow at a very early age. It is interesting that Virgil even describes Camilla performing a Parthian shot, the nomad horsewomen's feat of shooting arrows backward at enemies while galloping away. Many Etruscan bronze artifacts made in Italy show Amazon horsewomen executing Parthian shots.

There were multiple reasons for Virgil to decide to pit his great Roman heroes against bold women warriors. Inspired by both myth and history, his audience would certainly anticipate the appearance of Amazons in a rousing story of victory over an array of powerful enemies. Amazons were deeply admired as noble heroines even as they evoked ambivalent emotions. In the mythic world of Greece and Rome, Amazons always die young and beautiful. This is often seen as just another example of misogyny. But Amazons were foreigners—barbarians—and in patriotic mythologies of warrior cultures like Greece and Rome, the foe must be strong, fearsome, worthy of fighting and defeating. Otherwise, male heroes would earn no glory. It was natural, therefore, that Virgil would give Camilla a brave heart and an honorable death in battle, even as Aeneas ultimately triumphs. Camilla, though defeated, serves as an exemplary heroine whose robust native Italian roots will nourish and invigorate the new Roman era.

CHAPTER 25

Plato and the Amazons

WHAT DID PLATO HAVE TO SAY ABOUT AMAZONS? It is an unexpected question. The great Athenian philosopher might seem an unlikely commentator on the fierce, barbarian warrior women of Greek mythology. How could Amazons or warlike females figure in the great thinker's rigorous dialectical dialogues on politics, justice, love, virtue, education, laws, and metaphysics?

In fact, there is evidence that Plato (ca. 428–348 BC) devoted some thought to women's roles in ideal states. Published after his death, Plato's *Laws* features a remarkably admiring perspective on Amazons of myth and their real-life counterparts, the horsewomen-archers of nomadic steppe tribes around the Black Sea.

In this last dialogue of Plato, three unnamed interlocutors—an Athenian, a Spartan, and a Cretan—debate the best ways to raise citizens in an ideal state to be well prepared for both peace and war. Plato's Athenian notes that the Spartan system goes only halfway in equality: Spartan girls participate in strenuous athletics but do not share in military service (*Laws* 7.805e–806c). The Athenian suggests that at age six, boys "should have lessons in horse riding, archery, javelin-throwing, and slinging—and the girls, too, may attend the lessons, especially in the use of the weapons." On religious

Scythian equality: male and female archers, ancient gold plaque from Scythian grave, fourth century BC, British Museum. Drawing by Michele Angel.

and public occasions, continues the Athenian, both boys and girls should be "always equipped with arms and horses" (794c, 796c).

Notably, these training activities are not the military skills of traditional Greek hoplite warriors, who fought on foot with shields and swords. Instead, these skills mimic the expertise of mounted nomad archers of Scythia-Sarmatia, the vast territory stretching from the Black Sea to Mongolia, inhabited by nomads who were adept in riding and archery. By Plato's time, Scythia was notorious for warlike women who rode to battle alongside the men.

In his surprising proposal that Greeks should take up a Scythian lifestyle, Plato specifies that foreign teachers should be imported and paid to instruct the children to ride and shoot arrows in wide-open spaces created for the purpose (*Laws*

7.804c–805b). Plato states that "girls must be trained in precisely the same things as the boys"—in athletics, riding horses, and wielding weapons. As he points out, in an emergency Greek women should "dare to imitate Sarmatian women" by "handling a bow with skill, like the Amazons," and joining the men in battle against enemies.

This radical departure from traditional Greek male and female roles is justified by more than the ancient stories of mythic Amazons. Plato declares (805e), "I now know for certain that there are countless myriads of women (whom they call Sarmatians) around the Black Sea who have to ride horses and use the bow and other weapons just like the men." In their culture, Plato notes, it is an equal duty for men and women to cultivate these skills. Together, the men and women pursue "the same activities with one accord and with all their might." Although Plato does not mention his source, his readers would have been familiar with the vivid accounts of the Greek historian Herodotus (ca. 484–425 BC). Herodotus described in detail the Scytho-Sarmatians' egalitarian customs and the women's equestrian and battle skills.

Plato argues that these sorts of mutual cooperation and equal training of men and women are essential to a society's success. Indeed, declares the philosopher, any state that does otherwise commits a "surprising blunder." Why? Because without women's participation "a half-state instead of one twice the size" would result from the same cost and effort (805a–b). In this same section of book 7 of the *Laws* (794d–795d), Plato likens this all-inclusive, doubling approach to the Scythian archers' famous ability to shoot arrows with either the right or the left hand. Such ambidexterity is crucial in fighting with bows and spears, so every boy and girl should grow up versatile in the use of both hands. The example of Scythian women, says Plato, proves that it is possible and advantageous for a state to decide that "in education and everything else females should share very much with men" (805c–d).

Millennia before modern archaeologists and classical historians accepted the reality of Amazon-like women warriors among ancient Scythians and their relationship to Amazons of Greek myth, Plato not only recognized the link and understood the logic of their lifestyle; he also used it to justify having both men and women serve as soldiers in the ideal state (see also *Republic* 5.455–57). The philosopher challenged his fellow Athenians—and us—with a thought experiment: if barbarian women can fight like men, why not Greek women?

CHAPTER 26

The Brave Women of Argos

KING CLEOMENES AND THE SPARTANS thought their war against Argos was over. Victory was theirs! The Argive army was decimated, and a few survivors had fled the battlefield into a sacred grove for refuge. Those men were easily wiped out—burned alive when the Spartan soldiers set fire to the pine trees. Now all that remained was for the Spartans to march to Argos and take over the city renowned for music and poetry.

The ensuing battle for Argos (about 510–494 BC) was celebrated in Greek art and literature. According to legendary accounts recorded by Herodotus, Pausanias, Polyaenus, and Lucian, the Argive women saved their city from the Spartan attack. Inside the city, a distinguished poetess named Telesilla took charge. With all their soldiers killed in the battle, she sent old men, young boys, and household slaves to man key defensive positions. Meanwhile Telesilla and the women of Argos gathered up weapons and armor from houses and stored in temples. Dressed in men's clothes, the women massed where the Spartans were beginning the final assault on the city. Resolute and unfazed by the Spartans' terrifying battle cries, the Argive women met the Spartan charge with valor, stood their ground, and fought back with surprising strength.

Now Cleomenes and his men faced a dilemma. It would seem an inglorious kind of victory if they slaughtered such brave women. But, on the other hand, what a shameful disaster it would be if crack Spartan warriors somehow failed to defeat the women of Argos.

The Spartans withdrew and yielded the battle to Telesilla and her forces. Argos was saved.

Writing about six hundred years after the battle, the Greek traveler Pausanias visited Argos in the second century AD. He admired a sculpted relief near the the-

Ancient marble head of an Amazon, found in Argos, Greece. Drawing by Michele Angel.

ater and sanctuary of Aphrodite, and described it as honoring Telesilla, the city's poetess-warrior. Telesilla herself was shown donning a helmet, with her poetry books lying at her feet. That sculpture no longer exists, but tiny fragments of Telesilla's poetry do survive. She wrote songs for girls and poems on mythic topics.

It is intriguing that during the annual Hybristica festival of Argos, the Argive men and women traded clothing. According to the historian Polyaenus, this cross-dressing custom commemorated the success of Telesilla and the Argive women. They had put on men's clothing to fight the Spartans. Telesilla was also remembered in Rome. According to the early Christian writer Tatian (ca. AD 120–80), there was a statue of Telesilla in the Theater of Pompey. The statue had been plundered from Argos by Romans after the conquest of Greece in 146 BC.

The Argives, declared Pausanias, "had loved freedom from earliest times." Indeed, he noted, the local stream was called "Water of Freedom." Pausanias then recounted the tale of a self-possessed maiden of Argos who took revenge on her rapist, a cruel general named Bryas, by putting out his eyes as he slept. He had seized her while she was on her way to her wedding. Bryas was one of the Thousand, tyrannical oligarchs supported by the Spartans who overthrew the Argive democracy and oppressed the citizens (418–417 BC). The young woman escaped and found refuge with the Argive people, who defended her from the wrath of the Thousand. This incident precipitated a violent uprising against the Oligarchs, in which the Argive democracy was restored.

A woman of Argos was involved in yet another conflict, in 272 BC. Plutarch reported that during the nighttime street fighting in the Battle of Argos, between the forces of King Pyrrhus of Epirus, the Spartan king Areus, and the Macedonian king Antigonus Gonatas, Pyrrhus was knocked off his horse and killed by a roof tile hurled by an Argive woman.

It was said that the women of Argos must have worshipped Ares, the god of war. The same was said of the mythic Amazons of Themiscyra. Given the Amazon-like courage of Telesilla and her female recruits and the unnamed young Argive woman, perhaps it is no surprise that one of the reliefs on the Temple of Hera at Argos (late fifth century BC) featured a battle with Amazons. The head of one of the Amazons, with a calm but defiant expression, is now in the Getty Museum.

Cleopatra and Antony Go Fishing

CLEOPATRA HAD A THOUSAND WAYS of flattering Mark Antony, remarked Plutarch in his biography of the Egyptian queen's Roman lover. With a raptor's vigilance Cleopatra monitored Antony's moods day and night, and she was always thinking up some new diversion or novel adventure to distract and charm him. Cleopatra was Antony's drinking buddy and his gambling partner at dice. She accompanied him whenever he exercised, hunted, and practiced with weapons (see chapter 41). Dressed in disreputable disguises, the couple enjoyed rambling recklessly around Alexandria, Egypt, in the middle of the night like hooligans, pounding on people's doors and shouting insults at their windows.

Another time, Cleopatra bet Antony that she would invite him to the world's most expensive banquet. Antony took up the wager. The story goes that when he arrived for the luxurious dinner, she simply removed one of her dazzling pearl earrings, crushed it, and dissolved it in a goblet of vinegar-wine. According to Pliny the Elder, the pearls in her earrings were perfectly round, lustrous, enormous specimens acquired from some precious treasure of the East. Pliny guessed they were worth sixty million sestertii, about the equivalent of thirty million dollars today. She offered the other earring to Antony, but he was sufficiently impressed. Antony declined the aperitif and admitted that she'd won the bet.

One day Cleopatra took Antony fishing on the Nile on her fabulous barge, accompanied by a flotilla of smaller fishing boats. That day everyone on board pulled up a good number of Nile perch on their gilded hooks, everyone except Antony. Feeling humiliated in front of his lover and determined not to be skunked again, Antony devised a clever plan.

The next day he secretly paid several of the fishermen in the smaller boats to dive underwater and place their own freshly caught fish on his hook. Plutarch tells us that over the next hour or so, Antony pulled up fish after fish. The Egyptians on the barge marveled at the heap of silvery blue fish on the deck and wondered at the speed at which the perch were taking the Roman's bait.

Ancient Egyptians fishing.

Cleopatra immediately figured out Antony's ruse. But she feigned great admiration, exclaiming over what a natural fisherman he was. Declaring that his haul would surely be even more impressive tomorrow, she invited everyone back for another day of fishing.

The next day Cleopatra arranged her own cunning trick. As soon as Antony let down his line, some of her servants dove down out of sight. They attached a very large, very dead, salted fish from the Black Sea onto Antony's hook. Feeling the tugging on the line Antony quickly landed the heavy fish. As everyone stared at his catch, it was instantly obvious that he'd hauled up a big fish that was not only dead and dried but not even from the waters of the Nile. As his biographer Plutarch comments, you can imagine the guffaws and hoots that ensued. Cleopatra, giggling mischievously, diverted Antony's irritation with flattery: "Better to leave fishing to us poor Egyptians—your game is conquering kingdoms."

Nile perch (*Lates niloticus*) have a high fat content, so the Egyptians preserved perch by smoking instead of drying and salting. Cleopatra chose a different preserved fish for her prank. In those days, the Black Sea fisheries exported vast stores of salted fish all around the ancient Mediterranean world. The large salt-cured fish from the Black Sea "caught" by Antony in the Nile was most likely an enormous tuna.

Great schools of bluefin tuna (*Thunnus thynnus*) used to dominate the Black Sea, but they went extinct there from overfishing in antiquity. Today they are endangered for the same reason in the Atlantic Ocean. Bluefin tuna are very good eating. But we can imagine that instead of the bedraggled, twice-caught salted tuna, Cleopatra, Antony, and their friends would have dined on fresh Nile perch that day.

CHAPTER 28

The Poetess and the Queen of Amazons

THE YOUNG ENGLISH POET AND PAINTER Anne Killigrew was born in 1660. She died at age twenty-five, of smallpox. Her lifetime thus coincides with the duration of the Restoration of the Stuart monarchy, the reign of Charles II, 1660–85. When her poetry was published after her death, John Dryden compared her to the ancient Greek poet Sappho. Well-educated in Greek myth and history, Anne was a maid of honor to Mary of Modena, Duchess of York, who became queen of England in 1685. Anne Killigrew was encouraged to write poetry by Mary and a circle of early feminist intellectuals and writers who urged women to rebel against male domination.

Anne was also an accomplished painter, producing about fifteen paintings in her short life. Only four survive today. As in her poems, Anne highlighted strong women and mythology: two paintings featured the goddess Venus, one showed Salome with the head of Saint John the Baptist, and another depicted Judith killing Holofernes. She also painted a self-portrait.

Anne's first poem, "Alexandreis," was an epic ode to the meeting of Alexander the Great and the Amazon queen named Thalestris in 330 BC. Their encounter on the southern shore of the Caspian Sea was reported in detail by the historians

Left, poetess Anne Killigrew, engraving after her self-portrait; right, portrait of Thalestris, queen of the Amazons, J. Chapman, 1797. Photo 12 and The Print Collector / Alamy Stock Photo.

of Alexander's campaigns. Whether Amazons were real, and whether Alexander really interacted with an Amazon queen, aroused lively discussion in the seventeenth century. Notably, a French scholar, Pierre Petit, gathered literary and artistic evidence to argue that Amazons were historical, not fiction (chapter 29). The meeting of Thalestris and Alexander figures in Petit's treatise, published in 1685, the year of Anne's death. Anne and her readers would have been familiar with popular paintings, engravings, medals, and tapestries illustrating the two leaders' romantic idyll in Hyrcania.

Anne's poem begins confidently, with a verse full of praise for the young world conqueror. After two more verses declaring the modesty of her own talents and calling on ancient Muses for inspiration, Anne's poem finally takes off with an arresting scene.

The sun rises in azure skies over the exotic Hyrcanian desert and suddenly illuminates a formidable army, a vision of bright silver armor and scarlet plumes. Anne describes the troop's splendid appearance. Crescent shields and panther-skin capes are slung over their shoulders, bows and quivers "rattled by their sides," and each warrior carried a "well try'd Speare."

Only then do we discover that these impressive soldiers are not men but women! These are "Warlike Virgins" from their mythic Amazon homeland on the Black Sea. The host is led by Queen Thalestris, an eminent ruler seeking glory like her ancestor Penthesilea, the Amazon warrior queen who came to the aid of Troy in the legendary Trojan War (chapter 24). Tales of Alexander's noble courage and magnificent triumphs had fired Thalestris's "soul," filling her with longing to "see the Hero she so much admir'd." Thalestris dispatches a messenger to Alexander's camp.

Anne imagines their meeting, brimming with suspense. A "great cloud of Dust" and "Loud Neighings of Steeds and Trumpets" herald Alexander's arrival at the head of his own splendiferous army of "Burnisht Gold." Now the two armies, one silver and the other gold, come to a halt and face each other respectfully and expectantly. As they gaze in amazement at each other, a pregnant hush falls over the scene.

In the next verse, the "Heroick Queen" Thalestris advances boldly. "And thus she spake."

But here the poem breaks off. A note explains, "This was the first Essay of this young Lady in Poetry, but finding the Task she had undertaken hard, she laid it by till Practice and more time should make her equal to so great a Work."

The unfinished poem is an eloquent evocation of male and female equality. Why did Anne break off and set aside her first poem? We might venture some guesses. The Restoration court of Charles II has been described as notoriously libertine, cynical, and dissipated (see the bawdy origin of toasting, chapter 30). Anne's age when she began the poem is unknown. But some of Anne's poems are taken as critiques of the licentious court lifestyle. She expresses distaste for worldly joys and admiration for strong and outspoken but virtuous and chaste women. And she warns against the dangers of brief love affairs. In the "Alexandreis" poem, she has described Thalestris as the leader of "Warlike Virgins" and says that the Amazon longs to "see" the new conqueror of the world in person. But Thalestris's actual desire was earthier and blatantly erotic.

According to all the ancient historical accounts, the Amazon queen invited Alexander to have sex with her. Thalestris planned to make love for some weeks and then return to her own land to give birth to a child by Alexander. Alexander readily agreed to her invitation and devoted a fortnight to sexually satisfying Thalestris. The Amazon reportedly departed when she felt certain she was pregnant.

Despite Anne Killigrew's sophisticated education and the cultural climate of sexually explicit and rakish Restoration comedies, spelling out Thalestris's scandalous reason for her mission might have posed challenging contradictions for the young poet. In Anne's group of friends, the women circulated and critiqued their poems privately. Despite Anne's decision not to complete her poem, it is likely that the momentous meeting between the audacious Amazon and the willing Alexander was much discussed within the articulate circle of feminist intellectuals. Indeed, Anne's second poem even refers to her unfinished verses about Thalestris and Alexander. We might imagine that Anne Killigrew's fellow poet and age-mate, Anne Finch, and the other worldly women in her group would have helped her find a way to continue the poem. The successful contemporary playwright Aphra Behn (1640–89), for example, who was forty when Anne turned twenty, wrote easily about sexual matters. And Anne Finch penned ardent, intimate love poetry. If only Anne Killigrew had the chance to benefit from the science that developed smallpox vaccination a century later (chapter 36), her promising first poem might have blossomed into her best work.

Proving the Existence of Amazons in 1685

WERE AMAZONS REAL OR IMAGINARY? If warrior women did once exist in antiquity, was their society exclusively female? In 1685, the French scholar-physician Pierre Petit (1617–87) set out to prove the reality of warrior women, known as Amazons. Petit's original work *De Amazonibus* was written in Latin under the pseudonym Euthyphron ("Straight Thinker"). Petit's illustrated treatise was published in French and Latin and reprinted several times between 1685 and 1718. The subtitle, *Historical Treatise on the Amazons*, and the abstract explain that Petit "considers all the authors, ancient and modern, who have written for or against the existence of these heroines, and presents many ancient coins and artworks as evidence to prove that they did exist." A historian after my own heart!

Petit studied medicine and classics and wrote Latin poetry. His approach to Amazons was practical and rigorous, based on all the literary and archaeological evidence available in the seventeenth century. He included maps and numerous drawings of medals, coins, and statues of Amazons. I was fortunate to be able to consult a French edition of *Traité historique sur les Amazones* from 1718 in the Getty Museum's rare book collection in 2010. I noted that some of the medallions that Petit believed to be authentic Greek antiquities were neo-classical French forgeries, however, especially those showing Amazons with only one breast, something that no ancient artist depicted.

Petit began by gathering all the Greek and Latin sources describing Amazons known to him. Logic, he maintained, requires that the sheer number of ancient reports and images of various warrior women in barbarian lands should be taken seriously.

Next Petit reasonably dismissed the idea that the Amazons would have been a society of women only. It is this false notion that they lived without men, he wrote, that has led people to reject the historicity of Amazons. Petit cited the work of the Greek medical writer Hippocrates (fifth century BC) and his descriptions of steppe nomad women who rode horses, shot bows and arrows, and made war alongside their men. (Notably, the philosopher Plato also linked mythic Amazons with real women of the steppes; see chapter 25.) Petit also commented that contemporary European travelers of his day had observed warlike women in various cultures.

Petit then addressed the first-century BC geographer Strabo's skepticism: Strabo had compared the notion of Amazons to an impossible inversion, in which "men would have to be women and women would become men." But, as Petit pointed out, Strabo's doubts were grounded in biological determinism and arose from assumptions that we would today call gender bias.

Indeed, Petit's rational arguments and well-considered conclusions are surprisingly modern and refreshing to read. "Who can deny," wrote Petit, "that women have the same

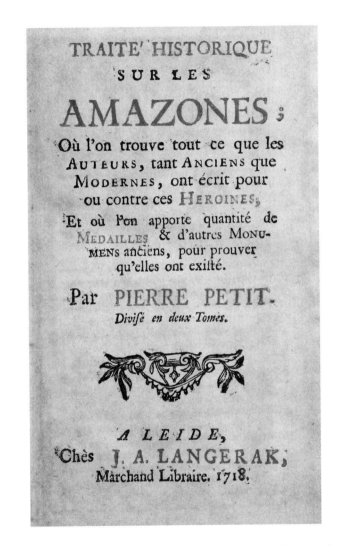

TRAITÉ HISTORIQUE

SUR LES

AMAZONES;

Où l'on trouve tout ce que les
AUTEURS, tant ANCIENS que
MODERNES, ont écrit pour
ou contre ces HEROINES,

Et où l'on apporte quantité de
MEDAILLES & d'autres MONU-
MENS anciens, pour prouver
qu'elles ont exilté.

Par PIERRE PETIT.

Divifé en deux Tomes.

A LEIDE,
Chès J. A. LANGERAK,
Marchand Libraire. 1718.

Historical Treatise on the Amazons, in which we find everything that the authors, both ancient and modern, have written for or against these heroines, along with a number of medals and other ancient monuments to prove that they have existed, by Pierre Petit, frontispiece, 1718 edition.

nature as men?" Since we cannot deny this natural equality, it follows that God endowed both sexes with the same ability to reason and act. Therefore, Petit concluded, women, like men, are capable of giving counsel, making decisions, governing, and fighting.

Wine Goblets and Women's Breasts

TO KICK OFF THE NEW ART SEASON of fall 1993 in SoHo, the *New York Times* "Styles" section featured photographs of socialites, celebrities, and art patrons attending a series of gallery openings and parties. In the lead photo, Gwendolyn Fisher wears a "cocktail dress with cutouts resembling champagne glasses" on the bodice just under the bust. Her companion, gallery owner Pablo Van Dijk, pretends to hold the stem of one of the cutouts, giving the impression of cupping Fisher's breast in his goblet. The setting is chic, sophisticated, but the image, as well as its conceit, is an updated, elite version of a cliché with roots in both low and high culture.

The art patron's witty cocktail dress with revealing cutouts that appear to support her breasts echoes a well-known photograph of another art-world celebrity taken twenty years earlier by Helmut Newton, known for his contrived images of artistic decadence. In the 1973 photo, the jewelry designer Paloma Picasso wears a designer cocktail dress and holds a highball glass strategically over her exposed breast. Picasso appears to be toasting her own bosom in a composition that is remarkably similar to the pose affected by Van Dijk as he pretends to toast the breast of Gwendolyn Fisher. Picasso's

Dress with champagne goblet cutouts, worn by art patron Gwendolyn Fisher, toasted by gallery owner Pablo Van Dijk, SoHo, New York, 1993. Drawing by Michele Angel, after photo in the *New York Times*.

glass is tall and cylindrical, but the visual simile conveys the same erotic conceit of a woman's breast suspended in a wineglass. The austere straight-sided tumbler complements Picasso's own bold, angular gold and silver jewelry designs. But more significant for our purposes, a straight-sided glass is the opposite of a curvaceous champagne glass, allowing Newton to impart androgynous ambiguity to the conventional breast/beaker association. Whereas a stemmed champagne glass would in effect display a breast on a pedestal, and its hourglass shape evokes a womanly form, Newton uses a tall columnar glass to play on this expectation. Indeed, one may discern the ghostly shape of a champagne glass in the chiaroscuro created as one views Picasso's breast through the glass. The dark nipple appears to float near the surface, giving a subliminal impression of a cherry in a champagne cocktail.

The photograph of Fisher's dress in the *New York Times* sent one reader, Larry Vinick, "scurrying to [his] ephemera file" for earlier fashion statements that played on the association between breasts and champagne glasses. In a letter to the editor, Vinick credited Broadway costume designer Miles

White with a "wittier" version, citing the "champagne glass bra, complete with a red satin cherry and sequin bubbles" worn by the showgirls in the 1949 stage production of *Gentlemen Prefer Blondes*.

But the association between wineglasses and breasts is even hoarier than Vinick suspected, embodied in language, literature, art, and artifact long before the socially acceptable burlesque *Gentlemen Prefer Blondes*. Among wine connoisseurs, the origin of the *coupe*, as opposed to the flute or tulip champagne glass (sometimes called "the inverted ballet-skirt"), has been linked to four delicate rose-white breast-shaped Sèvres porcelain cups that were created as a surprise for Marie-Antoinette. The cups were displayed in the queen's "Dairy Temple" at Rambouillet in 1787. In the flapper era of the Roaring Twenties, it was said that cultured gentlemen preferred a breast whose dimensions perfectly matched those of a champagne *coupe*.

In the 1950s, these sentiments were supplanted by *Playboy*'s expanded requirements for bosomy perfection. The magazine's heyday coincided with the preoccupation of the American male with rating a woman's desirability according to her bra cup size. Other periodicals in the so-called "men, sophisticated" category were more up-front about their fixation; for example, *Gent* (established in 1960) called itself the "Home of the D-Cup." "Cup" (from Latin *cuppa* and German *kopp* for drinking vessel) itself is a predictable unit of measurement, in view of the age-old tendency to identify breasts with beverage containers. The word *coupe*, for the saucer-type champagne glass, also derives from *cuppa*. Graduated cup sizing for bras originated in the 1930s, shortly after the late 1920s invention of the brassiere with separate cups created by sewn darts.

Among the items sold in twentieth-century gag and novelty shops was a big plastic nipple made to fit on the top of a beer can. This crude metaphor was made aesthetically palatable in more sophisticated settings in the association of bosoms with champagne and wine goblets. The appearance of this timeworn image at elite gallery openings, in elegant photographs, and in debonair Broadway shows could be read as an attempt to appropriate and refine popular coarse expressions in British and US slang from the 1700s to the present, comparing breasts to drinking vessels: "jugs," "cream-jugs," "dairies," "milk bottles," "teacups."

Perhaps in an effort to distance themselves from the vulgar associations of champagne goblets and breasts, one school of elite champagne devotees has long argued that the "tall-stemmed tapering" flute is more "soberly elegant" than the déclassé *coupe*, which came into middle-class fashion in the early Victorian era. Reasons for preferring the less mammi-form flute usually invoke the physical dynamics of gas bubbles, the bouquet, and other oenological desiderata. But the remarks of the literary critic George Saintsbury, in 1920, are revealing. In discussing the correct glass for wine, Saintsbury especially deplores the tumbler because "there is no stem for the finger tips to play with," and "a wine-glass without a stem is as bad as some other creatures without a waist." Saintsbury's sentiments not only participate in the metaphor of wineglass as woman's body, but they enhance the perversity of the aesthetic message of Helmut Newton's 1973 photograph of a woman posing with an angular tumbler.

Champagnologist Patrick Forbes admitted in 1967 that he was a "*coupe* man," despite its bourgeois reputation. His words are suggestive: "Even today . . . when one walks into a dining-room and notices *coupes* beside the ordinary wine-glasses, one experiences a momentary thrill of expectation [for] *coupes* have a most romantic ancestry." The modern wine expert Frank Prial told me in 1994 that flute aficionados "currently are in the ascendancy" because they "disdainfully associate the coupe glass with tacky weddings, shrimp cocktails, and road companies of *Traviata*."

As Patrick Forbes noted, in the 1950s and 1960s, the glossy magazine ads of the great champagne producers consistently featured "the beautiful girl in the beautiful dress" with a wineglass in her hand. From its inception in 1953, *Playboy* perpetuated the notion that its readers were worldly connoisseurs of beautiful women and fine wine, which justified advertisements, cartoons, and other images that juxtaposed ideal large-breasted females with oenological glassware. A recurrent icon was the drawing of a miniature busty brunette in black stockings who cavorted with a champagne glass on the *Playboy* "Party Jokes" page.

This synecdochical fetish, in which woman-as-breast becomes the intoxicant that fills the breast-shaped goblet, had long served as an expression of the breast/drinking vessel dynamic in both high and low culture. The painting of a classical Bacchante with bared breast and *coupe* goblet is a typical Romantic era image. A nymph entwined around or posed inside a wineglass was a respectable art nouveau and art deco theme in the nineteenth and early twentieth centuries, and Lalique crystal stemware featured women's forms. Meanwhile, illustrations of lingerie-clad women suggestively filling, holding, or offering wineglasses have been favorite icons in spicy pulp magazines since the 1930s. Cheap plastic swizzle sticks in the shape of shapely women allow everyman to have a nymph in his glass. The simile lends itself to ironic interpretation in the art world and mass culture alike. Just as Newton's aesthetically erotic photograph depends for its frisson on subtly subverting the expectations of his cultured audience, so images from vulgar men's magazines achieve churlish impact by playing on those same expectations.

"Wine and women, which have besotted myriads, go commonly together," wrote Robert Burton, in *Anatomy of Melancholy* (1621). Renaissance woodcuts of nude women and courting scenes commonly included wine goblets. Compositions that link women and wine, breasts and drinking vessels, abound in a series of sixteenth-century woodcuts created by the influential engraver Jost Amman. His patrons were aristocrats and patricians and affluent burghers who delighted in playful themes of a "hearty lasciviousness." Amman catered to their "ordinary tastes for large-breasted Venuses in suggestive poses," with "dynamic curves rather than Gothic angularity and austerity," conditions that resonate with the twentieth-century aesthetic-erotic oppositions noted earlier. This elevation of popular images enjoyed by "common people of low rank" into erotic aesthetics for elite connoisseurs corresponds to similar modern appropriations, by fashion designers, art photographers, and swank playboys. Amman, for example, superimposes a generous goblet over a woman's bosom and places a jug under one breast; in another image a woman holds a goblet on the same plane as her bared bosom, whose dimensions are visually quoted by the goblet. In yet another vignette, a topless woman pours from a jug a stream of wine that arcs across her nipple into a breastplate-like chalice.

Traditions about the origins of toasting also pair women's beauty and wine in ways that commingle refinement and gross vulgarity. Toasting was supposedly inaugurated when a beau pledged his love to a well-known beauty in the notoriously libertine court of Charles II (1660–85) with "a glass of water taken from her bath" (see chapter 28, and for the Roman emperor Elagabulus's bathwater, see chapter 50). But "to toast," *propino*, was already known in ancient Greece, and the antiquity of the gesture of "toasting" a women's breast with a wine-cup is suggested by typical erotic scenes painted on fifth-century BC drinking cups from ancient Greece. In fact, the classical Greek association of drinking alcohol from women's breasts is made crystal clear in the popularity of breast cups, *mastoi*, terra-cotta drinking vessels in the shape of a breast with an erect nipple.

In one of Amman's woodcuts, he places a large "double bumper" between a courting couple. A bumper is a wine chalice filled to the brim, often decorated with bulging bosses;

Ancient Greek *mastos* or breast cup for wine, 520 BC, Metropolitan Museum, New York, 1975.11.6.

"bumper" also refers to something unusually large or abundant (1600s on, from *bump*, to bulge, swell out, or be protuberant). By drawing the viewer's eye to the bumper's two bulging globes placed immediately next to the bodice of the elegantly dressed lady, Amman transposes and reveals the woman's bosom in the wine goblet.

"Bumpers" was British and US slang for breasts in the mid-1900s. The connotations of the word "cocktail" also draw together women and liquor, so it is particularly fitting that champagne-glass images should appear on the bodices of modern *cocktail* dresses, as in the photographs by Newton and the *Times*. The cocktail dress was invented in the 1920s, along with cocktails and cocktail parties. Champagne cocktails are one of many effervescent aperitifs served before dinner as a social lubricant. The typical cocktail dress was informal, up-to-the-minute, and cleverly revealing, in keeping with the era's hectic frivolity and naughty "fizz and bubble." Critics railed against the innovation, calling the cocktail a titillating "titivation" that makes "respectable and palatable" what should remain the vulgar "province of the worn-out spark." They likened the cocktail to "a decadent Picasso" and decried aristocratic ladies who dressed as barmaids to serve cocktails. According to the arch *Savoy Cocktail Book* (1930), the word "cocktail" was supposed to have derived from "Princess Cocktel, daughter of King Axolotl VIII of Mexico." Other versions mention "an Aztec princess, who was supposed to have given a drink to the king with romantic results." On the other hand, "cocktail" was also nineteenth-century slang for a harlot. Once again, low popular culture nurtures high culture's tastes.

If the compelling logic of equating perfectly proportioned bosoms and wine goblets is as unavoidable and pervasive as this brief review of the history of the cliché suggests, it should come as no surprise to discover the comparison explicitly expressed in ancient legends about the famous beauty Helen of Troy. This story takes the notion of the ancient Greek breast-shaped drinking cup to another extreme. According to Pliny the Elder, writing during the reign of the Roman emperor Nero in the first century AD, tourists visiting the island of Rhodes could admire an exquisite electrum wine-cup in the Temple of Athena. This celebrated silver-and-gold cup was said to have been dedicated to the temple by Helen herself. The vessel's real claim to fame, however, was not its precious metal or its antiquity, but the popular belief that the goblet had been fashioned to perfectly represent Helen's perfect breast (Pliny 33.81).

Let us conclude with a tale by Maurice des Ombiaux, the prolific French wine enthusiast of the 1920s. In his risqué narrative, "Le Sein d'Hélène" (The breast of Helen), the gods Dionysos and Apollo "decided to associate Helen with the enchanted juice of the grape . . . by raising to their lips a chalice molded from her breast." With the help of Venus, they summoned Helen's lover Paris to take a wax impression of her breast ("pink as the dawn, white as milk, with a nipple like a berry, and glowing like an alabaster vase"). "As the *coupe* was raised to the lips of Helen's suitors, each man could experience the divine illusion that he was drinking from the breast of the most beautiful woman in the world."

CURIOUS HISTORY
AND SCIENCE

Ghost Ships

IN 1932 THE ENGINE OF THE SCHOONER *John and Mary* exploded off New Jersey, and its crew abandoned ship. The empty schooner stayed afloat, however, and sailed upon the seas with sail still furled and a freshly painted hull. It was eventually found fifty miles south of Bermuda.

During a mast-snapping hurricane in 1944, the freighter *Rubicon* broke its moorings in Havana's harbor. With only a dog on board, it drifted from Cuba off into the Gulf Stream. Months later, the US Coast Guard retrieved the freighter near the Florida coast; the dog's fate is not recorded.

The schooner *Fannie E. Wolston* was abandoned for reasons unknown with a cargo of pine lumber in 1891. It covered nine thousand miles in its wanderings, circling aimlessly in the Atlantic's lonely Sargasso Sea. It was sighted forty-six times by other ships, last seen floating near Cape Hatteras, North Carolina, 1894, never recovered.

The circumstances of the unmanned brig that sailed ashore on Easton's Beach near Newport, Rhode Island, in 1750 were even more mysterious. Fishermen who boarded it found only a dog and a cat, alive. The table was laid, a kettle and pots of food were on the stove, but there was no trace of the crew. Records show that the ship had set sail from Newport several months earlier and had docked in Honduras, but then what?

There was no way of knowing when or why the crew vanished or what propelled the ship's strange homecoming.

The thick archives of ghost ships should also include HMS *Erebus* and *Terror*. The two ships and their crews vanished on the expedition to find the Northwest Passage in the Arctic, commanded by Sir John Franklin in 1845. The wandering derelict vessels were observed by Inuits, whose oral traditions were disbelieved but then helped searchers to locate the ships 170 years later, in 2014–16. Mysteriously, the ships were found sixty and ninety miles from where they were abandoned, carried by drifting ice floes (chapter 32).

A floating vessel that has been deserted by its crew is called a "derelict" under maritime law. Seaworthy derelicts, especially those with buoyant cargo such as timber, can float for years, carried by prevailing winds and currents for thousands of miles until they run aground or rot away. During the glory days of sailing, thousands of abandoned and disintegrating wooden ships of all descriptions drifted at sea, disabled by storms, fires, leaks, explosions, mutiny, or disease on board. Sailors sometimes saw the same decaying hulk several times—months or even years apart and in different latitudes. A floating or half-submerged wreck could loom up unexpectedly in fog or at night. The terrifying sight and the true danger inspired a mythology of malevolent "ghost ships."

According to sailing lore, a vessel involved in disaster can become a phantom, ceaselessly wandering and foretelling doom for all who encounter it. Such a tale is the *Flying Dutchman*, which comes in many versions. The apparition sometimes appeared to sail in the air, leading some to suggest that a marine mirage may have been responsible (chapter 32). The legend is thought to have originated during the heyday of the Dutch maritime empire in the eighteenth century; the earliest written report appeared in 1790. The several renditions have some features in common. An arrogant captain defies Nature or God, sometimes by making a pact with the Devil, and causes misery and death for his crew. Usually the mad captain drives his ship and sailors to inhuman limits to break speed records rounding Cape Horn or the Cape of Good Hope. Other versions tell of murder, mutiny, or dark deeds that doomed the cursed ship to an eternity of haunting the trade routes.

The grim ship looms suddenly alongside ordinary vessels, and the frightened crews often imagined that they saw ghosts or demons hauling on the ropes and at the wheel. A verse by Sir Walter Scott sums up the bad luck implied in encountering such a sight: "The Demon Frigate braves the gale / And well the doom'd spectators know / The harbinger of wreck and woe." When he was sixteen, the future king George V and his brother sailed around Australia, serving as cadets in the British Navy (chapter 9). In 1881, on a clear, calm night, they and the crew saw a ghostly brig, glowing red, suddenly coming up on their port bow. The next morning the sailor who first sighted the *Flying Dutchman* fell from the mast and "was smashed to atoms."

The Roman historian Suetonius recorded what appears to be the earliest documented case of a phantom ship in AD 68. A vessel full of weapons from Alexandria, Egypt, sailed into the harbor at the mouth of the Ebro River, below Dertosa (Tortosa), Spain. But the ship was discovered to have "no person to steer it, or so much as a single sailor or passenger on board." The ghost ship appeared as the governor of Spain, Galba, plotted to overthrow Emperor Nero, who committed

Phantom ship with skeleton crew, nineteenth-century engraving.

suicide in AD 68. The phantom ship loaded with arms was taken as a sign that the gods supported Galba. But the real reason was more mundane. It is likely that the crew panicked during a storm and abandoned ship. Wind and currents carried the vessel onward with its sails still up.

During the Black Death scourge of the Middle Ages, ships carried rats and fleas infested with *Yersina pestis* contagion to port cities throughout the Black Sea, the Mediterranean, and Atlantic. Between 1347 and 1351, it is estimated that worldwide deaths from plague reached at least seventy-five million. Entire ships' crews succumbed during voyages. The plague originated on the steppes and arrived in Europe around the time of the Tatar siege of Kaffa on the Black Sea in 1344–46. It was said that the retreating Mongols catapulted their own plague corpses over the city walls. Terrified citizens of Kaffa fled in ships bound for Sicily, Genoa, and Venice. When a dozen ships reached Messina in fall of 1347, the Sicilians were horrified to see the boats manned by dead sailors slumped over their oars. They pushed the ships of death out of the harbor, but the fleas and rats stayed behind. Plague soon engulfed all Italy.

The phantom ship legend is not solely a Western tradition. According to a Mamluk historian, a plague-infested ghost ship sailed into Alexandria, Egypt, in 1347. An Arabian text details a chilling curse cast on the bloodthirsty pirate Dahoul: "You shall wander on every sea until the end of time, at the will of the winds and the mercy of the waves. Your crew will exhaust itself in endless toil. Your passengers will be the drowned of the world; you shall never die nor will you ever reach shore." The curse is reminiscent of the European *Flying Dutchman* legend.

Other cultures have associated the idea of supernatural ships with guilt or death. Old English, German, Scandinavian, and Asian myths described magical ships that transported the souls of the dead. Medieval French and Italian histories tell of apparitions of boats seen on anniversaries of shipwrecks. The idea that something associated with violent death can become a ghostly harbinger of future tragedy seems almost universal. The *Flying Dutchman* legend probably arose from a mixture of superstitions about such ghosts and from sailors' early contact with other seafaring peoples who sent their dead out to sea in boats. Not surprisingly, wrecked, sunken, or deserted ships were the most common candidates for ghosthood.

The famous derelict brigantine *Mary Celeste* generated rumors of mutiny and foul play. The *Mary Celeste* sailed from New York for Genoa, Italy, in 1872, and its log reported a position one hundred miles west of the Azores on November 24. The *Dei Gratia* found it about two weeks later, completely deserted, with the crew's clothes hung out to dry, drifting about five hundred miles from the last reported position. The ship's papers, except for the logbook, were gone. No survivors were found. The captain of the *Dei Gratia* was an acquaintance of the *Mary Celeste*'s skipper; he hauled the derelict to Gibraltar and claimed a huge reward. Suspicions about his profitable discovery lingered for decades. And the *Mary Celeste* was plagued by bad luck until its final wreck in 1885. Philip Richardson of Woods Hole Oceanographic Institution says that "the Atlantic was literally strewn with ships like *Mary Celestes* in various stages of disintegration" in the late 1800s.

Sea-lore writer Peter Freuchen suggested that derelict vessels were featured in so many sailors' stories simply because "there is no more terrifying peril to meet on the Seven Seas than the almost invisible hull of a dead ship which can itself kill the living." The grave navigation hazards posed by derelicts were a constant problem in the nineteenth and early twentieth centuries.

The rescuers of the crew of the British coal ship *Rumney* had a hair-raising experience with a derelict in a dense Atlantic fog in 1884. The *Rumney* rescued the crew of the sinking French steamer *Frigorifique*. It had been listing steeply, and the engine room was flooded with water surging in through a huge hole amidships. As the *Rumney* was groping along in the fog at two knots with the survivors, a ship suddenly rose up dead ahead. The *Rumney* barely managed to dodge the phantom and continued on course. Again the same great ship bore down on the sailors from the gloom. This time everyone could see that the phantom was the *Frigorifique*, apparently risen from the deep. The *Rumney* was rammed and sank immediately. Fortunately, all hands escaped in lifeboats. The dangerous French derelict was discovered later, still listing badly but with one propeller turning and smoke still rising from one funnel. The wheel had been lashed, which kept the ship turning a wide circle—that was why it had twice crossed the British ship's course.

By 1883, mariners who encountered derelicts in the Atlantic began reporting their positions to the US Navy Hydrographic Office in Washington, DC. The derelicts' positions were plotted on a huge blackboard and updated in monthly Pilot Charts, issued free to navigators. Between 1887 and 1893, the office logged 1,628 sightings of abandoned ships. More than 400 derelict wooden sailing vessels were spotted after the fierce hurricanes of 1883 alone.

Such ghost ships, some floating upright, dismasted, overturned, or flooded to the gunwales, meandered for thousands of miles. Despite the attempts to record their positions, these treacherous ships were difficult to track down. Between 1887 and 1893, six ships were lost and fifteen were severely damaged in collisions with derelicts. Of the 1,628 derelicts known to be drifting during those years, only 41 were towed in, and 72 were destroyed by being set afire. The waterlogged three-masted schooner *Drisko*, loaded with lumber, was sunk with great difficulty by the USS *San Francisco* near Key West, Florida. *Drisko*'s bad luck had begun when it collided with a younger derelict in the Gulf of Mexico in 1891. *Drisko* then drifted for two years. In 1893, the *San Francisco* fired artillery shells and eight torpedoes, but the ragged ship kept afloat. The *San Francisco* ended up ramming the schooner and broke it in two.

Some sunken ships can rise from the ocean floor, like the *Frigorifique*. Peter Freuchen recalls a schooner that was seen by its own crew to sink out of sight off the coast of Portugal, but days later they saw their ship, resurrected, floating on its side. And off the Carolina coast, a series of photographs show the schooner *A. Ernest Mills* as it rose to the surface days after it had gone down in a storm. Experts suggest these two ghost ships might have been carrying cargoes of salt. Warren Wren, a ranger at Cape Hatteras, North Carolina, told me that "ships carrying commodities such as salt, sulfur, or phosphorus could have gone down in storms only to rise again after the cargo dissolved." Wren noted that ships that were "only swamped and then suspended just below the surface, or ships that sank but were never snagged on the bottom," might float up for a number of reasons: shifting shoals or strong currents, ship/cargo buoyancy, erosion or buildup of shorelines, and violent storms. "Even if it happened once every few decades, the mysterious sight would have made quite an impression," he said, especially along the perilous sea-lanes off the Carolina Outer Banks, known as the "Graveyard of the Atlantic." Sailors have claimed that vessels from every era of seafaring— Phoenician galleys, Roman triremes, Spanish treasure galleons, pirate vessels, frigates, clippers, steamers, packets, and yachts—haunted the Gulf Stream.

Such images have inspired art and literature. Richard Wagner's famous opera of 1843 was inspired by *Flying Dutchman* tales: Washington Irving and Edgar Allan Poe both wrote stories about spectral ships with demon crews. To write *The Rime of the Ancient Mariner* (1798), Samuel Taylor Coleridge drew on experiences of ships becalmed in the hot, dry windless horse latitudes, thirty degrees north and south of the equator. The horse latitudes were so named because sailors had to throw any horses they were transporting overboard to conserve drinking water. Coleridge had heard of actual sightings of ships with frozen corpses on deck and knew the true story of a privateer who was dogged by bad fortune after he shot an albatross while rounding Cape Horn in 1720. The *Ancient Mariner* tells how his ship was mysteriously immobilized in the doldrums because he had wantonly killed an albatross. The bird, a sign of purity, freedom, and the safety of land, then became a symbol of the mariner's guilt and Nature's reproach. The mariner, lone survivor of his crew, spots a frigate approaching: "At first it seemed a little speck / And then it seemed a mist." As it neared, "It plunged and tacked and veered." And then the copper sun set behind it, revealing the ribs of a skeleton ship.

Benjamin Franklin was one of the first to take a scientific interest in the positions of crewless ships in the Atlantic shipping lanes. After talking with experienced sailors in 1775, Franklin speculated about a continuous great current that could help or hinder a ship's progress. This current became known as the Gulf Stream. Today's oceanographers study past sightings of ghost ships reported at the turn of the century to clarify the dimensions, direction, and velocity of the Gulf Stream's surface.

At Woods Hole, Massachusetts, Philip Richardson analyzed the trajectories of two hundred derelict ships reported by name in the monthly Pilot Charts from 1883 to 1902. He superimposed maps of their routes in the Gulf Stream and discovered interesting patterns. After the lumber schooner *W. L. White* was abandoned in a blizzard in Delaware Bay in March 1888, it drifted south with all three masts and portions of sails still standing. Then it was taken up by the Gulf Stream and turned east-northeast. That summer and fall, "she looped and zigzagged east of Newfoundland directly within a major shipping lane," says Richardson. Nearly a year and six thousand miles later, the *W. L. White* finally ran aground in the Hebrides Islands, Scotland. During its journey, thirty-six other vessels passed it. The captains' reports trace its degeneration into a blackened hulk, with two broken masts, the deck rotted away, and the hull covered with sea grass and barnacles.

According to Richardson's data, it typically took about ten months for a derelict to drift clockwise from Cape Hatteras, North Carolina, to Europe, and "a complete circuit of the gyre" averaged three years. Many of the derelicts made tight turns or traced large loops; their crisscrossing, convoluted trajectories indicate a branching of the Gulf Stream near Newfoundland and suggest the presence of strong counter-eddies within the current.

Richardson points out that the number of derelicts declined after 1900, partly because of "the rise of iron, steel, and steam." Steamships were "abandoned less often and those that were abandoned tended to sink, not remain afloat as derelicts," he says. Efforts by naval vessels and the Revenue Cutter Service (forerunner of the US Coast Guard) to pinpoint derelicts and destroy them also contributed to the decline.

As steam eclipsed sails and the number of derelicts waned, so too did the legends attached to drifting hulks. Horace Beck, collector of folklore about the sea, noted that the *Andrea Doria*, the *Lusitania*, the *Morro Castle*, the *Titanic*, and the *Normandie*, all victims of great sea disasters, inspired no tales of ghost ships. When he asked old Caribbean sailors about haunted ships these days, they pointed out that ghosts and spirits prefer sails—and they detest engine fumes.

CHAPTER 32

Mirages at Sea

FATA MORGANA

SINCE THE MIDDLE AGES, people have marveled at a fantastic panorama of towers, arches, and castles sometimes seen shimmering in the mist over the sea, in the Strait of Messina between Italy and Sicily. Fabulous mirages that appear over water were called "Fata Morgana," because medieval crusaders imagined the illusions were the handiwork of Morgan le Fay, the enchantress of Arthurian romance.

Morgan le Fay, dwelling in a palace under the sea off southern Italy, was famous for her ability to create "castles in the air." According to medieval legend, seafarers who mistook her magical mirages for a safe harbor were led far off course and hopelessly lost. A typical account of the mirage written in about 1500 describes "an array of towers, pinnacles, and columns, palaces with balconies and windows, extended alleys with trees . . . a scene of architectural magnificence" hovering above the horizon until it seems to slowly melt away.

One of the earliest descriptions of the famous Fata Morgana of the Strait of Messina comes from 1634. From Reggio di Calabria, a port on the tip of Italy's toe, Father Angelucci was gazing out over the strait toward Sicily. Suddenly the priest saw what he called a "vision of paradise." Angelucci all his life had hoped to observe the wondrous mirage, and he strove to describe it scientifically in a letter to his friend Athanasius Kircher, the German polymath. "The ocean which washes the coast of Sicily rose up and looked like a dark mountain range," wrote the priest. Against this backdrop "quickly appeared a series of more than 10,000 whitish-gray pilasters," which "then shrank to half their height" and were transformed into "arches like those of Roman aqueducts." Castles with towers and windows also rose above the aqueduct; then the vision shimmered and disappeared.

Kircher, intrigued by the phenomenon, attempted to reproduce the ocean illusion in his laboratory by passing a ray of light through a heated vessel fashioned to mimic the shape of the strait and containing sand from Sicily. Encouraged by the partial success of this experiment, Kircher continued to work in optics. Ultimately, he was able to project a mirage effect on a screen that terrified and mystified his audiences. Kircher is credited with the invention of the magic lantern, the precursor of motion pictures—and inspired by illusions at sea.

In view of Kircher's optical experiments, it is interesting to find that in 1912 an article in *Scientific American* predicted that one should be able to obtain "good photographs of Fata Morgana . . . without difficulty." Indeed, by 1975 specialists in meteorological optics had successfully predicted and photographed a variety of marine mirages. Meteorologist Alistair Fraser, for example, determined the necessary atmospheric conditions, predicted, and then photographed several mirages in Puget Sound of boys "walking on water," ferryboats transformed into "castles," and images of Romanesque arches. According to Fraser, when the flat, evenly lighted surface of the sea is warmer than the air above, the air acts as a magnifying glass, distorting real features of the landscape or a boat into what appears as a mist or fog. Then gentle breezes "sculpt" the blurred image into spectacular castles, cities, mountains, or fancy bridges of the type so ornately described by the Italians.

About a century after Angelucci and Kircher's experiences, in 1773, a Dominican friar named Minasi published a dissertation on ocean mirages. Minasi was born near Reggio di Calabria and had seen the Fata Morgana in the Strait of Messina three times. At sunrise, he wrote, when the sea is calm, spectators, facing the sea and with the sun behind them, may suddenly see "various multiplied objects, such as numberless series of pilasters, arches, castles well delineated, columns, lofty towers, superb palaces with balconies and windows."

So far Minasi's description parallels Angelucci's. But eighteenth-century mirage-watchers tended to invest their visions with action-packed details. Besides cattle and sheep grazing in "delightful plains," Minasi saw "armies of men on foot and horseback, and many other strange figures, all in their natural colors and proper action, and passing rapidly in succession along the surface of the sea." His contemporaries at Manduria in the heel of Italy had described another mirage sometimes glimpsed hovering over the Gulf of Taranto. This illusion also featured animated panoramas, luminous palaces, grazing herds, and cavalry parades, all outlined with an iridescent glimmer. Mirage scientist Andrew T. Young confirmed to me that "superior-mirage displays" like those seen by Minasi "often look like moving crowds of people, soldiers, or herds of cattle and flocks of sheep to an inexperienced observer. The motion is supplied by waves in inversions and turbulence in inferior mirages."

Although marine mirages are sighted elsewhere, the Fata Morgana of the Strait of Messina was considered the classic example. A drawing included in Minasi's treatise became the standard textbook representation of an ocean mirage.

There have been many eyewitness accounts and discussions of the atmospheric details of Italy's great metropolis in the sky. Early in the twentieth century, a physicist from Reggio di Calabria, V. E. Boccara, made three sketches of the illusion. The first depicts the eerie streak of white mist that often heralds the Fata Morgana. The next shows the phantom city rising out of the sea against a magnified backdrop of mountains. The third illustration shows a three-tiered cityscape suspended over the water. Other writers have concentrated on the ideal conditions for sightings of the famous mirage. They agree that the best time is a hot summer morning, when the air is extremely clear, except for a thin veil of mist obscuring the coast of Sicily. The sea should be calm, with only a gentle northerly breeze.

MIRAGES IN CLASSICAL ANTIQUITY

There was no ancient term for "mirage," but if one reads carefully, one can discover descriptions of mirages on land and sea in ancient Greek and Roman writings. For example, Alexander the Great's biographer Quintus Curtius Rufus (ca. AD 40) recounted that a vast plain in Asia resembled a distant sea on an exceedingly hot day. This was probably an inferior mirage, like the typical phantom lakes that recede in the desert or illusory rainwater on hot asphalt roads. This sort of mirage may explain what Saint Anthony saw in the Fayyum Desert of Egypt. He described seeing a "very large silver disk" far away on the surface of the desert that "suddenly vanished like smoke."

The earliest mention of "looming" mirages is in Aristotle's treatise *Meteorologica* (about 350 BC), where he states that "distant and dense air . . . acts as a mirror . . . making promontories on coasts appear elevated above the sea." Diodorus of Sicily described superior desert mirages in Libya in about 30 BC. On very still days, marvelous shifting shapes of all kinds of animal forms, some of monstrous size, appear in the air. Diodorus said that the images keep retreating if one tries to pursue them. Diodorus also remarked that people of Libya are accustomed to these visions, while visitors to the desert are astounded. Pliny the Elder reported that in about 103 BC two "heavenly armies" appeared to engage in battle in the skies. This sounds a bit like the moving mirage described by Minasi, above. An account of a similar mirage by the historian Josephus (in AD 78) is more detailed. Many witnesses saw scenes of "chariots and soldiers in armor" advancing and surrounding great cities in the clouds.

MIRAGES LURED SAILORS
AND INSPIRED POETS

Particularly fanciful descriptions characterize the Irish tales of ocean mirages, called "fairy isles" or "fairy castles." As in the Morgan le Fay legend, the illusions were said to be responsible for beckoning sailors to misadventure. According to Giraldus Cambrensis, who wrote a *Topography of Ireland* in 1187, when a mirage of an enchanted isle appeared, it was the custom to throw a burning coal at it, since fire was thought to dispel phantoms. On the other hand, many believed that a phantom island could be occupied by mortals if a fire could be started there.

To explain the origin of this belief, Giraldus told the story of a fairy island that appeared off the west coast of Ireland one calm morning. At first observers thought it was a whale, but as it remained stationary, they decided it was land. Daring youths approached the spot in a boat, but as they drew near, the island vanished. The next day the apparition rose again to mock the sailors. They were able to land on the island only after letting fly an arrow tipped with red-hot steel.

A history of Ireland published in 1636 noted that seamen often encountered enchanted isles as they sailed west. These "temporary" islands were sometimes perceived by people who lived on the western coast too. In the late seventeenth century, historian Roderick O'Flagherty recorded that to inhabitants of the island of Arran in the Firth of Clyde, northeast of Ireland, "often appears visible that enchanted island, called O'Branil, and in Irish Beg'ara." The chronicler described the place as a "wild island of huge rocks" that occasionally rises in the sea. At times one could also see "a great city far off, full of houses, castles, towers, and chimneys." Suddenly the mirage would become an animated cavalcade of "blazing flames, smoke, and people running to and fro." At other times one saw "a number of ships, with their sails and riggings" suspended over the ocean. Sometimes, seamen were treated to sights of lively fairs in progress, while others saw great bridges spanning the sky over the sea. One fairy island was more mundanely populated by women busily hanging out laundry.

Superior mirage of ships observed off coast of Greenland, 1822, engraving. World History Archive / Alamy Stock Photo.

An Irish memoir written in 1748 told of an enchanted island that could sometimes be seen floating beyond Giant's Causeway, on the north coast of Ireland. In the summer of 1812 several sightseers there were amazed to see images of "castles, ruins, and tall spires darting rapidly across the surface of the sea, which were instantly lengthened into considerable height."

About sixty years later, over the Firth of Forth (along the east coast of Scotland), in the early summer of 1871, "scarcely a day passed without several instances of atmospheric phenomena of vivid and interesting character." The "extraordinary optical illusions" over the sea were reported in great detail in the sober pages of *Symon's Monthly Meteorological Magazine*. The most spectacular display occurred on a warm Saturday afternoon.

First, a mirror image of Balconic Castle on the Fife coast appeared about forty-five degrees up from the horizon. Tiny May Island "suddenly shot up in the form of a huge perpendicular wall, apparently 800 or 900 feet high." A long row of rocks east of the island "assumed the most diversified and fantastic shapes." Once they appeared as a "beautiful columnar circle, 20 to 30 feet high"; then they changed to a grove of trees that rapidly expanded to a "plantation." An arch spanned the trees and the island; then dozens more arches appeared in quick succession. Meanwhile "jagged rifts and ravines" opened in the face of the high wall, and a series of towers, columns, and archways sprang up and disappeared. Astounded witnesses watched this incredibly active panorama for four hours. The spectacle ended when the island shrank to a thin blue line above the horizon and a drenching rain began.

The 1914 *Royal Meteorological Society Quarterly Journal* carried an account of a mirage that appeared off the Cornish coast near Land's End, England. Along the sea horizon suddenly appeared a line of coastal scenery, complete with woods, fields, and hedges. Before long the witness recognized the scene as a reflection of his own location. He was able to identify several church spires, the river, and the harbor of Falmouth. Soon he saw Pendennis Head with its castle and military buildings. The mirage lasted for several minutes and was "reversed as though in a looking glass and slightly magnified."

French legend tells of an ancient submarine city, Ys (or Lyonesse), which can be glimpsed in the Bay of Douarnenez. This mirage has an aural facet—some travelers say they can hear the tolling church bells of Ys. Edgar Allan Poe might have been thinking of Lyonesse when he wrote his poem "The City in the Sea" (1845). In those "kingly halls" far beneath the melancholy and serene deep, "the light from the lurid sea / streams up the turrets silently." Some legends of cities that appear to be submerged below the sea could be inspired by what Minasi had classified as "marine" (as opposed to "aerial") mirages. In modern terminology, the cities beneath the sea correspond to "sinking" inferior (as opposed to superior) mirages. These refractions occur when the air temperature decreases in relation to the height above the ocean surface.

Fantastic landscapes shimmering over the sea have inspired other poets. In a famous verse by Wordsworth, a spectacular city with "alabaster domes and silver spires" and "bright pavilions" appears in the sky. "Towers with battlements" and "terraces upon terraces" are repeated endlessly and constantly transformed upon the screen of clouds until the "vapors recede" and the scene vanishes. Wordsworth's Romantic description is remarkably like Father Angelucci's dramatic vision.

Many of the supernatural images in the poetry of Samuel Taylor Coleridge were mirage inspired. Coleridge was an avid reader of the memoirs of the early polar explorers, who often encountered mirages. In one of his verses, a mysterious island appears over the sea, its "o'er-hanging cliffs glassed in the ocean," and "warriors coursed o'er the sky and battled in mid-air." And in Xanadu of "Kubla Khan," published in 1816, Coleridge imagined how "high in air a stately palace rose . . . the shadow of the dome of pleasure floated midway on the waves . . . a miracle of rare device / a sunny pleasure dome of ice!" The surreal images of green ice floes, the desolate spires of icebergs, and the dazzling mirages described by polar explorers inspired Coleridge's vivid celestial visions, and even the ghost ship, described in his *Rime of the Ancient Mariner* of 1798 (see chapter 31).

ILLUSIONS IN ICE

In the icy vast seas of the Arctic and Antarctic, mirages are common. The dry, dust-free air makes it possible to see for miles, so distances are very deceptive. Owing to complex atmospheric conditions, the ocean sometimes appears concave, bending upward toward the horizon. Was this sort of polar mirage involved in the sinking of the *Titanic* in 1912? It has been suggested that atmospheric conditions as the ship sailed into the cold Labrador Current might have created a mirage of a false horizon, obscuring the fatal iceberg.

In a type of superior mirage that occurs when the air temperature increases with height above the surface, land masses, icebergs, or ice fields beyond the horizon seem to loom ominously near, or a mountain range far inland may suddenly appear to be on the coast, spectacularly magnified with distinct features. Another type of polar mirage, the Novaya Zemlya ("New Land") effect, gives the impression of a fiery sunrise, when the sun is still out of sight beyond the curve of the earth during the polar night. These extraordinary illusions mystified explorer Willem Barents and his sailors in the Arctic in 1594–97.

"Magnification" or "looming" mirages have been recorded in ships' logs around the globe. They are especially common in polar oceans. In 1939, the captain of the *Morrissey* traveling between Greenland and Iceland saw clearly recognizable mountains and landmarks of Iceland that appeared to be only thirty miles off when they were actually three hundred miles away. From Cuxhaven on the northern coast of Germany, an image of Helgoland, an island with red sandstone cliffs thirty-seven miles north, has been observed "hanging upside down" over the sea's horizon. The Royal Meteorological Society has reported such "looming" phenomena from distances of six hundred up to two thousand miles.

In 1818 the British explorer Captain John Ross, searching for the Northwest Passage to the Pacific, was defeated by a polar mirage. Sailing up Lancaster Sound, the actual entrance to the Northwest Passage, on his lead ship, *Isabella*, he saw the entire end of the sound blocked by a formidable mountain chain, which he named the Croker Mountains. Dismayed by what was actually a realistic mirage of a continuous land mass, he abandoned his search for a passage to the Pacific.

At the South Pole, great controversy arose over the findings of the US Exploring Expedition (1838–42) under Charles Wilkes and the voyages of the *Erebus* and *Terror* (1839–43) under Sir James Clark Ross, during the exploration and mapping of the Antarctic continent. Ross accused Wilkes of placing mountains along the coast that were two hundred miles inland, but Ross made similar errors. In some places where he charted the coast, later explorers found only water. Both had been misled by polar mirages.

The two rugged, ice-proven ships and their crews of 133 vanished in 1845, near the North Pole. They were last seen near Baffin Bay in the Arctic, during another search for the Northwest Passage, led by Sir John Franklin (see chapter 31). Amazingly, the missing ships were discovered 170 years later, in 2014–16. But the mystery deepened, because *Terror* was sixty miles and *Erebus* ninety miles south of their last reported locations. Was it possible that mirages were involved?

Probably the most famous geographic delusion orchestrated by an Arctic mirage is the case of Robert E. Peary's Crocker Land, "discovered" in 1906. Trying to reach the North Pole, Peary saw a spectacular expanse of snow-capped mountains, valleys, and hills, which he judged to be about 120 miles west of his vantage point, on the northern tip of Axel Heiberg Land. He again observed the same "land" from Cape Columbia on Ellesmere Island and mapped it at about 83°N, 103°W. Despite his Arctic experience, even Peary was not immune to the sorcery of the mirage and the yearning it aroused. He wrote that as he gazed at the beautiful "snow-clad summits above the ice horizon," his "heart leaped the intervening miles of ice." He looked "longingly at this land, and, in fancy, I trod its shores and climbed its summits, even though I knew that that pleasure could be only for another in another season."

Not until 1914 was Peary's error revealed. Financed by the American Museum of Natural History, a party led by Donald B. MacMillan set out in 1913 to explore Crocker Land with sledges and dog teams. MacMillan and Fitzhugh Green set off from Cape Thomas Hubbard over the polar seas made treacherous by blowing snow, "stretching and bucking" thin blue ice, and temperatures of –25°F. At last, "this morning Green yelled in through our igloo door that Crocker Land was in sight," wrote MacMillan in his diary. "We all rushed out . . . Sure enough! There it was as plain as day—hills, valleys, and ice cap, a tremendous land extending through 150 degrees of the horizon." MacMillan crowed, "Great Heavens, what a land!"

The group pressed on, catching tantalizing glimpses through fog and blowing snow of the "mountain range glittering in the sunshine." After seven days they calculated that they had gone at least 137 miles over the polar sea, far beyond where Crocker Land should have been. MacMillan scanned the horizon with binoculars—the skyway now a "deep cloudless blue and all the mist had disappeared." No land was in sight. They had been pursuing a hyperborean looming mirage.

CHAPTER 32

USEFUL ILLUSIONS

Some historians suggest that "looming" and "magnification" mirages may actually have helped ancient sea explorers, such as the Vikings, to discover lands that lay beyond the true horizon. The mirages would enable them to see over the curve of the earth and use looming images of islands as stepping-stones across unknown seas. At least two modern polar explorers have acknowledged that they used the "looming" effect in this way: Carsten Borchgrevink of Norway, in 1895–99, whose party was the first to land on Antarctica; and Englishman Robert Falcon Scott in Antarctica in 1901–10.

The *Marine Observer* of 1938 reported that on a regular run of the ship *Hauraki* from Suva to Papeete in the South Pacific, Tahiti appeared to be only 35 miles away—in fact it was 250 miles distant. Similar looming mirages of islands may have aided intrepid Polynesian canoe explorers in the South Seas.

As we've seen, marine mirages have inspired countless legends of "lost islands," "castles in the air," "kingdoms in the sea," and "flying ghost ships" around the world. Many of these images appear to be based on recognized mirage phenomena: fairy islands or celestial castles that appear and disappear to tantalize homesick sailors, and ghostly ships sailing the skies, could be attributed to looming superior mirages, and kingdoms in the sea to inferior mirages. Some scientists have suggested that an understanding of ocean mirages may be useful in exploring the alien atmospheres of other planets, where optical illusions could abound. Atmospheric conditions on Venus, for example, might cause the horizon to appear to bend upward, like the inside of a bowl, creating a looming mirage similar to those encountered in Earth's polar oceans.

Yet the astronauts' psychological reactions to other-worldly mirages will be just as important as their scientific understanding of them. No matter how well we understand the mirage's atmospheric physics, it is the link between the viewer's imagination and the mirage that remains elusive. Future interplanetary explorers will do well to remember how Morgan le Fay's "castles in the air" lured seafarers to pursue dreamlands and spelled frustration for mapmakers.

Mirages at sea have always enchanted ocean voyagers, inspired poets and legends, and sparked the curiosity of scientists. The editors of the *Journal of the Optical Society of America* claim that scientists who study meteorological illusions are really "natural philosophers" lured by the intrinsic fascination of the mirage, a phenomenon that bewitches anyone who gazes out over a still sea on a hot summer morning.

CHAPTER 33

Winds in Ancient Myth and History

Greek wind gods have colorful and lusty legacies, and winds
have played decisive roles throughout history and legend.

IN THE FIRST CENTURY BC, the Macedonian astronomer Andronikos of Kyrrhos built a "weather station" for Athens with
a clock, sundials, and weather vane, at the octagonal Tower of
the Winds. The tower is still a well-known landmark near the
Roman Agora in Plaka, at the head of Odos Aiolou, a street
named after Aeolos, the legendary King of the Winds in antiquity. Each of the eight façades of the tower is decorated with
a sculpted relief personifying the wind from that direction.

In Andronikos's day, the figure of a huge bronze Triton
revolved on the roof to point out the face of the prevailing
wind on the frieze below (for Tritons, see chapter 2). The per-
sonified winds are shown flying counterclockwise, in the pattern that typically occurs when a violent storm passes through
the Aegean region. In Homer's *Odyssey*, Odysseus described
just such a cyclone, a word derived from the ancient Greek
for "coil of a snake." Odysseus ran into the storm as he was
departing Calypso's island: "The South Wind and the East

Tower of the Winds, ancient Athens, engraving, 1880. Old Books Images / Alamy Stock Photo.

Wind clashed together and the bitter-blowing North Wind and the West Wind rolled up a heavy sea. Storm blasts from every direction were crowding in. They snapped the mast and whirled our little boat in circles!" The winds played a sort of keep-away game with Odysseus's craft, finally blowing him far off course for yet another adventure.

The four winds from the cardinal directions were given vivid personalities by the ancient Greeks.

The North Wind, Boreas, is the prevailing wind in the Mediterranean and was usually portrayed as a blustery, impetuous ruffian. Ancient Greeks liked to say that the fleetest race horses were the offspring of Boreas and swift Thracian mares. On the Tower of the Winds, Boreas wears a thick mantle and high-laced boots, and he blows a conch shell to signify the howling northerlies that can bring winter's cold and snow. In one of Aesop's fables (sixth century BC), Boreas challenges the Sun to a contest of strength. The Sun agrees and cleverly selects the goal: to see who could induce a traveler to remove his coat. Naturally, the chilly North Wind loses.

The ancient Athenians appreciated the North Wind because he was so important for their sea trade. Boreas had had a strong mythological connection with the city of Athens ever since he ran off with Oreithyia, daughter of the city's first king. Ranging over Attica from his cave in northern Greece, Boreas had spied the princess gathering flowers on a hillside. In the myth, the North Wind was smitten. But he was not the type to court her with soft sighs or soothing caresses. True to his nature, he simply swept her away. Ancient Greek vase paintings of the event reveal Boreas to be a rather uncouth character with unruly, disheveled hair and beard. Boreas and Oreithyia had two sons, Calais and Zetes, who joined Jason and the Argonauts on their epic quest for the Golden Fleece (chapter 3).

The Athenians had a special reason to be thankful for Boreas. The North Wind helped weaken the Persian fleet in 480 BC, after the Battle of Artemisium off the northwest coast of Euboea. Before the battle, an oracle had suggested that if prayers and sacrifices were made, the North Wind would do a good turn for the Greeks. The naval battle was a draw, but a late summer gale was rising. The Greek ships made it safely into harbors, but the Persians lost at least four hundred vessels in the gale. The storm raged for four days, until finally the Persian magi cast some counterspells to lull the wind. The Greeks of Euboea called this timely northeasterly wind the "Hellespontias." The grateful Athenians thanked Boreas and erected altars to the North Wind. One Athenian colony actually voted to make the North Wind a citizen of their town and allotted him land and a house. A collector of modern Greek folklore discovered that in some parts of Greece in the early twentieth century people still addressed the North Wind as "O Kyrios Boreas"—Sir Boreas. Today Boreas is known as the "Tramontana," and Athenians appreciate him for his ability to relieve scorching summer heat.

Next to Boreas on the Tower of the Winds is the stern, cold and wet Northeast Wind, emptying a shield full of hailstones (or are they ripe autumn olives, as some believe?). In winter the tempestuous Northeast Wind, known as the Euroclydon in antiquity, can make sailing in the Aegean dangerous. This northeasterly is sometimes called the Gregale, the "Greek wind." It plagued Odysseus, driving him farther from home, and it once caused Heracles to be shipwrecked on the island of Cos. It was the Euroclydon that caused Saint Paul to be shipwrecked off the island of Malta in late September of AD 59. Paul had booked passage on a ship transporting prisoners to Rome from Asia Minor. The ship's captain was hugging the southern coast of Crete seeking a safe winter harbor when the northeasterly struck. For two harrowing weeks the ship was tossed upon the seas, with neither stars nor sun visible. The ordeal was described by Paul in a section of Acts that has been called the Bible's "mini-Odyssey."

Another northeasterly wind, called the Bora in Italy, whistles down the Alps and bursts out violently along the Adriatic coast in winter, whipping up steep waves and forcing ships to flee south for safety. Fishermen describe the shrill scream of this scourge of the Adriatic as a desperate wail that chills a seafarer's heart.

In Athens, northeasterlies can bring cool, clear weather. On such days, air pollution lifts and visibility is fine. We have noticed that from the Acropolis one can even see the harbor of Piraeus and ships in the Saronic Gulf. Charles Kingsley, a robustly anti-Romantic poet, praised the invigorating Gregale in 1873: "Welcome North-Easter! / Shame it is to see / Odes to every zephyr / Ne'er a verse to thee!"

Next on the Tower of the Winds comes Apeliotes from the east, bringing ripe fruit and gentle rains. Today the East Wind is called the Levant; it is usually hot in summer and cold in winter. Next, the sultry southeasterly Euros (now called the Souroko or Sirocco) is shown threatening a storm. Notos, the South Wind, empties an urn of water. The South Wind was associated with drenching storms in antiquity. The Roman poet Ovid described Notos as "all darkish . . . with water streaming down his hair." The Southwest Wind holds onto a ship's stern ornament, promising a rapid voyage. Not all ancient cultures found the southwest wind so benign. Ancient Mesopotamians were in awe of the demon Pazuzu, lord of the wind demons. Pazuzu rode the southwest wind, scourging the land with famine, drought, and plagues of locusts.

On the west face of the Tower of the Winds is Zephyros, bearing spring blossoms. Byron and countless other Romantic poets rhapsodized over the way the West Wind, Zephyros, glides over still water, "just kissing" the surface, "caressing" flowers and gently stirring maidens' tresses. Greek myths connect Zephyros with Flora, goddess of flowers and spring, and with Iris, the rainbow. Since Homer's day, the first spring zephyrs signal the beginning of the good sailing season in the Aegean. As Homer wrote, "Gray-eyed Athena sent the sailors a favorable breeze, a fresh west wind singing over the wine-dark sea." It was said that the West Wind was once as churlish as his brother Boreas (see chapter 34). But Zephyr mellowed when he fell in love with a beautiful nymph who was trans-formed into the "windflower," the anemone, a wildflower that graces the Greek countryside, nodding in the soft, pleasant breezes that the word "zephyr" has come to denote.

Skiron personifies the Northwest Wind on Andronikos's tower, carrying a bronze charcoal brazier to symbolize his ability to dry up rivers in the summer. The northwesterlies, or "Etesian" (seasonal) winds, can be a blessing or a curse. These periodic cool winds, today known as the Meltemi, rise on summer afternoons as air is sucked from the Balkans to-ward the Sahara Desert. Despite a clear sky, the Etesian wind can whip the Aegean into a choppy froth. Strabo, a Greek geographer of the first century AD, described Skiron as an "impetuous and terrible wind that displaces rocks and hurls men from their chariots and strips them of their weapons." Strabo may have been thinking of the night in 371 BC when the Spartans were retreating after the Battle of Leuktra. Hurrying single file, in heavy battle gear, down the shoulder of Mount Kitheron above the eastern end of the Gulf of Corinth, the Spartans were suddenly assailed by such violent blasts of wind that it whipped their shields away. One summer, Josh and I hiked along that same route as a Meltemi wind came up. Stay-ing on the narrow path clinging to the mountainside above the sea was daunting. This region is still susceptible to sudden northwesterly gusts in late afternoons. On the island of Spet-ses, the local name for sudden Etesian winds is "table-turners." Josh and I have observed blasts strong enough to blow over wooden tables and chairs at cafés along the seashore.

Shortly after Boreas participated in the battle at Artemisium, a timely Etesian wind aided the Athenians in the naval battle of Salamis, in September 480 BC. The Athenian commander

CHAPTER 33

Themistocles waited until about noon to draw the Persian fleet into battle. As the line of Xerxes's 1,400 ships became disorganized in the narrow strait, Themistocles gave the signal for his 310 warships to burst out at full speed just as the Northwest Wind came blasting down from the hills of Attica. Themistocles knew that this powerful, gusty wind usually hits its stride just after noon in late summer and autumn in the Aegean. But the Persians were totally unprepared for the combined onslaught of ramming triremes and strong gusts in the confined waters. They lost decisively in the chaos of oars and splintering boats.

Odysseus was constantly harassed by untimely, contrary winds during his ten-year attempt to sail home from Troy to Ithaca—even though he spent a month as the honored guest of Aeolos, the Ruler of the Winds. According to myth, deep in bedrock caverns below his palace on the floating island of Aeolia, King Aeolos kept the winds of the world imprisoned. Visitors to the barren island "who please the king are given large ox-skin sacks filled with violent winds. But these sacks are best left unopened." In the *Odyssey*, King Aeolos presented Odysseus with just such a bulging leather bag. The bag confined all the winds except Zephyros, the warm breeze that would blow him home. Ten days later, in sight of their own island, Odysseus's crew untied the mysterious sack, expecting to find treasure inside. Immediately, the released winds swept into a terrific gale that propelled the ship far from Ithaca again.

Two thousand years after Homer wrote the *Odyssey*, the French satirist Rabelais claimed that Aeolos's windbag had been transferred to Windy Island. In this island, the inhabitants live on wind. The rich obtain abundant nourishment from their fancy windmills, while the poor must subsist on puffs of air that they raise with paper fans. Naturally, Windy Islanders suffer from diseases originating from flatulence. But fortunately, the islanders can cure themselves of the most serious of these ills by inhaling a bit of the original wind remaining in Aeolos's ox-hide sack, which their king preserves like the Holy Grail. At banquets, the wealthy blowhards spend hours debating the qualities of various winds, like wine connoisseurs discussing vintages. Perhaps they reminisce about famous old winds and their dispositions, wind cults of yore, and those brave souls who actually set out to do battle with the wind in antiquity.

Herodotus, the fifth-century BC historian, described a Persian army that was engulfed in a sandstorm, driven by a *simoom*, or "poison wind." In 1917, T. E. Lawrence vividly recounted a similar experience with a ferocious *haboob* in Arabia. The vortex tore off his men's cloaks and lifted their camels off the ground. Such desert dust storms are caused by strong downbursts creating a tall and wide wall of dust that can travel between twenty and sixty miles an hour. Herodotus also reported that a North African tribe, called the Psylli, once declared war against the South Wind. The hot wind had dried up all their crops and evaporated their water holes. The Psylli warriors marched out in battle array, beating drums and cymbals, to confront the whirling hot blast. The entire army vanished into a cloud of red dust.

In antiquity, kings, sailors, and farmers dreamed of controlling the wind. Setting off for the legendary Trojan War, for example, King Agamemnon sacrificed his own daughter Iphigenia to obtain favorable winds for his fleet. The Roman natural historian Pliny the Elder advocated a less dramatic method for preventing the wind from damaging crops. Pliny suggested simply burying a toad in a new clay pot in the center of the field. Pausanias, a travel writer in Greece during the second century AD, reported that not far from Epidauros he saw two farmers racing around their vineyards each brandishing half a white rooster. The farmers hoped to keep the North Wind from desiccating their new grapevine shoots. Pausanias also reported that on a windswept ridge near Corinth, priests sacrificed at an altar of the winds. They made secret offerings at four pits in the ground, singing the same spells that the sorceress Medea had used to bind winds in the mythic epic of Jason and the Argonauts. Another myth tells how the Greek hero Aristaeus once made a sacrifice on the island of Kea to summon the Etesian winds so he could sail south. Another hero, Menelaos, offended the Egyptians by sacrificing two children to dispel contrary northerly winds.

During the historical reign of Constantine the Great (AD 272–337), a man was actually executed for casting a spell on the South Wind. It happened when calm, windless days delayed the fleet of ships bringing desperately needed grain from Egypt to feed the people of Constantinople. The hungry Byzantine masses had gathered in the theater, and their mood grew ugly. Some courtiers, jealous of a court philosopher named Sopater, accused him of chaining the South Wind by magic. Reluctantly, Constantine ordered Sopater's execution, and by and by the ships came in.

During the medieval Crusades, Saint Nicholas miraculously quelled a tempest that threatened a boatload of pilgrims in the Aegean. Around the time that Andronikos built the Tower of the Winds in Athens, there were actually official guilds of "wind-lullers" based in Athens and Corinth. These professionals used magical incantations and blood offerings to propitiate the winds.

Travelers in the Aegean today might wish that the wind-lullers' guilds were still in business when the Meltemi or Euroclydon cancels ferryboat trips and makes island travel unpleasant. Because of its varied topography and indented coast, Greece has a wide range of interesting wind patterns. Autumnal winds rush down mountainsides, heating up and drying out as they descend. On summer evenings, cool breezes are drawn from the sea by the rising hot air of the sunbaked land. After sunset and before midnight, the *apogeios* wind blows out to sea from the shore. As in antiquity, the first fresh breeze of dawn is still called an *aura*. The strong northerly Etesian wind that aided the Greeks against the Persians at Salamis, the Meltemi, blows between June and October, most often in July and August. In May the Etesians are weak and steady—the ancient Greeks called these forerunners the *prodromi*.

Both ancient and modern observers agree that the Southeastern Wind from the Sahara, the hot, dry dragon's breath called the Sirocco, has a debilitating, disagreeable influence. Classical Greeks claimed that when it blew, strings of musical instruments and human nerves snapped, and joints both human and wooden cracked. Unlike the exhilarating North Wind, the South Wind often seems to make one feel dull and irritable. Travelers in the Ionian islands in the eighteenth century noted that the South Wind "seemed to extinguish every passion." Modern research shows that this type of hot, dry, incessant wind can indeed make some people anxious and melancholy. It saps energy and patience, causes static in communications and relationships, and increases the incidence of traffic accidents. The northerlies are the prevailing winds in the Aegean; the South Wind is an occasional spring phenomenon. Perhaps it's just best to remember the old proverb that "wind in one's face makes one wise."

Legend says that King David used to hang his harp above his bed at night to be soothed by the wind's own melodies. In the third century BC, a Greek engineer devised a large musical wind organ driven by four sails. Many centuries later the Aeolian harp was invented to play ethereal tunes as the wind glided over its strings. The invisible wind has always evoked lyrical responses from poets: Homer sent Zephyros singing over the wine-dark sea. Shakespeare alluded to Boreas's trumpet-blast. Lord Byron heard whispering west winds. Longfellow detected "celestial harmonies" in the wind. Keats heard a "lovely sighing . . . a half-heard strain, full of sweet desolation." Long ago, Aristotle had remarked on the "bird winds" of spring, which coincided with the return of migrating flocks—and the modern poet John Masefield was moved to write, "It's a warm wind, the West Wind, full of birds' cries; / I never hear the West Wind but tears are in my eyes." In his nostalgic longing for home, the sailor Odysseus would agree.

Death by Bronze "Frisbee"

A MURDEROUS GUST OF WIND killed the beautiful youth Hyacinthus in ancient Greek myth. Zephyr, the West Wind, was usually depicted as a gentle spring breeze that ruffled the petals of his lover, the flower nymph Anemone (chapter 33). But the West Wind was also blamed for the death of Hyacinthus, a handsome Spartan youth beloved by Apollo.

Apollo liked to take Hyacinthus for rides in his chariot drawn by swans. The god taught the boy how to use a bow, and they often exercised together. The West Wind, Zephyr, was also attracted to the youth and vied with Apollo to win his love, but Hyacinthus preferred the radiant god of music.

One spring day Hyacinthus and Apollo were taking turns tossing a discus. Zephyr was consumed by jealousy when he happened on the two friends playing. Impulsively he blew a strong, sudden gust of wind just as Apollo tossed the discus. The gust caught up the discus and caused it to boomerang back at Hyacinthus. The edge of the metal Frisbee struck the young man on the forehead, killing him instantly.

How strong was that deadly gust? According to the modern Beaufort scale (developed in 1805) for measuring wind force, winds are rated from 0 to 12. At Force 0, smoke rises vertically and gossamer (fine spider silk) floats in the calm air. This weather condition was beautifully described by the philosopher Aristotle, who watched tiny spiderlings on fine webs wafting over a meadow one splendid summer morning in the fourth century BC.

At Force 4, "moderate breeze," one's hair is ruffled and skirts flap, and mosquitoes stop biting.

Between Force 6 and Force 7 (25–38 miles per hour), you would find walking into the high wind difficult. Umbrellas turn inside out, and trees toss and sway. Bees, butterflies, and most birds seek shelter.

By Force 9, "strong gale," dragonflies are grounded, small children are blown over, tiles are blown off roofs, outdoor tables are overturned, and the only birds still airborne would be swifts.

Adult men and women are toppled and trees uprooted at Force 10. Hurricane warnings are issued when winds reach Force 12, over 70 miles an hour.

In antiquity a bronze discus weighed about 4.5 pounds; a modern discus weighs about 4.4 pounds. The force and angle of Apollo's discus is unknown, but today's Olympic discus throwers aim for about 55 miles an hour. It seems reasonable to declare that Zephyr's fatal gust of wind would probably rate a Force 9 or 10, with wind speed of 47–63 miles per hour.

When the accident happened, Apollo was horrified and tried in vain to revive his friend with ambrosia, the nourishment of the immortal gods. The god created a flower in his memory. The beautiful deep purple flower (probably the larkspur rather than the hyacinth), sprang up from the youth's blood, and Apollo, in mourning, marked its petals with AI, "Alas."

As early as the Bronze Age, a cult arose around Hyacinthus, at Amyclae, southwest of Sparta, where the young man was said to be buried in a mound nearby. The Spartans celebrated the annual Hyacinthia festival in early summer, beginning with a day of mourning for the tragedy, followed by a second day of singing, dancing, and racing, and a third day of mystery rites.

Remarkably, this was not the only death by discus in Greek myth. The story begins when King Acrisius of Argos locked his daughter Danae away in a bronze tower. He intended to keep her childless, because the Delphic Oracle had predicted that Acrisius would be slain by her son. But Danae was impregnated by Zeus in the form of a shower of gold and gave birth to Perseus. Acrisius believed he was safe after throwing Danae and her newborn son into the sea, but they survived. The hero Perseus grew up and killed Medusa. With her frightful head, he rescued the princess Andromeda from a sea monster. One day Perseus went to Larissa to participate in funeral games. By chance, his estranged grandfather, King Acrisius, was also attending the games. A discus thrown by Perseus accidentally struck Acrisius on the head and he died, fulfilling the oracle.

The role of wind is not mentioned and this misfortune was an accident, unlike the murder of Hycinthus. But taken together the two mythic incidents suggest that the sport of hurling a heavy bronze disc through the air was recognized as dangerous and may have actually killed in antiquity. Such accidents are rare but not unknown today. For example, the University of North Carolina's National Center for Catastrophic Sport Injury Research reported four fatalities from thrown discuses, hammers, and shot put balls in high school track and field events between 1992 and 2012.

Could Aristotle Guess Your Personality from Your Face?

READING SOMEONE'S PERSONALITY and temperament by looking at his or her face, a "science" known as physiognomy, was accepted by philosophers in classical antiquity. Indeed, the great natural historian Aristotle (fourth century BC) was one of those who believed that facial features indicated personality type.

According to little-known passages in the *History of Animals*, Aristotle included physiognomy principles in his detailed descriptions of human faces based on his own observations. He started with the forehead: those with high foreheads were "sluggish," notes Aristotle, while those with broad foreheads were "excitable." People with small foreheads were "fickle," and a bulging forehead revealed a quick-tempered individual. Straight eyebrows were "a sign of a soft disposition" but eyebrows that curved out toward the temples signaled a mocking and evasive personality. Eyebrows curving down toward the nose indicated a harsh temper. People who blinked a lot were indecisive and unstable, but those who could stare without blinking were deemed impudent. Aristotle thought ears were especially revealing: large, projecting ears were a sign that the person indulged in a lot of silly chatter.

The earliest professional phyiognomist was Zopyrus in Athens. According to a story reported by Cicero (*De fato*), Zopyrus read Socrates's character after observing the philosopher's face, but without ever meeting him. The reading he gave was so far off the mark that Socrates's friends in Plato's Academy burst out in guffaws. According to Zopyrus, Socrates's physiognomy supposedly revealed that he was stupid, dull-witted, and lecherous toward women. But Socrates

Socrates. Drawing by Adrienne Mayor.

came to his rescue, stating that indeed Zopyrus was correct. Socrates explained that he was naturally inclined to be slow and stupid and addicted to women, but that he had—with the help of reason and determination—overcome these character defects.

The ancient idea that faces reveal personality brings to mind the nineteenth-century pseudoscience of phrenology, reading character from bumps on the head, and the notion that "born criminals" could be identified by physical anomalies, a theory perpetrated by Italian criminologist Cesare Lombroso (1835–1909). More recently, professor of behavioral science Alexander Todorov has studied the cutting-edge science that lies behind people's first impressions based on faces (*Face Value*, 2017). Everyone has made snap judgments about others' trustworthiness, competence, friendliness, honesty, and so on based on how they look. But it turns out that these decisions reveal our own biases and stereotypes.

The First Anti-Vaxxers

THOSE WHO RAILED AGAINST Edward Jenner's brilliant idea of injecting material from cowpox, a mild disease suffered by milkmaids, to protect people against smallpox thought it was a shocking notion. It may seem counterintuitive to voluntarily take a small dose of a toxic or contagious substance into one's body to defend against a concentrated attack by that same toxin or disease. But this is how our immune systems learn to recognize danger and marshal defenses.

In the first century BC, Mithradates VI of Pontus, the first experimental toxicologist, followed his hunch that ingesting a concoction of minuscule amounts of toxins on a daily basis would bestow immunity to poisons. His cleverly conceived "universal antidote," based on a concept that anticipated vaccinations, kept him in robust health well into his seventies at a time when assassination by poison was rife and the average life span was about forty-five. His original recipe of more than fifty ingredients was lost, but his idea was marketed as "Mithridatium" during the Roman Empire and the Middle Ages, up through early modernity. The elixir was sought after and trusted by royalty and ordinary folk alike.

In 1706, Onesimus, an enslaved African, joined the household of the Puritan leader Cotton Mather in the Massachusetts Bay Colony. In about 1716 he explained to Mather the method used in his homeland to confer immunity to smallpox. He showed Mather the scar where smallpox material had been rubbed into a scratch. Several other Bostonians had heard about the operation from other Africans in their households. Intrigued, Mather did some research and learned that similar methods of achieving immunity to smallpox had been used in ancient China and India, and the Ottoman Empire.

The procedure, called variolation, was disgusting and it could be dangerous. Pus from a smallpox victim was rubbed into an incision or pricked into a person's skin, in the hope that the resulting case would not be fatal and would confer immunity.

When Mather and a doctor in Boston used the method during a devastating smallpox epidemic in Boston in 1721, it proved to be statistically effective. But many Bostonians refused to undergo a nasty operation invented by "ignorant" African slaves. The local newspaper mocked Mather, and someone even threw an incendiary through his window.

George Washington, who had survived smallpox in Barbados in 1751 when he was nineteen, understood the potential devastation of the contagion and the wisdom of inoculation. When he took command of the revolutionary army in 1775, he realized that the British soldiers already possessed herd immunity to the smallpox virus, which was endemic in Europe. The lethal disease was raging among Native Americans, colonists, and Washington's recruits. Washington had heard of the crude and risky method called variolation, practiced by slaves from Africa and taught to Cotton Mather. But was the method safe and worthwhile? Washington waffled. He wrote out the order, then rescinded it. Finally, Washington overcame his doubts and determined to protect his troops by ordering mass inoculations for all his men.

A little while later, in England, Edward Jenner realized that milkmaids were mysteriously immune to the ravages of smallpox (chapter 28). The "father of immunology" theorized that cowpox, a similar but less virulent disease contracted by humans from cows, somehow protected the milkmaids. He tested his hypothesis successfully in 1796, and vaccinations began soon thereafter.

But great controversy and fear swirled around inoculations with cowpox in England. Opponents of vaccination spread scare stories about Jenner's method.

The most sensational claim was that the introduction of infectious material from cattle into humans would cause people to develop bovine features. Many lurid cartoons warned of the dire effects. One cartoon captioned "The Wonderful Effects of the New Inoculation" by satirist James Gillray was published by the Anti-Vaccine Society in 1802. The grotesque scene depicts vaccinated men and women in London's St Pancras Hospital. Horns are erupting on their foreheads, and bulls, cows, and calves burst out of their mouths, eyes, ears, noses, arms, and buttocks. A painting on the wall shows the Israelites worshipping the Golden Calf.

Dr. Benjamin Moseley, at the Royal College of Physicians, issued dreadful warnings implying that the cowpox vaccine contained bovine venereal disease. "Can any person say what may be the consequences of introducing the *Lues Bovilla* [syphilis of oxen], a bestial humour, into the human" body? Moseley's 1800 anti-vaccination tract also contained dark allusions to ancient Greek mythology, specifically the myth of Pasiphaë and the Minotaur. Pasiphaë was a queen of Crete who formed a perverse desire to mate with a bull. In the myth, Pasiphaë's lust was satisfied, and she gave birth to a monstrous infant with a bull's head and a human body—the Minotaur.

"Who knows," continued Moseley, but that "the human character may undergo strange mutations" replicating the nature of cattle? Moseley went on to suggest that a vaccinated lady risked becoming a "modern Pasiphae to rival the fables of old." He called up shocking scenes of vaccinated British women wandering in cow pastures hoping to have sex with bulls. Another physician, Dr. Thomas Rowley, went so far as to claim that an "ox-faced baby boy" had been born to a vaccinated woman. Another anti-vaxxer cartoon showed an alternative scenario, a midwife presenting a newborn calf with a baby's head.

"Effects Arising from Vaccination." A midwife presents an infant with a calf's body, allegedly born to a woman vaccinated with cowpox. Robert John Thornton, *Vaccinae Vindicia* (London: Symonds, 1806).

Ultimately, wiser minds prevailed and the insightful under-standing, based on millennia of experiments and keen obser-vation, of how to immunize people against horrid contagions by means of a small dose of the disease was widely accepted by the 1840s. Jenner's insight is often said to have saved the lives of more people than any other medical discovery.

Poison Honey

A sip of toxic nectar could kill a horse, render a soldier senseless, and maybe even inspire the Delphic Oracle.

IN 401 BC THE GENERAL XENOPHON was leading ten thousand Greek mercenaries back home after having fought with distinction against the grand army of the king of Persia. As they hurried through Asia Minor toward the Black Sea, battling local folk and plundering along the way, a mystifying event befell them. While making camp and looking for food in the territory of Colchis, they noticed extraordinary numbers of swarming bees. After feasting on honey raided from the beehives, wrote Xenophon in his history the *Anabasis*, the soldiers suddenly became "like intoxicated madmen" and soon collapsed by the thousands.

Xenophon reported that his troops were sprawled over the ground like victims of a terrible rout. As though under a spell, the warriors were immobilized and a "great despondency prevailed" until they began to recover a few days later. Still feeling weak, they continued west to friendly territory. Unknown to Xenophon and his soldiers, the culprit was naturally toxic honey, produced by bees that collected nectar from rhododendron blossoms. Inhabitants of the Black Sea region knew all about the beautiful yet baneful rhododendron, but strangers in their land eagerly devoured the tempting honeycombs.

The land south and east of the Black Sea was notorious in antiquity for its poisonous plants and minerals. This was the realm of the legendary sorceress Medea of Colchis and of King Mithradates VI of Pontus, both famed keepers of poisons and antidotes. It was also the haunt of Dionysos, god of madness, and his maenads, to whom honey was sacred. Nearly four centuries after Xenophon, the Roman general Pompey was campaigning against Mithradates on the southern shores of the Black Sea, in the Third Mithradatic War (73-63 BC). The geographer Strabo describes how Mithradates's allies, the Heptakometes, placed toxic honeycombs along Pompey's route. They were not as fortunate as Xenophon's men. Three Roman squadrons succumbed to the delicious poison and were wiped out. In AD 946 Russian foes of Olga of Kiev fell for a similar ruse in the same region when they accepted several tons of fermented honey from her followers. All five thousand were massacred as they lay in a stupor. In 1489 some ten thousand Tatar soldiers were slaughtered by Russians after stopping to gulp down huge casks of mead in an abandoned camp not far from where Olga's enemies had fallen.

Classical honey connoisseurs appreciated the distinctive flavors of nectars from exotic places. After Xenophon's experience they became aware of the effects of "mad" honey and its value as a *pharmakon*, or drug. Greek and Roman medical authorities thought that it might reverse the madness of the insane. The Roman naturalist Pliny extolled the qualities of excellent honeys from around the Mediterranean but warned against *meli maenomenon* ("mad" or "raving" honey) from the Black Sea coast. He was the first to attribute toxicity to the rhododendron, azalea, and oleander, plants known locally as "goat-bane," "lamb-kill," "cattle-destroyer," and "horse-killer." Some honey was so pernicious that Pliny advised immediate antidotes: fine old mead, honey in which bees had died, or rue and salt fish as an emetic. He also noted that sometimes only part of a honeycomb was bad, and that honey was hazardous only after wet springs. Musing on the paradox that the "sweetest, finest, most health-promoting food" could be so randomly lethal—and pointing out that nature had already armed bees with venom—Pliny concluded that such honey must be intended as a natural curb on human greed.

It took a while for modern science to catch up with Pliny. The *Encyclopedia Britannica* of 1929 scoffed at the very idea of poison honey: "In all likelihood the symptoms described by these old writers were due to overeating," or to eating honey "on an empty stomach." In modern times, as in antiquity, it was foraging soldiers' encounters with poison honey that led scientists to try to understand the toxic process. In 1875 Dr. J. Grammer, a former Confederate surgeon, recorded in *Gleanings in Bee Culture* numerous incidents in which Southern soldiers were poisoned by honey. The effects were like those experienced by Xenonphon's men: first a "queerish sensation of tingling all over," then blurred vision, and finally "an empty, dizzy feeling about the head and a horrible nausea." Lurching about with no voluntary muscle control, the soldiers seemed "entirely overpowered" and "dead drunk." Their senses returned in two or three days, but Grammer remarked that "fatal consequences have been known to follow a too free indulgence."

In 1891 the German scientist P. C. Plugge isolated a toxic compound in honey from Trebizond (northeastern Turkey):

andromedetoxin (now called acetylandromedol, a type of grayanotoxin). Pliny had been correct: the toxins occur in Mediterranean oleander (*Nerium*, dogbane) and in members of the heath family (Ericaceae), which includes *Rhododendron ponticum*, azaleas of the Black Sea and Caucasus, and *R. maximum* (*Kalmia*, mountain laurel) of the eastern United States and Pacific Northwest. Modern toxicological studies identify grayanotoxins as breathing inhibitors and hypnotics that act dramatically on the central nervous system. Depending upon the amount consumed, one experiences tingling sensations and numbness, dizziness, psychedelic optical effects such as whirling lights and tunnel vision, giddiness and swooning, and impaired speech in which words and syllables are uttered out of sequence. Symptoms may progress to vertigo, delirium, nausea and vomiting, respiratory difficulty, very low pulse rate, a ghastly blue skin color, muscle paralysis, unconsciousness, and even death, Recovery time—hours to days—depends on dosage.

Since Xenophon's first description, honey poisonings have been reported in Anatolia and southern Russia, the Himalayas, the eastern United States, the Pacific Northwest, and other locales where Ericaceae plants thrive. But not all Ericaceae honey is dangerous—Scottish heather, sourwood, and blueberry honeys, for example, are highly esteemed. Moreover, outbreaks of intoxication seem to occur in cycles. About a hundred years after Pompey's disastrous encounter with honey, the Greek physician Dioscorides, the great pharmacologist of antiquity, wrote that only in certain seasons was Pontic honey dangerous. He noted that the toxin was signaled by an acidic taste, profuse sweating, and violent sneezing. In a 1929 article in *Bee World*, a beekeeper in the Caucasus described the unpredictability of his region's persistent poison honey problem. In his experience, dry spells at high elevations produced the most dangerous honey, and a single honeycomb could contain both lethal and good honey, something Pliny had noticed.

What accounts for honey's variable toxicity? Individual experiences and expert opinions have been maddeningly conflicting since antiquity. Pliny blamed rainy spring weather, while others mention drought. Some say mad honey is red and watery. Others say it smells odd or tastes bitter; still others claim it is indistinguishable from good honey. Some believe that aging or boiling makes mad honey safe; others even claim that one can get used to it. Physician and botanist Benjamin Barton noted in 1794 that Scottish heather honey made him feel as though he had taken "a moderate dose of opium," while Scottish Highlanders denied any strange effects.

Almost all intoxications occur in springtime. Ancient Greek and Roman writers associated toxic honey with early spring and referred to maddening "fresh" honey. Longus, a novelist of the second century AD, compared a lover's kiss to the "madness of new honey." These clues accurately point to the conditions that permit or prevent the development of poison honey. According to John T. Ambrose, the state apiculturist of North Carolina, where honey poisonings occur sometimes in spring, honeybees usually bypass Ericaceae plants in favor of flowers with a higher sugar content and more nectar. But rhododendrons are vigorous early bloomers, and in some regions they are the predominant native flora. When these are the only blossoms available, the first honey of the season is often toxic, especially if it is "green" (unripe), from cells not yet "capped" with wax. This explains the ancient descriptions of mad honey's watery consistency and why only part of a comb may be harmful.

Grayanotoxins do not pose a problem in commercially produced honey because most toxins are neutralized in the hive by dehydration during the ripening process, and because large beekeeping cooperatives blend massive quantities of honeys and monitor the results. Small-scale beekeepers in areas with toxic plants are usually familiar with the dangers of spring honey. Consumers who seek the "exotic tastes of imported honey" or who, "in the quest for natural foods," obtain unprocessed wild honey or buy "from farmers who have only a few hives" should be aware of the hazards, says Kenneth Lampe of the American Medical Association (AMA). Prompted by a spate of intoxications in northern Turkey and mindful of the long history of mad honey there and in parts of the United States, the AMA recently warned that "today, cases of mad honey poisoning should be anticipated everywhere." And, as Xenophon and Pompey discovered, one should always be cautious when sampling honey in exotic lands.

Did the ancients deliberately ingest mad honey as an intoxicating drug? According to Pliny, properly aged *meli maenomenon* made a fine mead. The intoxicating properties of Pliny's mead were probably not due to its alcoholic content alone: horticultural historian David Leach found that for centuries the people of the Caucasus have "added small quantities of Pontic azalea honey to alcoholic drinks to intensify the effect." Known as *deli bal* in Turkey, a spoonful of toxic honey in milk is a traditional tonic; a dollop in alcohol gives an extra kick. Whether the honey is an intoxicant, pain-killer, or deadly poison depends on the size of the dose, says Leach. *Deli bal* was a major Black Sea export in the eighteenth century: twenty-five tons of toxic honey, known to Westerners as *miel fou* (crazy honey), were shipped each year to Europe to be added to drinks sold in taverns. And America had its own *miel fou*. Noting that Indians used the leaves of mountain laurel as a drug, Benjamin Barton described some Pennsylvania beekeepers who became inebriated "to a great degree" by ingesting honey from its flowers. These "adventurers" then turned a profit by adding liquor and selling the elixir in New Jersey under the name "metheglin." The high began pleasantly enough but could suddenly turn "ferocious," according to Barton.

Clues from ancient Greek texts allow us to speculate that grayanotoxins might have inspired the trances of the Pythia at Delphi and other oracles whose cryptic utterances were translated into prophetic verse by interpreters. Roman writers stated that laurel leaves were burned or chewed by the Pythia to induce a hypnotic state in which she predicted the future. Plutarch adds that Pythias often died young. He describes a trance that went horribly wrong in the second century AD, when the Pythia became "dreadfully disordered," rushed about shrieking, collapsed, and died. Yet most classical scholars discount the Roman accounts on the basis of the experience of T. K. Oesterreich, an expert on voluntarily induced trances who personally tested the Roman theory about laurel in the 1920s. He reported that chewing laurel foliage produced "no results of any interest."

Ancient and modern confusion over the identity of what we now call laurel, rhododendron, and oleander probably accounts for the lack of effects reported by Oesterreich. "Laurel" (*daphne* in Greek) was indeed traditionally associated with Apollo, but we cannot be sure what plant it was. Oesterreich probably chewed the edible leaves of *Laurus nobilis* (the sweet bay used in cooking), which, like those of rhododendron and oleander, are dark, glossy, and evergreen. But some species of the genus *Daphne*, also native to Greece and known as laurel, are poisonous, causing stupor, convulsions, and death. To compound matters, what the ancient Greeks called rhododaphne or rhododendron is now called dogbane or rosebay, or even oleander, a word that conflates the Latin for laurel and rhododendron. Oleander contains grayanotoxins, as do rhododendrons and azaleas (whose names are often used interchangeably), but they too are sometimes called rosebay. Laurel and bay are common terms for similar-looking but diverse species with evergreen leaves, as in mountain laurel for rhododendrons native to the United States.

If the Pythia was under the influence of a plant, some member of the Ericaceae family or related species seems the most likely. Quite possibly, Roman authors (and Oesterreich) got the story half right: a plant was the source of the Pythia's trance, but they got the plant wrong and perhaps misunderstood how its toxin was ingested. The key may lie in the *Homeric Hymn to Hermes*, written sometime between the eighth and sixth centuries BC. It describes mysterious bee-oracles or *melissai*, young women who revealed the future while under the influence of "maddening" fresh honey. They lived below the cliffs of Mount Parnassos and fed "on *meli chloron*, food of the gods / Divinely maddened, they are inspired to speak the truth / But if they are deprived of the divine honeycomb / they cannot prophesy." Classicists usually translate *chloron* as "golden" or "liquid" and assume that the authors are simply speaking metaphorically or referring to ordinary mead. But *chloron* can mean not only the color green, but "green" as in fresh or uncured, as in "green" wood or honey. If we take "green honey" to mean unripe, uncapped spring honey that causes intoxication, then the maddening *meli chloron* eaten by the bee-oracles must refer to mad honey made by bees feeding on rhododendrons or related species.

Indeed, the *Hymn* further likens the raving of the bee-oracles to the frenzy of the maenads, Dionysos's female followers. According to the fifth-century BC playwright Euripides, maenads waved "wands flowing with honey" and drank an intoxicating concoction of honey and alcohol. Thus maddened, says Euripides, these maenads could even tell the future—just like the bee-oracles. The Pythia at Delphi was also called a bee-oracle (*melissa*, after the nymph who invented mead), and she predicted the future under the influence of an intoxicating substance. Could mead spiked with mad honey have been the secret inspiration of the Delphic Oracle?

We have seen that in ancient times women intoxicated with mad honey engaged in religious rites ranging from bacchic frenzies to mantic trances. The writings of an eccentric British novelist, Rose Macaulay, suggest that mad honey can also inspire the literary imagination, Macaulay's fantasy-memoir, *The Towers of Trebizond* (1956), recounts a tipsy trip through Asia Minor. After a Greek friend named Xenophon introduces Rose to the local delicacy of azalea blossoms and yogurt, she sets off with her camel as the "May breezes were blowing." Along the way she chews the flowers of lush rhododendrons. So does the camel, and it ends up galloping up paths, roaring drunk and acting lovesick.

Near the place where Xenophon's army fell under the spell of mad honey in 401 BC, a sorcerer gives Rose Macaulay a mysterious "green potion," a strong, sweet elixir "more marvelous than mere wine." Feeling "dizzy and strange" after three sips, the young woman stops to rest in a mossy glade. She swoons, falls into a coma, and has an enchanting, hallucinatory dream, imagining that she "wandered in the woods eating azalea honey." For the rest of the novel, she is continually swigging *deli bar* and slipping into trances, while her frisky camel companion forages for *Azalea pontica*. At the end of her "long, delirious journey," Rose vows to return some day to Trebizond and "lay in a good stock of the stuff." It's fitting conclusion for a novel described by reviewers as an "inspired, hypnotic frolic with a haunting aftertaste" set in the land of maenads.

CHAPTER 38

Who Was the First Foot Fetishist?

A FOOT FETISH IS A SEXUAL ATTRACTION to naked feet. Of nongenital body parts, it seems that feet are the most fetishized. Not only is foot worship—podophilia—surprisingly prevalent, but it is a very ancient phenomenon. A passage in Homer's *Odyssey* describes the hero Odysseus gazing at the comely feet of dancing boys in the first bloom of youth, who performed for him at the court of King Alcinous. Notably, ancient Greek vases in the shape of pretty feet were used as drinking cups and perfume jars. From Roman poets, we know that a small foot was a desired attribute of one's lovers, and we hear that Mark Antony liked to caress Cleopatra's feet (see chapter 41).

The so-called Greek foot, in which the second toe is longer than the big toe, appears in ancient Greek and Roman statues of men and women, from the Caryatids to Venus, from fauns to old boxers. Even Michelangelo's *David* has "Greek feet." The characteristic is genetically determined, found in about 20 percent of the world's population today. In classical antiquity, this configuration of toes was considered aesthetically pleasing to the ancient Greeks and Romans. Notably, the ideal ancient Egyptian foot had a long big toe and the other

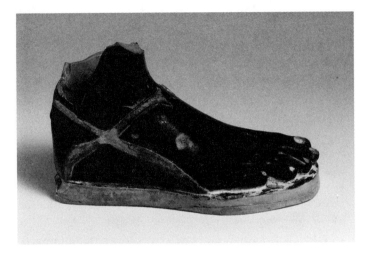

Vase in the shape of a foot, fifth century BC, Metropolitan Museum, New York, 21.88.31, Rogers Fund, 1921.

toes tapering gracefully to the little toe. But it was the Greek foot that was idealized and enshrined in Western art. Some scholars speculate that the Greek love of what they called the "golden ratio" governing divine proportions in nature led them to admire the long second toe.

In the literary world, evidence for ancient sexual podophilia stands out in a series of sixty-four brooding, obsessive Roman "Love Letters" composed in the second century AD. Authorship is uncertain, but the work is sometimes attributed to Philostratus. The letter writer is bisexual, addressing both women and male youths.

Letter 18, "To a Barefoot Boy," for example, insists that only the elderly, lame, and infirm should wear slippers, sandals, and boots. Moreover, leather footwear tends to pinch, blister, and disfigure one's feet. "Why don't you always walk barefoot? . . . Let nothing come between your naked foot and the earth." The dust will welcome your tread, declares the lover, who vows to kiss the youth's footprints. The writer goes on to rhapsodize about the perfect shape of the beloved's feet, comparing them to "new and strange flowers sprung from the earth."

"Do not ever wear shoes!" the lover demands in Letter 36, "To a Woman." Don't even wear white clothing, lest you obscure the pale purity of your feet, he pleads. Leave your feet bare like your neck and face, without any cosmetics or adornments, not even chains of gold or silver. Be like the silver-footed goddess Thetis and the newly born Aphrodite, the goddess of love barefoot on the seashore. "Do not torture your feet, my love, and do not hide them. Walk softly and leave prints of your lovely feet behind you, for those who would love to kiss them."

Strangely enough, an obsession with eroticized feet is a persistent thread in the so-called pagan poems of the Romantic poets Keats and Swinburne, a fetish that drew on their fascination with the literature and sculpture of classical antiquity. Keats, for example, compares the feet of the goddesses Diana and Venus in *Endymion* (1.624–26, 123): Diana's "hovering feet [are] more bluely vein'd / More soft, more whitely sweet / Than those of sea-born Venus."

The Roman-era fetishist compared his beloved's feet to flowers. This calls to mind the fact that in China "Lotus" was the poetic name for the torturously tiny bound feet of Chinese girls and women. The ideal size, "Golden Lotus," was three inches; four-inch feet were "Silver Lotus," and woe to those with "Iron Lotus" feet. The craze for eroticized foot binding began among concubines in the court circles of the

Song dynasty (AD 960–1279) and spread to urban elites and across China until it was commonplace by the 1800s, fading away only in the early twentieth century. Sex manuals of the Qin dynasty (1644–1912) detailed forty-eight forms of erotic play with bound feet.

Sigmund Freud considered Chinese foot binding a foot fetishism perversion on a vast cultural scale. True to his own personal obsessions, Freud believed that sexualization of feet arose because they looked penis-like. But some modern brain studies point to a neurological explanation for foot fetishes. In the human brain's body-imaging map, it happens that feet and genitalia are adjacent areas. According to neuroscientist Vilayanur Ramachandran, director of the Center for Brain and Cognition, University of California, San Diego, foot fetishes appear to result from "cross-wiring in the brain between the two body parts."

CHAPTER 39

"Giants" in Ancient Warfare

OUT OF THE RANKS of the Philistines strode the champion warrior Goliath of Gath, a mountain of a man standing almost ten feet tall. His bronze helmet, chain mail, and greaves weighed 150 pounds. He carried a javelin with a wooden shaft like a beam; the bronze spearhead alone weighed almost 20 pounds. For forty days Goliath spewed insults at the Israelites, defying them to send out their best warrior. No one stepped forward until the young shepherd David vowed to kill the giant of Gath. The Israelites piled a helmet and coat of mail on David and handed him a sword, but the armor was so heavy he could not move. Throwing off the armor, David selected five smooth stones and took up his sling. The young man let fly a stone that struck the huge Philistine, and Goliath crashed down dead.

David and Goliath . . . Odysseus and the Cyclops . . . Jack the Giant-Killer. Powerful stories, but aren't they just symbolic fairy tales illustrating the triumph of the righteous underdog over towering evil? What would happen if average men found themselves pitted against actual "giants"? Modern military thought generally ranks opposing forces in terms of numbers of combatants or technological superiority. Throughout much of history, however, there has been another important factor: stature differences among combatants.

David and Goliath. Chronicle / Alamy Stock Photo.

Classical Greek mythology peopled the ancient world with giants; Homer's superheroes of the Trojan War supposedly averaged fifteen feet in height. Titans fought against the Olympian gods in great gigantomachies. The heroic strongman Heracles wrestled the giant Libyan ogre Antaeus to death, and the clever Homeric hero Odysseus figured out how to blind the oversized, one-eyed monster Cyclops in his cave. An Egyptian text (late Eighteenth Dynasty, ca. 1580 BC) in the tomb of Horemhab at Saqqara reveals that the ancient Egyptians considered the people of Sudan and Libya to be much taller and more robust than themselves, and a Nineteenth Dynasty

(1292–1189 BC) account describes nomadic Bedouins as ter-rifying enemies: "They are fierce of face, and some of them are 4 or 5 cubits [7 to 9 feet] from their nose to their toes."

The Egyptians "sometimes exaggerated the size of their foreign foes," remarks Egyptologist Henry Fischer, but their assessments may not be wildly off the mark. Studies of more than two hundred Egyptian skeletons from ancient sites along the Nile River show that the males of the New Kingdom era had an average height of five feet, two inches. Comparative data are lacking for the ancient people of Sudan and Libya, and in view of population movements since antiquity, aver-age modern heights may not tell us much. But it's interesting that one of the tallest National Basketball Association players to ever play the game, Manute Bol, stood seven feet, seven inches tall and hailed from Sudan. And the tallest player of all time was Suleiman Ali Nashnush, an eight-foot Libyan.

It seems possible that not all men labeled "giants" were the stuff of myth. Centuries after the Hebrew chronicler told how David overpowered Goliath in the tenth century BC, Greek and Roman writers recounted historical battles with oversized adversaries from India to Great Britain. Their descriptions give a sense of what it was like for soldiers to confront en-emies whose size and strength far exceeded their own. The Greeks and Romans were initially terrified when confronted with towering opponents, but they found that stature alone could not always predict victory or defeat.

Because ancient history is a mixture of fact and legend, it is useful to know that the tallest man documented in the twen-tieth century measured just over eight feet, eleven inches, and his hand span was twelve inches. His height was due to a pathological condition, gigantism or acromegaly (see chapter 47). But the historical accounts gathered here deal with healthy strongmen who just happened to be much bigger than most people of their day or else belonged to genetically tall societies. They are not extremes on the scale of miniature Lilliputians versus the skyscraping Brobdingnagians, as described in Jonathan Swift's fantasy *Gulliver's Travels*. Instead, imagine today's tallest and heftiest basketball stars pitted against world-class soccer players in a life-and-death struggle. Visualize both sets of athletes as highly trained battle-hardened soldiers in peak condition, fitted out with bronze armor and shields and wielding swords and spears.

In the Old Testament, the Hittites, Amorites, and Canaanites were about the same size as the Israelites. However, Hebrew sources attributed intimidating stature to certain tribes, such as the Anakim or Rephaim, the cave-dwelling Avvim, and the Philistines. People of phenomenal height are described in Genesis, Numbers, Deuteronomy, Joshua, Samuel, Chronicles, Amos, Baruch, Judith, and the Midrash. Other sources, such as the *Ras Shamra Texts* (cuneiform writings from Ugarit, Syria, twelfth century BC) and the *Egyptian Execration Texts* (a series of curses from 1900–1700 BC), refer to the same groups.

In the Dead Sea Scrolls, Goliath was described as a warrior of six feet, four inches, an imposing opponent in the eyes of an average ancient man of just over five feet. According to Israeli antiquities authority Joe Zias, biblical copyists added a cubit here and a span there, until Goliath towered ten feet tall. In the Jewish necropolis at Jericho, Zias reported that archaeologists discovered a casket containing the skeleton of a six-foot-tall man buried in the first century BC or AD. The casket was inscribed with the nickname "Goliath," demonstrating that six-footers were considered giants in the time of Josephus. More recent excavations of the ossuaries at the monumental family tomb revealed more inscriptions identifying five members of a single family as "Goliath." The longest inscription is in Greek: "Salome, wife of Yoezer, of Goliath / and her son Ishmael, of Goliath and her son Yoezer." This ancient "Goliath" family included very tall people for their day.

By the time Moses led the twelve tribes of Israel out of Egypt (twelfth century BC), lore about giants was already established in Jewish tradition. When Moses sent out spies to gather intelligence about the inhabitants of the Promised Land, his scouts brought back sightings of warlike people of terrifying size. Their sobering report is found in Numbers, chapter 13: "We saw the sons of the Nephilim. We are like grasshoppers compared to them." The Nephilim, a composite species of primeval monsters and fallen angels who dwelt outside the Garden of Eden, were believed to have mated with mortal women and produced superhumans. It is not clear whether the spies had observed settlements of extra-tall people or encountered some very tall individual leaders. But fear of fighting giants may have been one of the things that kept the Israelites wandering in the desert for forty more years.

When the Israelites finally attacked the alleged sons of Nephilim, the formidable Og of Bashan was one of the first giants to fall. Og had few equals in height or might, and the historian Josephus noted that he was admirably proportioned and well coordinated. Og's stronghold was an impregnable subterranean city. The book of Joshua suggests that the Israelites routed Og's forces by releasing swarms of hornets into his underground fortress. After the victory, "people could get a sense of Og's strength and magnitude when they found his sleeping quarters," said Josephus. "His bed was 4 cubits wide and 9 cubits long!" (Deuteronomy 3 gives the same figures.) Depending on how much leg- and headroom the legendary giant preferred, the bed suggested that Og could have measured fifteen feet tall. Og's great iron bed was a popular attraction at Rabbah until the sixth century BC, an impressive relic of the Jews' crucial early victory in the Promised Land.

David became a folk hero for killing Goliath, but for the Israelites there were more immense adversaries to come. A few years later, one of David's companions, Benaiah, killed two oversized warriors from Moab. Meanwhile, in the Philistine city of Gath, Goliath's enormous colleagues burned for revenge. Lahmi was just as mighty as his brother Goliath and carried a spear as thick as a tree trunk. Another unnamed giant of Gath was distinguished by six fingers on each hand and six toes on each foot. Yet another, Ishbi-benob, wore a 150-pound suit of bronze armor.

On the battlefield at Gob, near Gezer, David's army confronted the Beelzebub-worshipping Philistine behemoths. In the battle, Elhanan, son of Jaare-oregim, felled the towering Lahmi. Sibbecai the Hushathite destroyed the oversized Philistine Sippai. The Israelites then advanced to attack the city of Gath, and the fearsome six-fingered ogre came out to taunt them. David's nephew Jonathan took up his challenge to duel, and another Philistine giant was slain.

In a separate battle, David was pursuing the fleeing Philistines when Ishbi-benob suddenly recognized the killer of Goliath. The huge warrior wheeled around to face the flagging David. Too exhausted to fight, David dropped his shield and collapsed just as the giant rushed him. But David's companion Abishai ran up to cover the fallen leader with his own shield and turned to face Ishbi-benob. He managed to slay the big

Philistine, but the Israelite soldiers were so upset by David's narrow escape that they made him swear never to accompany them on the battlefield again. Fortunately, giants were no longer a significant threat in the land.

Believed to be vestiges of the huge humans of yore, individual giants still occasionally appeared in the Middle East during the Roman Empire. But they had moved from military threat to curiosity. Josephus, for example, reported that a seven-cubit-tall (about ten feet) giant from Palestine named Eleazar was sent as a diplomatic gift from King Artabanes of Persia to the Roman emperor Vitellius. Other emperors also displayed living giants; Gabbaras, an Arabian giant of almost nine feet tall, was a presented as a spectacle during the reign of Claudius.

The apocryphal Jewish Book of Baruch claims that the "famous giants from olden times, of great stature, experts in war," died out "for want of wisdom, doomed by their stupidity." Here we have an early forerunner of the later medieval stereotype of the giant as an aggressive but dull oaf clad in animal skins and dragging a club. But the historical accounts of the Greeks and Romans suggest that the gargantuan warriors they met on the battlefield were nothing like the slow-witted, lumbering giants of fairy tales.

In 326 BC, Alexander the Great encountered a memorable adversary in the last great conquest of his career. In one of the most audacious engagements in history, Alexander's men crossed the raging Hydaspes River (the Jhelum) in a violent lightning storm to surprise the vast Indian army commanded by King Porus. The Macedonians, already intimidated by Porus's two hundred war elephants, were awestruck by the prodigious height of the Punjabi ruler. Plutarch says that Porus's "great size and huge physique made him appear as suitably mounted on an elephant as an ordinary man looks on a horse." Alexander was not tall, perhaps five feet. By most accounts, Porus stood just under seven feet tall. The turbaned monarch's majestic bearing amplified the impression of grandeur, as did his seat on the back of an extra-large Indian elephant.

The Macedonian charge routed Indian soldiers on both flanks. Falling back on their panicked elephants in the center, the Indians rallied around Porus. "Stubborn hand-to-hand struggle ensued" for eight more hours, according to Plutarch. High on his elephant, Porus fought bravely. But by the end of the day Porus's troops were defeated. Out of thirty-five thousand men, Porus had lost a staggering twenty-three thousand; Macedonian losses were a few hundred. Alexander asked his king-sized prisoner how he wished to be treated. Porus's booming reply—"Like a king!"—was so full of pride that Alexander gave Porus command of his former kingdom (as a vassal) and threw in five thousand newly conquered towns for good measure.

The giant Porus may have been the inspiration for Alexander's psychological ruse after the Battle of the Hydaspes. "To impress the inhabitants of the region," said Plutarch, Alexander had his smiths forge weapons and gear "which far exceeded the normal size and weight." He left these huge items scattered around the countryside to discourage potential attackers. Ultimately, however, the country of India itself proved far vaster than the Macedonians had imagined. Not long after the defeat of Porus, they began the long march home.

Alexander was not unfamiliar with giants; he had already encountered them on the other side of the world. The Celts and Germani, a cultural array of tribes known variously as

Gauls, Cimbri, Teutons, and Britons, occupied lands stretching from Central Asia across northern Europe. Many ancient writers remarked on their uncommon height. The Greek historian Arrian wrote that in 335 BC Alexander established good relations with "these people of great stature and arrogant disposition" along the Danube River and Adriatic Sea. Hoping to hear his own name, Alexander asked the Celts what their greatest fear was. Their reply, that the sky might fall on their heads, sounded like an arrogant allusion to their own skyscraping height. Alexander went away muttering that the Celts thought too highly of themselves.

Not every Celt or Gaul was a giant, but the average warrior probably stood a foot or so taller than an ordinary Roman soldier, and a substantial number of them approached seven feet tall. A Celtic tomb near Milan excavated in 1977, for example, contained the skeleton of a warrior measuring six feet, five inches. Many other examples of surprisingly large skeletons, suitably proportioned armor, and very large weapons have come to light across northern Europe. According to Diodorus Siculus, a historian of the first century BC, Celtic warriors were "tall and terrifying, with very white skin and rippling muscles." During the next four centuries, the Romans would learn to dread these grim, blond Goliaths.

When Julius Caesar's men attacked the Gallic capital in 57 BC, the Celts laughed at the sight: How could such little men do any harm? To Roman ears, the Gauls' language sounded harsh and belligerent. They were terse but loud, wrote Diodorus, always shouting "in superlatives extolling themselves and belittling all others." To Ammianus Marcellinus, Celtic voices were powerful and threatening, whether they were in a good mood or angry. Almost all of them are of a lofty stature, fair-haired with ruddy complexions, and pale, stern eyes, he wrote, and they are proud, loud, and quarrelsome. The "women are strong, too, with thick necks and huge white arms. When they gnash their teeth and rain punches and kicks like catapults no one can restrain them."

Diodorus was impressed by the wild hairstyles of these strapping men. In contrast to the Romans' military haircuts, the Celts yanked their hair into unruly topknots that slipped to the sides of their heads. Their locks were as coarse as a horse's mane and too flaxen to be believed—Diodorus assumed the wheat color was achieved by bleaching with caustic lime. Soon after the first contacts with Celts, dyed blonde tresses became the rage for women in Rome. The Celtic warriors' shaggy red and blonde mustaches "strained whatever they drank and got entangled in their food." They thought nothing of fighting on a full stomach, unlike the Romans, who liked to eat, sleep, and fight at regular intervals. Even during meals, the pugnacious Celts would "seize upon any trivial matter and recklessly challenge each other to single combat."

Julius Caesar described the Gauls' grisly human sacrifices. Their Druid priests "construct enormous wicker-work figures and fill them with living men. They set the huge straw images on fire, and the men trapped inside perish enveloped by flames." Diodorus told of an even more gruesome custom. Among Celtic soldiers it was an "age-old practice to plunge a dagger under someone's ribs and then stand around reading the future from the victim's gushing blood and twitching limbs."

When the Romans first faced armies of Gauls or Celts, they were immediately struck by their great height. The warriors' size was exaggerated by frightening helmets shaped like the gaping jaws of wolves and monsters, and decorated with horns, antlers, and feathered plumes. Around their necks Gauls and Celts wore thick torques of twisted gold or silver, a habit verified by many archaeological finds in Celtic lands. The men's shirts and trousers were dyed in wild patterns and colors, and they fastened their plaid woolen cloaks with heavy buckles. According to the Roman historian Florus, the Gallic tribe the Senones were fearsome owing to "the very massiveness of their bodies and their huge weapons." The Celts carried immense swords and shields as tall as an ordinary Roman, and they seemed to have no fear of death.

But the giants were not invincible. The historians Tacitus and Livy remarked that the oversized northerners did not seem to know how to conserve their energy. Plutarch pointed out that they originated in a land of deep forests and frigid shade where the whole year was divided into one long night and one short day. In the warm, sunny climate farther south, the northerners gained weight because they drank and ate as if they were at home. Unaccustomed to the heat and strong sun, they bolted for shade whenever possible. They were "superhuman in size, with the spirit of wild beasts," noted Florus, but describing them in the heat of battle, he slighted them by comparing them to "the snow of their own Alps." After the first attack, "They are no longer supermen, but break into a sweat and melt."

Julius Caesar discovered that the Celts' tendency to fight among themselves worked to his advantage during the bloody Gallic Wars of 58–51 BC. And the Romans had learned how to breech the Gaulish lines with a barrage of javelins and then at close quarters chop and stab with their short swords around the bigger men's shields. The trick was to get close to the giants, inside the swinging range of their heavy, unwieldy swords. So even when they lost battles, the disciplined and dogged Romans still inflicted heavy casualties with their lighter, stubby swords.

Sculptures such as *The Dying Gaul* and *The Teutonic Prisoners* not only give a vivid impression of the barbarians' impressive physical stature and strength, but they also capture the awe and respect the Romans felt for their formidable enemy, the wild and noble giants of the north.

In Britain, Caesar found warriors "taller and more gangly than the Celts." Mere lads towered a foot over the tallest Roman, marveled the geographer Strabo. Boudicca, the queen who led the British revolt against the Romans in AD 60, was described by Dio Cassius as "enormous of frame, with a terrifying visage, and a rough, shrill voice." Boudicca wore "a huge twisted torque of gold and a tunic of many colors, with a thick mantle held by a brooch. A great mass of brilliant red hair fell down to her knees." When this British Amazon "grasps a spear, it strikes fear into all who see her." Tacitus told how she led multitudes of wild Britons to torch Colchester, then stormed St. Albans and London, slaughtering some seventy thousand Roman troops. In the end, Boudicca took poison after eighty thousand Britons fell to overwhelming Roman reinforcements. In 1712, a skeleton more than seven feet long was unearthed near the old Roman camp at St. Albans, and some identified it as one of Boudicca's lanky warriors.

The Germanic Teutons and Cimbri were even "wilder and taller" than Gauls and Britons. The Gauls warned Caesar about the "enormous physique, incredible valor, and extraordinary military prowess" of the Germani, who believed that sexual abstinence was the secret of their great size and muscular development. Plutarch estimated that each

Germanic berserker could attack with the speed and force of five Romans. "Nature has made Germany remarkable for armies of very tall men," complained Columella, while Vegetius moaned, "What could our undersized men do against the exceedingly tall Germans?" Hegesippus declared that the Germans were "superior to other nations by the largeness of their bodies and their disdain for death." The ancient authors indicated that the Germani concurred with these sentiments. As many modern historians have noted, the early Latin descriptions of Teutonic tribes would later be used to justify an ideology of cultural and racial superiority in German nationalistic writings of the early twentieth century.

In 113 BC, waves of some three hundred thousand hulking Teuton, Ambrone, and Cimbri warriors and their families migrated across the Danube River. A Roman legion (about five thousand soldiers) sent to stop them was totally crushed. Four years later, another Roman army went out, only to be swatted away like a gnat. Four more years passed, and two more Roman legions faced the giants, this time at the Rhone River. The Romans were exterminated, with only twelve survivors to tell the tale.

The threat posed by the Germanic tribes mobilized Rome. The commander Gaius Marius realized that organization and discipline were essential if the Romans were to offset their stature deficit. Marius spent the next several years forging the Romans into a crack army. He made soldiers run miles and lug their own baggage. His soldiers came to be called "Marius's mules." By 102 BC he was ready to march out to meet the Cimbri and Teutons in southern France. He ordered every Roman soldier to spend time on the walls observing and getting used to the awesome size and savage yelling of the Germanic brutes massed on the plain. "Their numbers appeared to be infinite," says Plutarch, "they were hideous to look at, and the din was outrageous." But soon the Romans became accustomed to their appearance, and they began to agitate to attack. The Romans noted that the northerners presented bigger, less agile targets; they relied on their sheer size and valor to terrify and overpower enemies. The warriors did not pace themselves in battle and were not trained to fight in formation but threw themselves into disorganized, headlong rushes at the enemy. Tacitus remarked that they tended to "flee shamelessly with no concern for their commanders."

Intensive drill and discipline paid off for the shorter Romans. They were trained to fight in waves of thin lines in close order, which meant that "all available manpower could be brought into direct action along the line," commented Roman historian Arther Ferrill. Morale was high in Marius's army, wrote Plutarch, especially when the men spotted their two tame vultures with bronze collars soaring overhead (see chapter 8).

In the course of battle, Roman soldiers would depend on reinforcements. Ferrill points out that the Romans were "not expected to fight to the death"; they knew "in the depths of their souls that their comrades-in-arms would not leave them in the lurch." The psychological advantages of their system offset the reckless ferocity of the bigger Celtic and Germanic berserkers as long as the Romans were not taken by surprise or forced to fight on unfavorable terrain.

Marius refused to be drawn out when the Ambrones thrice stormed the walls of his fortified camp; his men simply rained down missiles on the tall men below. After that, the multitude of Ambrones began to march. For six days they walked in a steady stream past the Roman camp, heading for the Alps.

Relying on topography and surprise, Marius stalked the huge army with short marches and took a position above a riverbank at Aquae Sextiae (in southeastern France). The Romans watched patiently as the robust Ambrones feasted and cavorted in the hot springs by the river. Marius then provoked the Ambrones to attack. "Gorged with food and intoxicated with strong drink," the big men grabbed up their weapons and rushed up the riverbank. The Romans fell upon them from the higher ground and forced them back down into the stream where the water soon ran red with blood. The soldiers pushed the Ambrones all the way back to their camp. Suddenly the Ambrones' women surged out like Valkyries, slashing with axes at the Romans and their own fleeing men alike.

Despite the great victory, the Romans passed a nervous night in a weak position, kept awake by the howling of thousands of dying Ambrones and the fear that the Teutons would attack. The next morning, Marius lured the Teutons into charging furiously uphill, where his men waited. Again, the Romans rushed down and drove the giant warriors back into an ambush, for more infantry waited in a wooded glen. The confused Teutons were forced to fight stumbling backward on broken terrain. Trying to strike upward with their weighty swords, they had little force against the Romans hurling javelins from above. As the infantry in the glen attacked from the rear, Marius and his men shoved the bigger Teutons with their shields, thrusting and hacking with their trusty short blades.

The Romans took heavy casualties in the close fighting, but Plutarch says they slaughtered or captured one hundred thousand of the Teutons. Plutarch also remarked that the farmers of the region later fenced their vineyards with the Teutons' sizable bones. They also enjoyed extraordinarily rich vintages for years, their grapes having been fertilized with layers of rotting bodies.

Teutobochus, king of the Teutons, was captured and taken to Rome for Marius's victory parade. A warrior of colossal height even among his own men, Teutobochus towered head and shoulders over the Germanic trophies displayed in the triumph. Spectators were dazzled by his feat of leaping over the backs of six horses abreast.

Now only the dreaded Cimbri remained. In the Alps they had terrorized Catulus's pursuing legion with "quite unnecessary exhibits of strength and daring." The towheaded titans "pranced naked in blizzards and came tobogganing down snowy crags and crevasses on their shields." Then, "like giants from Greek myth, they tore up entire trees by the roots and great fragments of cliffs to dam a river." Plutarch says Catulus's troops were sorely demoralized by these antics.

But Marius arrived to meet them on the plain at Vercellae in northern Italy in the middle of August 101 BC. He found 180,000 Cimbri warriors in a square formation almost four miles long on each side, with their families at the rear in wagons. The Germanic groups commonly used what the Romans called *cuneus*, a wedge-shaped battle formation, but in practice it was far from a genuine wedge formation. It seems that the warriors simply massed in deep, roughly square columns, and then worked themselves into a frenzy, so that they resembled a roiling sea of bodies. They attacked en masse, with the wildest berserkers rushing ahead of the others.

With the wind and rising sun at his back, Marius approached confidently from the east. He had devised a secret weapon against the Cimbri. A weak wooden pin had replaced one of the iron nails that secured the point to the shaft in every soldier's javelin. On impact with the enemy's shield, the weakened javelin's shaft would twist downward and drag on the ground. The javelins could not be hurled back, and they impeded the Cimbri's forward movement.

A great cloud of dust enveloped the two marching hosts. This was good for Roman morale, claimed Plutarch, since no soldier was able to see the enormity of the enemy ranks but simply focused on fighting whichever massive German loomed up before him. The day was stifling, and the fierce summer sun beat down on the Romans' backs and directly into the faces of the Cimbri. The denizens of "the ice-bound forests" were "disheartened by the heat, covered in sweat, and panting," while "not a single Roman was short of breath or perspiring." Choking and squinting in the heat, dust, and glare, the all-too-human giants instinctively lifted their shields to shade their eyes—and that is when the Romans moved in for the kill.

The "best of the Cimbri were immediately cut to pieces," related Plutarch, "for they had linked themselves together with long iron chains passed through their belts in an attempt to preserve an unbroken front." Romans claimed that more than 120,000 Cimbri died that day and only 60,000 survived as prisoners. Romans who pursued the fleeing remnants to their wagons witnessed "an appalling spectacle," as the Cimbri women hacked down their own men, then killed their children and themselves amid the stampeding horses. In the words of historian J.V.P.D. Balsdon, "The carrion-crows [and Marius's lucky vultures] had never feasted on such gigantic corpses as when Marius defeated the Cimbri."

Much later, in AD 363, Jovian, a simple eight-footer of Celtic ancestry who served as a bodyguard for the emperor Julian, was accidentally made emperor of Rome. Historian

Ammianus Marcellinus, who was there on that day in 363, said there was a coup, and the soldiers took up a cry for a new emperor. According to Ammianus, the men were shouting "Julian," but the generals misunderstood and placed the purple mantle on Jovian's broad shoulders. His reign was brief, only seven months, but notorious in Roman annals because he was tricked by the Persians into abandoning all five Roman provinces beyond the Tigris River without lifting a sword.

Jovian was one of the last of the Celtic warrior-giants, although a few physically imposing individuals would rise to power in the old lands of the Gauls and Germani. Most prominent of these were Charlemagne (742–814) and the Holy Roman emperor Maximilian I (1459–1519).

Medieval romances magnified Charlemagne's strength, claiming that he could pull four welded horseshoes into a single iron bar, lift a man wearing full armor like a flour sack, and kill wild bulls single-handedly. According to contemporary biographers and portraits, the founder of the Holy Roman Empire was a tall, powerfully built man with a thick neck, hawk-like nose, pleasant expression, and a surprisingly soft voice. He was beloved even by the Saxons he conquered. If he was seven times as tall as the length of his foot, as his biographer claimed, then Charlemagne stood nearly seven feet tall, an impressive height for the son of Pepin the Short.

In the Middle Ages, knights in shining armor were stock figures of romantic epics. In Carolingian lore, the Spanish giant Ferragus killed four of Charlemagne's knights before Sir Roland slew him in a duel. Incidentally, the Roman historian Sallust had reported that in 75 BC, a Spanish warrior "far surpassing normal height" had wounded the Roman general Pompey the Great.

The legendary knights of King Arthur's Round Table defeated their share of armored giants. The prodigy of valor Sir Guy of Warwick, for example, overcame two mighty giant foes. First he slew what may have been the last giant left in the Holy Lands, a Saracen warrior called Amarant. Then Sir Guy returned to England in 937 to find King Athelstan desperate for a champion to face the monstrous Danish knight Colbrand. Sir Guy took up the giant's gauntlet and mowed down Colbrand in a jousting duel at Winchester. Relics of Sir Guy and Colbrand were enshrined at Warwick Castle, and a special guard was paid two pence a day to polish Sir Guy's twenty-pound sword and thirty-pound shield. A giant breastplate was also displayed, but modern historians have identified it as chest armor manufactured for a horse. The monumental three-hundred-pound bronze bowl said to be Colbrand's porridge pot turned out to be a caldron from a sixteenth-century mess hall.

The "Last of the Knights," Maximilian of Germany (b. 1459) claimed direct descent from the Cimbri. The founder of the Hapsburg dynasty developed his nearly eight-foot physique with constant exercise, and he delighted in cornering wild bears in their dens barehanded. Renowned for cunning strategies and rash valor in battles against the Italians, Maximilian forged his own king-sized armor and sword. He could always be seen marching ahead of his men with a colossal lance on his shoulder, mounting his great horse only when battle was imminent. It was during Maximilian's reign that German nationalists first articulated their belief in the superiority of the Aryan people as heirs of the ancient Cimbri and Teutons. But the era when entire armies of real giant warriors marched against Roman legions was over. The Cimbri and other larger-than-life peoples had been destroyed or assimilated into the Roman Empire.

The soldier-king Frederick William I of Prussia (1688–1740) was obsessed with trying to recapture the days when giant Germans stalked the earth. When he first began collecting living giants for his grand Potsdam Grenadiers, he started modestly, recruiting local tall men. But soon his agents were scouring the world for really big men. Like maniacal basketball scouts, they cajoled and kidnapped one hundred giants a year for Frederick's three battalions of seven- and eight-foot grenadiers. The regiment was an enormous money pit. The king's agents paid thousands apiece for star giants, and their custom-made fancy uniforms, muskets, and rations were very costly. The grenadiers were made to marry tall women in the hope of breeding a race of giants. Later, Frederick's son abolished his father's regiment of titans and for the same price established four regiments of ordinary-sized soldiers.

Basketball agents seek out today's athletic giants, but at least military recruiters leave them alone. Men the size of the Potsdam giants, Teutobochus, Jovian, or Maximinus (see chapter 47) would be too tall to serve in most armed forces. The height limit for US Army soldiers today is between five feet and six feet, eight inches for men, and between four feet, ten inches and six feet, eight inches for women. According to army recruiter Sgt. 1st Class Cletis Kirkpatrick, the rationale is standardization of equipment and physical training; the average American man is about five feet, nine inches tall. In today's world, where armies of children carry automatic weapons, mobs with machetes attack unarmed civilians, and technology deals swift death from afar, mere physical size is of dubious value in warfare.

Sweating Truth in Ancient Carthage

A NEW APPRECIATION OF FLAUBERT'S PUNIC FEVER DREAM

THOSE WHO DISCOVERED the phantasmagoric novel *Salammbô* (1862) at an impressionable age—prior to studying conventional histories of the Punic Wars—know how difficult it is to shake Gustave Flaubert's intoxicating vision of the doomed Carthaginian Empire. Brimming with visceral images of war and lust, vast riches and bizarre rituals, violence and tragedy verging on melodrama, Flaubert's sensational novel about the North African power that rivaled Rome in the third century BC received mixed critical reviews but was an instant best seller.

In sharp contrast to the bored, provincial Emma Bovary, Flaubert's new heroine was Salammbô, a powerful high priestess of exotic Punic rituals. This femme fatale of Carthage inspired operas by Rachmaninoff, Mussorgsky, and Fénelon. She was celebrated in voluptuous art nouveau and symbolist paintings by Rochegrosse and Alphonse Mucha and featured in silent films and plays. Salammbô influenced the novelist Thomas Mann, Rodin's erotic sketches, and even inspired a Parisian fashion craze: "le style Carthaginois."

In the sumptuously illustrated 1927 edition, with a gilded and embossed cover, that I pored over at age fourteen, Mahlon Blaine's diabolical Aubrey-Beardsley-on-Ecstasy drawings rendered Flaubert's evocative tale even more eidetic.

Largely forgotten now, *Salammbô* still has the power to scandalize critics, yet the book continues to thrill certain audiences. Should you find yourself in Tunisia, you can order a cocktail or book a deluxe room at the Club Salammbo Resort. And consider the video game *Salammbô: Battle for Carthage* (2003), created by award-winning French graphic artist Philippe Druillet. Druillet's 1980–86 trilogy *Salammbô, Carthage*, and *Matho*, a science-fiction appropriation of Flaubert's novel, was rereleased in 2019.

Penned during the French colonization of North Africa, Flaubert's Carthaginian chronicle has been criticized by modern scholars as an over-the-top imperialist fantasy that denigrates indigenous cultures: "A roller-coaster ride of sexual sadism, extreme cruelty and repugnant luxury [that] played to every western-European stereotype . . . about the decadent Orient," declares Richard Miles in his history of Carthage (*Carthage Must Be Destroyed: The Rise and Fall of an Ancient Civilization*, 2010). Ancient Rome's triumph over Carthage provided a historical "blueprint" to justify French domination in North Africa, writes Miles, and *Salammbô* was "the most famous product of these colonial assumptions."

No doubt. Yet Flaubert's aims and achievement were deeper and more complex than that. His attempt to reconstruct Carthage is certainly outdated and shocking to contemporary sensibilities. But Flaubert chose to focus on Carthage, not on Rome's victory. The novelist's endeavor to write from *inside* the lost empire, to bring an ancient culture to life from

Illustrations for Flaubert's *Salammbô* by Mahlon Blaine, 1927 edition. Clockwise from top left: child sacrifice to Baal/Moloch; Salammbô curses those who desecrate the goddess Tanit; Salammbô and the eunuch priest of Tanit; "Thus died Salammbô, Hamilcar's daughter."

the ruins and artifacts buried for millennia in the sands of Tunisia, to visualize the Carthaginian world on its own terms—*without* Hannibal, Rome, or the Punic Wars as his focus—was admirable. Telling Carthage's story through his heroine created mesmerizing narrative fiction. And *Salammbô* was an amazing feat of literary archaeology. What is rarely appreciated today is the depth of scholarship that informed Flaubert's masterpiece of romantic realism.

After reading Miles's dispassionate, fact-packed *Carthage Must Be Destroyed*, I revisited Flaubert's *Salammbô*. I expected the novel's charms to have faded; instead I found myself swept into Flaubert's fever dream of erudite "Orientalism." But this time, I could appreciate the novelist's grasp of the Greek and Latin sources on Carthage and his knowledge of French archaeological excavations of the ancient city, begun by Charles Beulé in the 1850s. Notably, it turns out that even Mahlon Blaine's drawings of 1927—Salammbô's diaphanous gown and towering headdress, the horned helmet of the Punic god Melqart, the priests sacrificing a child to Baal—were influenced by contemporary French archaeology at Carthage.

Flaubert embarked on his Punic project in 1857, after the obscenity trial of *Madame Bovary*. Flaubert was acquitted but disgusted by the censorship of his novel. He devoted the next five years to obsessive research on his ancient historical project. To reconstruct Carthage and the daily life of the Punic world of 241–238 BC, Flaubert studied the accounts of Carthage by Polybius and a host of ancient writers. In his own reckoning, Flaubert consulted more than a hundred volumes, including contemporary monographs (scholarly knowledge of Carthage has advanced apace since then, of course).

In his epic struggle to make his book "sweat truth," Flaubert—a notorious perfectionist in his realism—immersed himself in Tunisian botany and natural history, local traditions, geology, and geography. He sought out photographs of Tunisia, and gathered descriptions of Punic costumes, fortifications, rituals, and the flora and fauna of North Africa. He was keen to examine the artifacts emerging from Carthaginian archaeological sites. In his study, he surrounded himself with amulets, arrowheads, copper objects, and other Carthaginian relics. Finally, in 1858 he sailed to Tunisia and explored the countryside, visiting the ancient ruins in Tunis, Utica, Hippo (Bizerte), Sicca (El-Kef), and other sites, soaking up every detail and sensation, communing with the ghosts of Carthage.

Writing at the dawn of modern Carthaginian archaeology and scholarship, Flaubert could hardly avoid being influenced by the two millennia of lurid negative images of the powerful Phoenician trading empire. But nineteenth-century archaeology was often concerned with testing the truth of ancient sources. It is fascinating to realize that Flaubert's contemporary was Heinrich Schliemann, who discovered and excavated the ancient site of Troy. Excavations at Carthage seemed to confirm ancient Roman accounts of their archenemy. Modern archaeology is continuing to illuminate—and complicate—the Greek and Roman literary evidence about the great North African empire.

With the exception of Aristotle, who singled out Carthage for admiration in the *Politics* ("Many of the Carthaginian institutions are excellent. The superiority of their constitution is proved by the fact that the common people remain loyal to it"), most Greek and Latin writers portrayed Carthage as a decadent, ruthless, barbarian empire that deserved annihilation. In the first century BC, Virgil's epic paean to Rome's foundation, the *Aeneid*, described the suicide of the Carthaginian queen Dido after her lover Aeneas abandons her to fulfill Rome's glorious destiny. The historian Livy assured the Romans that as a little boy, Hannibal had vowed to destroy Rome. Early Christian fathers detailed horrifying accounts of children hurled into a pit of fire as offerings to the bloodthirsty Carthaginian god Baal. Hannibal, in his audacious trek over the Alps with war elephants, intent on enslaving all Italy, became an icon of danger preserved in Roman *cris de guerre*: "Hannibal at the Gates!" and "Carthage Must Be Destroyed!"

Carthage taught the Romans fear, but Romans liked to believe they were predestined to triumph, crushing Hannibal at Zama (202 BC). Yet the Punic Wars continued. After the bloody siege and sacking of Carthage in the Third Punic War (150–146 BC), Scipio Aemilianus burned the magnificent city to ashes and sold the fifty thousand survivors into slavery. His intention was to obliterate the memory of Carthage, except as a parable of overweening power and debauchery that brings about its own destruction. The claim that he sowed Carthage's fields with salt was a modern flourish, however, inspired by an incident in the Old Testament.

Remarkably, Flaubert decided to ignore these famous zero-sum duels between Carthage and Rome. Instead of setting his tale during the Punic Wars, he chose to set it during an obscure internal conflict in North Africa that occurred during Hannibal's boyhood. After losing the First Punic War, Carthage was unable to pay its diverse army of Libyans, Numidians, nomads, and other warriors of the Maghreb, northwest Africa. The Mercenary Revolt of 241–238 BC was led by Mâtho, a Libyan, and a former Greek slave named Spendius. Carthage's elite, including Hamilcar (Hannibal's father), Hanno, and the powerful eunuch priests of Baal, retaliated against the veterans' rebellion. Treachery, torture, mayhem, cannibalism, and a plethora of violent passions ensued in the war, described by Greek and Roman historians of Carthage, who had access to Punic chronicles.

Flaubert brought his heroine Salammbô to life from a brief mention of Hamilcar's unnamed daughter, sister of Hannibal. He imagined the historical Libyan warrior Mâtho seized by mad love for her. Unforgettable scenes of excess in the novel include Salammbô's sensual interlude with a gigantic serpent and the frenzied mass sacrifice of Carthage's children to a colossal bronze idol of Moloch/Baal. Mâtho steals the forbidden veil of the Carthaginian goddess Tanit. He and Salammbô become secret lovers. They suffer agonizing deaths amid barbarian splendor.

The Roman historians Livy and Polybius, who was a friend of Scipio and eyewitness to Carthage's destruction, were Flaubert's chief sources. But he also relied on Herodotus, Xenophon, Cornelius Nepos, and Procopius, among others. For geography and fortifications, Flaubert turned to Appian and Diodorus of Sicily, and he read Aelian for military ruses and tactics. He mined Pliny, Theophrastus, and other sources for Carthaginian magical lore and religion. Athenaeus provided the description of Tanit's fabulous veil, while the indelible image of innocent infants burned in Baal's fiery furnace was culled from Strabo, Cicero, Plutarch, Saint Augustine, Eusebius, and Tertullian. I would guess that Salammbô's pet python arose from Valerius Maximus's account, based on Livy, of a battle between a Roman legion and a monstrous snake in the First Punic War, as well as Flaubert's knowledge of snake-charming traditions in North Africa. To refute contemporary critics who questioned the historicity of his details, Flaubert released a public dossier of his bibliography.

Flaubert's ancient documentary sources are the same texts that Richard Miles relied upon in his modern description of the Mercenary War. Indeed, the labor the novelist had set for himself, to reconstruct a systematically demolished ancient culture from enigmatic remnants and history written by its worst enemies, is the same task that the historian Miles takes on. Flaubert's lush novel was the first modern attempt to portray Carthage realistically in all its glory, while Miles's levelheaded, sweeping scholarly study is now the last word on the glory that was Carthage. Both the novelist and the historian were seeking to recover an independent Carthage, to know the city outside the "long shadow of Rome," each writer amassing every scrap of evidence available to him to place Carthage on center stage.

Flaubert's descriptions of gruesome violence were based on surviving historical accounts of the savage Mercenary War. And in his own discussion of the appalling atrocities reported during the Revolt of the Mercenaries, even Miles acknowledges the hair-raising violence of this "war without pity," marked by "infamous brutality," "hideous" tortures, and "butchery." Echoing the words of Polybius, Miles comments that this war "far excelled all wars we know of in cruelty and defiance of principle." Yet Miles presents Greek and Roman—and Flaubert's—emphases on Carthaginian cruelty as examples of casting the "Other" as savage and exotic. When Flaubert was writing, the so-called Orientalist framework was not as deeply analyzed and derided as it came to be 150 years later. Miles was bound to respond to this framework because of his authorial time period, but Flaubert was writing in a period when critics had different fixations. It was a bold decision for Flaubert to select such a vicious episode in Carthaginian history.

French critics blasted Flaubert for writing about a trivial duel between Tunis and Carthage when "everyone knew" that the only significant event was the great Punic War that Rome ultimately won. But Flaubert's choice allowed him to present Carthage in a purely Carthaginian context, of interest in and of itself, in a battle with other North Africans, with Rome and even Hannibal relegated to the background. Although his methods are very different, the historian Miles, too, wants us to comprehend the importance of Carthage in its own right, without assimilating it to the victor. Yet—unlike Flaubert who could chose his setting—Miles, as historian, cannot escape the need to constantly refer to Rome and "the West."

Aside from artifacts and enigmatic inscriptions, very little of Carthage's own history survived Rome's devastation. After the early French discoveries, it is mostly British and American archaeological excavations in Carthage that provide the current state of knowledge. We know the city originated as a North African trading outpost, established by the Phoenicians, who moved their center of gravity to the western Mediterranean in response to pressure from the Assyrian Empire. Artifacts recovered from Punic sites shed light on the Carthaginian lifestyle. Ceramic sherds recovered from the ash layer, for example, tell us that South Italian pottery, painted with scenes of Greek mythology, was in vogue when Scipio burned the city. The stunning Sabratha mausoleum reveals a lively fusion of Egyptian, Greek, and unique Punic artistic styles.

Flaubert was enthralled by the ships filled with Punic treasures that arrived in France. There is a great collection of stone inscriptions now in the Louvre, which help reconstruct Carthaginian culture. The story of how these valuable artifacts came to be available to modern scholars is amazing. In 1878, the French flagship *Magenta* exploded in the port of Toulon, on the French Riviera. Its precious cargo of 2,080 steles and inscriptions from Carthage sank in the harbor. They remained submerged in the sea for 125 years. Only in 1994 did French divers and archaeologists finally locate the wreck and begin bringing up inscribed tablets and statues.

Those thousands of monuments recorded votive offerings to the god Baal and the goddess Tanit. They are crucial to untangling the most enduring question about Carthage, namely, the sacrifice of aristocratic children to Baal (or Moloch, derived from *mlk*, "offerings of children"). The Near Eastern practice of *mlk* was described in the Old Testament, and many Greek and Latin writers accused Carthage of this cruel rite. Was this really routine Punic practice? Or was it only a desperate last resort in extraordinary situations? Historians relate that Baal's priests ordered the Carthaginians to burn their children alive to turn the tide of the Mercenary War. In his novel, Flaubert suggests that young Hannibal (his name means "Grace of Baal") survived the holocaust of children because his father sent a poor boy in his place. Did elite families of Carthage really substitute poor children for their own offspring? In this, Flaubert was following a claim by the historian Plutarch.

In the 1920s, an electrifying French discovery in the ruins of Carthage was reported. The precinct of the *tophet* (cemetery/site of child sacrifices) had been found. Other *tophets* exist in Punic colonies, for example on the island of Sardinia. The archaeologists unearthed thousands of urns with burned remains of young children, stone tablets carved with the Phoenician letters MLK, Punic inscriptions dedicating sons to Baal, and a stele with the inscribed image of a priest holding an infant. All these finds confirmed the identification of the *tophet*. Centuries after child sacrifice had faded away in the Near East, the evidence shows that Carthage's elite continued the ritual, especially to avert calamity, not in secret but as a matter of civic pride and preservation. In view of the archaeological evidence, Richard Miles concludes that the accusations of child sacrifice in the ancient Greek and Roman sources can no longer be brushed aside as bias and "anti-Punic slander." Controversy persists, however, with some scholars still disputing the meaning of the evidence.

According to the Roman historian Livy, Hannibal's father held him over Baal's great furnace and compelled the boy to dedicate his life to fighting the Romans. For some reason Miles ignores Livy's account, even though it supports his thesis, based on many other examples, that Carthage was essential to Rome's own development and self-image. According to Roman legend, both great powers were founded in the same year, 753 BC. By insisting that evil Carthage inculcated its children with eternal hatred and vows to destroy Rome, Romans justified their own compulsion to crush Carthage as their most dangerous enemy. In fact, as Miles makes clear and as even some Romans recognized, Carthage was too important to Rome's destiny to forget: Carthage was truly "the whetstone on which Rome's greatness had been sharpened."

Both Rome and Carthage understood the importance of mythology, as demonstrated in their tug-of-war over possession of the mythic hero Hercules/Heracles. Rome liked to claim the Greek champion Hercules as an ancestor. His famous travels and exploits around the ancient world, from the Caucasus and Scythia to Greece and Italy, across North Africa to the Pillars of Hercules (Gibraltar), reflected their own imperial ambitions. According to Greek myths, Hercules even traveled across North Africa, and he defeated the giant Antaeus in what is now Morocco. But the Roman Republic's imperialism was driven by military invasion, occupation, looting, slavery, and harsh taxation of defeated subjects. Exploration for its own sake was not valued. In contrast, exploration was highly prized in Carthage, and Carthaginians made peaceful voyages of discovery down the coast of West Africa and established mutually beneficial trade relationships with these Africans. It was natural for the Carthaginians to assimilate the wandering Greek hero Hercules to their own Punic god Melqart. Hannibal, master propagandist, turned the tables on Rome by successfully appropriating Hercules as his own guardian-guide. To Rome's great consternation, Hannibal's conquests retraced Hercules's mythical sea and land routes, justifying Carthaginian dominance in North Africa, Spain, and Italy itself.

Carthaginian culture, recovered from its own artistic, architectural, archaeological, and literary evidence, demonstrates extraordinary eclecticism and shows openness to new ideas and influences. Carthage's founders, the seafaring Phoenicians, had invented the alphabet and the dominant oared warships of classical antiquity. As early as the eighth century BC the Phoenicians established colonies in the western Mediterranean (Sicily, Sardinia) and North Africa. And they sailed beyond the Pillars of Hercules into the Atlantic, establishing the trading city of Gades (Cadiz, Spain, where *garum*, Rome's notorious rotten fish sauce, originated). Carthage perfected the use of elephants in warfare and innovated naval technology. As sea adventurers, Carthaginians had no equals.

There is ancient evidence for two fifth-century BC Carthaginian expeditions along the Atlantic coasts of Europe and West Africa. Himilco's voyage went north, making contact with peoples of Spain, Portugal, France, Ireland, and Cornwall. Hanno's expedition went south, a flotilla of sixty-five oared ships, transporting thirty thousand men and women and supplies from Carthage to Morocco and Mauritania, establishing settlements along the way. Continuing south past the Canary Islands, modern Senegal, Ghana, Nigeria, and Gabon, the explorers encountered remarkable sights, animals, and peoples.

The purpose of the Carthaginian Atlantic expeditions is debated, but it seems clear that trade was a priority. A striking passage in Herodotus (ca. 460 BC), describes in detail the unique system of barter based on mutual trust and fair exchange developed by the Carthaginians to facilitate trade with various West African tribes. Upon reaching this land, "the Carthaginians unload their goods, arrange them in orderly fashion along the beach, and send a smoke signal." The West Africans, writes Herodotus, come out to examine the goods, and "place on the ground a certain quantity of gold in exchange," then retreat. The Carthaginians "come ashore and assess the gold. If it is a fair price for their wares, they collect it and depart. If the amount of gold seems too paltry, they go back to their ships and wait for the natives to add more gold." The system is "perfectly honest," remarks Herodotus, "for the Carthaginians do not touch the gold until it equals the value of the goods and the natives never touch the wares until the gold is taken." Herodotus's report of the bartering ritual suggests that both Carthaginians and Africans expected return visits.

Carthage's fair foreign relations with indigenous groups provide stark contrast to the power politics of Rome's plunder and subjugation policies. Carthage created a kind of middle ground of cooperation for Phoenician, Greek, and indigenous populations. The ancient and intense hatred between Carthage and Rome arose from profound cultural differences, amplified by bitter propaganda, combined with Rome's intolerance of peaceful coexistence with a powerful rival and the Carthaginian response to that intolerance.

As Miles points out, the symbolism that each culture assigned to fire gives us insight into the cultural gulf dividing Rome and Carthage. For Romans, fire's power was negative, destructive—hence Scipio's immolation of Carthage. Ironically, in Phoenician belief, fire was restorative, purifying, necessary to generate rebirth. Note that sacrifices to Baal were burned in his great furnace. The legacy of Carthage is suffused with irony. As proof of their own grandeur, the Romans themselves had to constantly polish and keep alive the memory of the city they had torched. The legendary empire of Carthage would continue to smolder and flicker for more than two thousand years. To draw readers close enough to Carthage to appreciate its radiance—that is really what the novelist Flaubert and the historian Miles, in very different ways and times, wanted to accomplish.

To understand Carthage's complex legend and elusive reality, one can learn much from both the historian and the novelist. One might say that, thanks to Miles, fortified by his rigorous, alexipharmic scholarship, it is now safe to indulge in the guilty pleasure of rediscovering Flaubert's long-reviled historical fiction. In *Salammbô*'s pages, a discerning reader can appreciate Flaubert's bold embrace *and* simultaneous evasion of Greco-Roman Orientalism, while catching a whiff of the fear and awe that we know Carthage evoked for Romans. Miles's cool analysis neutralizes the noxious clouds that long obscured Rome's rival, burnishing Carthage's tarnished reputation at last. The only dilemma is deciding which book to read first—the poison, or the antidote?

TRAVELERS, TATTOOS, AND TYRANTS

CHAPTER 41

Tourists in Classical Antiquity

AGES BEFORE MODERN TOURISTS flocked to Greece to enjoy its sun, sea, antiquities, and adventure, people of the Roman Empire descended on Greece for the same reasons. Antony and Cleopatra headed for a romantic island tryst on Samos; the emperor Tiberius preferred Rhodes. Some Romans attended the famous philosophy schools and drenched themselves in Greek history; others came for the Olympic Games; still others were attracted by the sensational—a chance to gawk at the egg hatched by Leda after her affair with Zeus in the guise of a swan, to dip a toe in the spring where Helen had bathed, or to gasp as professional divers jumped off the notorious "Lover's Leap" of Leucadia, a two-hundred-foot promontory where Sappho was said to have ended her life. And they all lugged home souvenirs: terra-cotta statuettes, trinkets, pots of Hymettian honey, silk scarves from Cos, gnarled walking sticks from Sparta, copies of racy Milesian love stories, and entire temple columns and thousands of statues.

Greek hospitality was renowned long before the Roman sightseers arrived. People who traveled often had "guest-friends" in Greek cities, and as early as the fifth century BC innkeepers let rooms in towns and along roads. Famous temples and sanctuaries provided public accommodations run by the host city or by other cities for their own citizens visiting the shrine. The fourth-century politician Demosthenes mentioned a hotel popular with ambassadors near the Temple of the Twins in Pherae on the northern coast of Greece, and the remains of an ancient hostel for visitors to Athens was found in Plateia in modern times.

Herodotus was one of the first ancient writers to travel purely for curiosity and pleasure in the fifth century BC. His books related the many strange customs and marvels he saw and heard about on his tours (see chapters 1 and 21). By the fourth century BC, foreign travel was becoming more common, as diplomats, messengers, mercenaries, tradespeople, merchants, poets, philosophers, musicians, artists, actors, and athletes all traveled for business, education, or pleasure. Ordinary and rich folk alike made journeys to attend festivals and religious celebrations.

Out-of-towners arriving in ancient Athens were required to register with the *proxenos*, like a modern consul, of their hometown. The *proxenos* was an Athenian citizen who had either family or friends in another town; he acted as the official host of visitors from that town while they were in Athens. Like the Greek Tourist Police of today, the *proxenos* was responsible for helping tourists in trouble.

Thebes and Sparta were more dubious about the benefits of tourism. The city fathers of Thebes once fined their native son Pindar ten thousand drachmas for praising the charms of their rival city, Athens, in a poem. A travel book written in the first century BC by Herakleides described Theban men as "rash and argumentative" with strangers and cautioned that disputes there were settled with fisticuffs. On the other hand,

Theban women—blonde, dressed in white with snazzy purple sandals—were said to be "the tallest, prettiest and most graceful in all Greece." Herakleides recommended Thebes as "one of the best places to pass the summer" because of its lush gardens, refreshing breezes, and cool water (winter there was out of the question, however, owing to "blizzards" and "much mud").

In the fifth century BC Sparta allowed visitors only short, rigidly supervised tours of its sights and restricted the travel of its own citizens. By Roman times, however, Sparta had become a sort of "theme park," a must-see on every tourist's list, where Old Sparta's myths, legendary austerity, and harsh discipline were glorified. Gullible tourists could view Leda's Egg (out of which Helen of Troy hatched; sophisticated travelers dismissed the large beribboned egg as that of an ostrich). Those familiar with the verses of the popular Roman poet Ovid probably hoped to see beautiful Spartan women wrestling in the nude, but they had to settle for statues of clothed female runners or women warriors brandishing swords. Tourists could watch endurance contests in which stoic Spartan teenagers were flogged, in the theater built by Roman entrepreneurs to accommodate hundreds of spectators. Or they could witness puppy sacrifices, exciting boar hunts, and brutal mock battles; visit the cave where criminals were confined, the altar where human sacrifices took place, and the notorious gorge where weak children were left to die. They could admire "vicious Laconian hounds" paraded on leashes; and wander through the impressive "victory" colonnade displaying Persian spoils and columns in the forms of chained captives.

Many of the bloodthirsty images of ancient Sparta current today actually come from descriptions of these commercialized sideshows created to entertain the Roman tourists.

Romans buying souvenirs in Greece. Drawing by Adrienne Mayor.

Members of the Roman leisure class began to take cruises to Greece in large numbers in the first century BC. The famous senator Cicero vacationed in Greece twice and came to study oratory and philosophy. In his letters home he marveled how one "cannot take a step in Athens without treading on history!" He wrote, "Athens delights me much—the town and the decking out of the town—I indeed love the city greatly." He sent his son to study in Athens, as did many other rich Roman senators and businessmen. Poets, like Horace, came to Greece for inspiration; others, like Propertius, hoped to get over a sad love affair. Many a Roman tourist with a literary bent made pilgrimages to see the iron chair where Pindar sat to compose; the cave on Salamis from which Euripides used to gaze out to sea, contemplating the mysteries of life; the beach at Piraeus where the comic playwright Menander drowned; or the temple on Poros, scene of Demosthenes's dramatic suicide (by sucking poison from his own pen). Tombs and portraits of classical literary figures were on view in every major town.

Greek antiquities were shown to tourists by a special class of guides called *mystagogi*, later known as *cicerones*, after the eloquent Cicero, the first foreigner to deplore the plunder of Greek art by his own Roman countrymen. Travelers stayed at inns along roads, near the city gates, or in the town center. Then, as now, the comforts of these lodgings varied enormously. In the cheapest, travelers had to provide their own food and linens, and they could expect to encounter hard beds, bedbugs, mosquitoes, little privacy, shady characters, and brawls. Wealthier tourists avoided these quarters and booked accommodations in luxurious converted mansions, with garden patios or dining rooms catering to Romans used to reclining during dinner. Wayfarers could buy simple snacks and wine at a modest café called a *kapilos*. All inns of the day provided sexual companionship of varying standards and costs.

Rich, famous, and powerful globe-trotters, such as Cleopatra and Antony, who cruised the Aegean in 40–30 BC, traveled first class. In April of 32 BC the pair sailed from Ephesus to Samos, bringing with them a retinue of popular actors, comedians, and musicians. For three weeks their revels were the talk of Greece: the island resounded with the sounds of pipes and lutes; there were sumptuous drunken banquets and all-night performances. Cleopatra's souvenirs from Samos included life-size bronze statues of Zeus, Athena, and Heracles taken from the Temple of Hera. She also took home scores of paintings and thousands of books. Antony bought Greek costumes for himself. Cleopatra was hoping to persuade Antony to get a divorce from his wife in Rome. But he was preoccupied with the upcoming showdown with Octavian (future emperor Augustus) in the Adriatic. The couple sailed from Samos to Athens, alternately bickering and making up all the way.

The tempestuous affair continued in Athens, where the city raised statues to both lovers on the Acropolis and hailed Cleopatra as the Goddess of Love and Antony as Dionysos. There were more riotous drinking bouts, torchlight parades, and outrageous behavior. Antony dressed up in a Dionysos costume. Cleopatra bought tablets of onyx and crystal, had them inscribed with love letters, and sent them to Antony. Antony caused a scandal by caressing her feet in public (see chapter 38). The lovers moved their celebrations to the city of Patras, but by September of 30 BC the party was over. They both committed suicide after their fleet was defeated by Octavian at Actium in the Gulf of Preveza.

After the battle, Octavian/Augustus himself headed for Samos to savor his victory, then journeyed to Eleusis to be initiated into the Mysteries. We know that Augustus, who sunburned easily, always wore a broad-brimmed straw hat. He loved to quote Greek proverbs, although his Greek was not fluent. His successor, Tiberius, retired to Rhodes for about seven years: he had cherished happy memories of that beautiful island since his first trip to Greece as a child (which had included a stop in Old Sparta). In Rhodes, Tiberius enjoyed what sounds like an ancient version of Elderhostel (now Road Scholar), the educational travel program for retirees. He stayed in a modest townhouse and an unpretentious country villa; he rode horses, took strolls, chatted with ordinary Greeks, and attended philosophy lectures.

Julius Caesar, Pompey, and Saint Paul all visited Lesbos, an island famed for its superlative annual beauty contest. But Rhodes and Cos were generally billed as the prime island getaways in the ancient world. The jet set of Rome, from emperors to best-selling poets, sang their praises. The physician Asclepius had advised his sons to spend their summers in mild and healthful Cos, and the Ptolemies and other prominent Alexandrians took this advice too. Roman women prized the chic transparent silk gowns one could obtain on Cos. According to the imperial biographer Suetonius, "No Roman general or magistrate sailing the Aegean failed to break his journey at Rhodes," celebrated for its lovely climate and flowers, flourishing philosophy schools, and active literary and artistic scene. And until an earthquake toppled it in 227 BC, the Colossus of Rhodes was one of the Seven Wonders of the Ancient World. Even after it collapsed, the broken ninety-foot statue was a prominent tourist draw for centuries, until the bronze pieces were shipped off to Syria and melted down. The writer Pliny counted two thousand statues, one hundred of them "colossal," still to be seen in Rhodes in the first century AD.

A Roman sightseer's list of not-to-be-missed destinations reads like the itinerary of today's traveler: Athens and its harbor Piraeus, Delphi, Corinth, Sparta, Olympia, and Epidauros. The Olympic Games and those at Nemea, Delphi, and Isthmia continued full bore, and there were Greek theatrical, literary, oratorical, and musical events galore. Local folk dances and festivals drew spectators, and energetic tourists, such as the emperor Hadrian, climbed mountains for the spectacular views (see chapter 43). Strabo, the geographer of the first century BC who described the diving shows that took place at Sappho's Leap, was very impressed with the sunset panorama visible from the great Acropolis of Corinth.

Nero, Rome's most philhellenic emperor, chose Greece as his only foreign expedition in about 67 BC. He learned Greek and undertook a whirlwind tour in which he participated in a multitude of athletic, musical, and acting competitions. Among Nero's Greek souvenirs were lyres, a marble statue of Eros from Thespiae, the eighteen hundred wreaths he'd won in musical contests, and Greek costumes. His most prized costume was a purple mantle spangled with gold stars (similar items are on sale in Greek tourist shops today). Nero raced a twenty-horse chariot in the Olympic Games and made a special trip to consult the Oracle at Delphi. But Nero skipped Sparta, because, he said, its reputation for discipline and austerity went against his grain. He also skipped Athens—was it because Orestes had been tried there for murdering his mother? That was the sly comment by a critic, alluding to Nero's own matricide.

In about AD 160, Pausanias wrote *A Description of Greece*, the first guidebook and the model for all subsequent efforts. Pausanias's Greek vacation lasted between ten and twenty years. Some speculate he began his trip to forget an unhappy love affair, as had Propertius, whose grand tour to Greece was undertaken to "erase the scar in my heart." Pausanias's guidebook, written for philhellenic sightseers and still relied on today, is jam-packed with information on history, sights, road conditions, time-saving hints, and curiosities throughout the Greek world.

By the time Pausanias began his excursion, the Roman Empire was maintaining and policing roads (many of which are still extant) and regulating inns, mules, and carriages in Greece. Carts could be hired in one city and left in the next, like modern rental cars. The emperor Hadrian had widened the road from Athens to Corinth to accommodate two lanes of chariots, and the great Via Egnatia connected the northwest coast of Greece with Constantinople. Nero and other investors built inns along the Via Egnatia. Large public latrines

Pausanias touring Greece in his horse cart. Drawing by Adrienne Mayor.

were constructed near the Agora in Athens to accommodate visitors. At famous sites, *cicerones* offered their services and guidebooks were hawked, along with souvenirs and art reproductions. In the Agora, for example, one could buy miniature busts of Socrates near the "very spot where he drank the hemlock." The Oracle at Delphi, once consulted by kings and emperors on foreign policy, had become a Guru to the Stars—wealthy private citizens, including Cicero and Nero, now made the journey to have their fortunes told. Other oracles and fortune-telling concessions proliferated—Pausanias described dozens of them, featuring dice, mirrors, lizards, birds, dream interpretations, and magic potions.

Pausanias sought out places of historical or romantic interest, and he was always on the lookout for antiquities. Like Herodotus, Pausanias sometimes made a nuisance of himself with his curiosity, pestering and contradicting local guides and arguing with other tourists over fine points of ancient Greek religion. He usually traveled by horse cart, going on foot when the route was narrow and "only fit for an active man." Complaints about steep footpaths and bad roads pepper his book, but Pausanias always lets the reader know whether the sight is worth the trouble. At Delphi, for example, he had to scramble up a rocky path to visit what turned out to be "the most worthwhile grotto" he'd ever seen. Later that day Pausanias negotiated yet another precipitous and craggy path, this time "difficult even for an active man." Happily, he was able to pronounce the water from the Kastalian Spring at the summit "delicious." Guides at another town pointed out two lumps of reddish clay supposed to have been left over when the human race was fashioned. Pausanias's description of them so intrigued later travelers that people were still searching for the clods of dried mud in the eighteenth and nineteenth centuries.

On Mount Helicon, Pausanias climbed up to the pool where the young man Narcissus had pined away for his own reflected image, a myth that Pausanias considered "absolutely stupid." More interesting to him were the lair of the riddling Sphinx, the field where Kadmos had sown the dragon's teeth that sprouted into fully armed men ("if you believe it"), and the exciting cockfights he saw near Thebes. In Levadia, Pausanias consulted the Oracle of Trophonios, which involved drinking from springs labeled "Forgetfulness" and "Memory." In Chaeronea, he recommended the renowned perfumes distilled from roses, iris, lily, narcissus, and orrisroot ("said to alleviate human distress").

Near Plato's Academy in Athens, Pausanias lingered at the "Lover's Leap" and the altar dedicated to "complicated love." In Megara, he was especially taken with the Harp Stone at the city wall. When tourists threw pebbles at it, it twanged like a harp—supposedly because Apollo had once set his own harp on the wall during its construction. "I was amazed by this," says Pausanias. The Lion Gate, royal tombs, and the "secret staircase" at Mycenae; the display of the war belt Hercules stole from the Amazon Hippolyte; the battlefield at Marathon (where one could still detect the ghostly sounds of battle); and the marble quarries with unfinished statues on Mount Pendeli were all de rigueur tourist destinations in Pausanias's day.

Local guides pointed out so many "Hercules slept here" places and "Helen bathed here" pools that Roman tourists must have pounced on Pausanias's rating system with sighs of relief. His ratings ranged from the superlative "you'll gasp," "I was amazed," "my favorite," "very worthwhile," and "delightful," to downright "silly," "stupid," "utterly idiotic," and "waste of time." In his many years of touring Greece, Pausanias was shown countless Helen's Pools and Hercules Passed Here attractions. Epidauros, for instance, boasted an olive tree "twisted by Hercules himself." He admired myriad springs bubbling up where Pegasus Stamped His Hoof (there was one in Corinth), places where Medusa Was Slain (Argos had one of these), springs where Hera Renewed Her Virginity (one near Eleusis and another at Nauplion), shady glades where Dionysos Stopped for a Drink or Zeus Met a Maiden (ubiquitous), grottoes where Pluto Abducted Persephone to the Underworld (at Nauplion, Troezen, Hermione, Boeotia, etc.), caves of Various Lions Wrestled by Hercules (Tiryns, Nemea, Mount Kitheron), and dozens of rival birthplaces and graves of heroes and gods.

Classical Greek statuary and paintings were greatly admired by Romans, who were avid souvenir collectors. Centuries before Lord Elgin raided the Parthenon marbles, Sulla (who sacked Athens in 86 BC), L. Mummius (who looted Corinth in AD 146), Verres (who plundered Samos in 82 BC), and other wealthy Romans were stripping the Greek world of antiquities to decorate their Italian villas. Cicero expressed great dismay at the plunder of Greek religious shrines. It apparently began when Sulla's theft of two great columns from Athens's Temple of Zeus began a rage in Italy for Corinthian antiquities. The lists of the plunderers' acquisitions would have made J. Paul Getty drool. Even mythical Greek creatures were exported: Sulla acquired a live satyr from a cave in Thessaly; the emperor Claudius owned a baby centaur preserved in honey. Pausanias was shown a merman in Boeotia that he pronounced mind-boggling, but it wasn't for sale (see chapter 2). By the second century after Christ, Greek sculptors were busy trying to meet the insatiable Roman demand for ancient Greek marbles by making copies of classical statues and inventing new ones.

Pausanias viewed hundreds of paintings of battles, warriors, and myths, endless statues of famous boxers, wrestlers, and runners, and myriad portraits of poets, playwrights, and musicians. To aid overwhelmed tourists, he singled out a few "really memorable" artworks "worth going out of the way for." At the top of the list were the magnificent thirty-nine-foot statue of Athena in the Parthenon, a gold-and-ivory statue of Dionysos in the Agora of Athens, and sculptures of Pegasus and a sea monster in Corinth. Incidentally, Corinth was a city renowned for its lovely prostitutes. Saint Paul wrote about this particular tourist attraction in his letters from Corinth, where he stayed with tent makers who made canopies to shade spectators at the Isthmian Games. Near Olympia, Pausanias gave very bad ratings to a famous statue of Zeus ("made like a pyramid") and a companion piece of Diana ("like a pillar")—both sculpted "without the slightest skill at all."

On the Corinthian Gulf near Patras, Pausanias found "a delightful place for idling in the summer." He noticed that Patras itself had twice as many women as men, and "if ever women belonged to Aphrodite, they do!" These women were expert weavers of cotton and flax, and their decorative hairnets and dresses were popular souvenirs of Patras. Pausanias consulted no fewer than three fortune-telling oracles near here, and he was enchanted by the story of a man who fell hopelessly in love with a faithless mermaid in the Selinous River (chapter 2). Bathing in the river, the guides assured Pausanias, could make one forget an unhappy passion. "If true, the river water is worth more to mankind than any amount of money," he remarked. His discovery of the delights of the coast near Patras, like Tiberius's fondness for *voltas* (evening strolls) with villagers in Rhodes, and Strabo's ascent of Acrocorinth for the thrilling view, remind us that, besides the glorious antiquities and stirring history, it is this glimpse of the real and present Greece, the unique out-of-the-way experience, that every visitor hopes to treasure as a personal souvenir.

By the third century AD, worsening economic and social conditions, not to mention barbarian hordes, made gadding about the Mediterranean for the pure fun of it simply too adventurous for most people. After three centuries of relatively safe travel guaranteed by the "Roman peace," more than a thousand years would pass before philhellenes would again make Grand Tours to Greece to satisfy curiosity and to seek history and adventure.

Grand Tourists in Greece, from Lord Byron to Sigmund Freud

THE FIRST SUNGLASSES were purchased for a trip to the sunny Mediterranean sometime in the early 1700s. And by 1814 the word "tour-ist" had been coined to describe the flocks of Europeans and Americans who capped off their Grand Tours with a trip to Greece. Whether the visitors (the *milordi*, as the Greeks referred to them) traveled with twenty-nine mules loaded with baggage, as did Lord Byron, or roughed it, with a single horse and a tent, all agreed that their hosts were generous to a fault; that the honey and coffee were delicious, but the wine tasted most peculiar; the insects were execrable; pirates and fevers were tiresome; and the antiquities were spectacular but sadly "dilapidated."

After the fall of the Roman Empire, except for a few reports from Crusaders on their way to the Holy Land, Greece's scenery, antiquities, and famed hospitality were virtually forgotten by the rest of the world until the late fifteenth century. It was an Italian, Cyriac of Ancona, who revived Europeans' interest in traveling to Greece. Cyriac, the Renaissance "father of archaeology," devoted himself to recording ancient inscriptions and

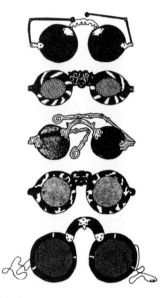

The first sunglasses, 1700–1900. Drawing by Adrienne Mayor.

describing ruins in the mid-1400s, two centuries before the modern era of archaeological plunder began.

His is the earliest surviving drawing of the Parthenon, and his sketch of a statue in Samothrace became the model for portraits of Aristotle. Cyriac visited Mistra in southern Greece while it was still ruled by the Byzantine Despot of the Morea. In Athens he enjoyed a lovely sunset from a still completely intact Philopappos Monument (built in AD 114). At the Temple of Olympian Zeus he counted 21 columns still standing with their architraves (originally there were 104 columns; today there are only 13).

Cyriac was a merchant as well as a tourist, and others followed his lead. By Shakespeare's time Greece was famous for its malmsey, a strong sweet wine exported from Monemvasia in the Peloponnese. In *Richard III*, Shakespeare has the Duke of York drown in a butt of malmsey.

A few travel and phrase books were published in the sixteenth century, and a trickle of travelers began to dally in the Aegean region. In his diary of 1599, a British visitor named Dallam made an ominous reference to souvenir hunting in Troy: "I brought home a piece of white marble pillar, which I broke off with my own hands, having a good hammer with me."

Treasure hunting among the ruins had begun with the Romans but abated in the Middle Ages. It had become a mania again by the early 1600s, with the shipment of four hundred statues stripped from the Cyclades islands for King Charles I. Lord Arundel sent his agents to scavenge all the movable antiquities they could obtain: they hacked apart colossal statues and columns to be transported to England for "safekeeping." These ancient marbles became "follies" in stately gardens. Column drums served as rustic seats or as rollers for bowling greens. Sarcophagi made novel planters or horse troughs. Beautiful friezes were even pulverized into gravel for cemetery walks.

On a more modest scale, but typical of most early travelers, Jacob Spon and George Wheler took an inscription from Delphi in 1675, "lest it be lost." By the time Lord Elgin arrived in 1802 and made away with the Acropolis friezes, the ransacking frenzy had been going on for two hundred years. Not until 1834, after the Greek War of Independence from the Ottoman Empire, was the first law passed forbidding random excavating and export of Greece's heritage. I found that the 1894 *Baedeker's* guidebook warned tourists that it was forbidden to remove antiquities in one's luggage.

Many European visitors expressed dismay at the pillage (a Frenchman at Delos in 1750 wrote, "My heart was pierced . . . to see the devastations made among such glorious edifices." Yet everyone wanted to take home keepsakes or leave their mark somehow. Lord Byron's Grand Tour of 1809–11 included Greece, and many a tourist since has admired his signature carved into a column of the Temple of Poseidon at Sounion.

Besides relics from antiquity, eighteenth- and early nineteenth-century tourists also acquired *chibouques* (long

Turkish pipes), walking sticks carved from Parnassian black-thorn, and fancy Greek and Ottoman costumes. Young John Morritt's letters home in 1795 talk of buying fine turbans and ermine robes *à la turque* for himself and a blue silk Maniot costume for his sister. Patterns for Grecian dresses were requested by sisters and girlfriends back in England, and "Grecian knot" hairstyles were a popular fad. It even became the vogue for young women to affect a "Grecian" slouching posture, hunching their shoulders like modest goddesses in nude ancient sculptures.

A portrait of oneself decked out as an "Evzone" or a "Pasha" was another popular souvenir. Lord Byron's costume portrait can be seen today in the Benaki Museum, Athens. The portrait of the dashing Earl of Sandwich, John Montague, who at twenty was the first European to include Greece in his educational 1738 Grand Tour, shows a beturbaned young man with a dagger in his belt, contemplating a goblet of local wine. Lady Hester Stanhope's likeness (early 1800s) shows her in silken robes and sashes, turned-up slippers, and turban, smoking a long *chibouque*.

Byron deplored Lord Elgin's vandalism. When he saw the crates of the Parthenon friezes on the docks at Piraeus, Byron compared Elgin to the barbarian hordes that sacked Rome. Byron himself was more interested in contemporary Greece and Greeks than in collecting curios. Still, we do learn that Byron once thrilled Sir Walter Scott with a gift of a large urn containing "deadmen's bones found in certain sepulchers within the long walls of Athens." When he departed Greece in 1811, Byron's only personal souvenirs were "four skulls dug out of sarcophagi in Marathon," a "phial of Attic hemlock," and "four live Grecian tortoises" (see chapter 6). Earlier he had considered buying the island of Ithaca, and he was offered the plain of Marathon for about nine hundred pounds. "It is astonishing how far money goes in this country!" exclaimed Byron.

Unwittingly, Byron began a rage for another kind of souvenir. After the publication of his poem "The Maid of Athens," based on his flirtation in 1809 with twelve-year-old Theresa Makri, the daughter of his pension-keeper, it became fashionable to "fall in love" with Theresa or one of her sisters, Katinka and Mariana. Everyone made the pilgrimage to no. 11 Theklas Street in Plaka, where the three young women held court. Breathlessly describing this living tourist attraction in diaries and letters home, each young man imagined he could detect melancholy beneath Theresa's gay demeanor.

The Makri house was one of the best-known pensions during the heyday of the *milordi*. One of the first American tourists, Nicholas Biddle of Philadelphia, stayed at the Makri pension in 1806 when the "Maid" was still a child. Biddle especially enjoyed the shady spring-watered courtyard ("haven from dust and noise") and the Greek servants who seemed to understand his Italian.

Throughout the Greek countryside travelers could stay in *khans*, inns that might consist of a loft above a stable or a series of rooms arranged around a courtyard. Retsina, olives, cheese, bread, eggs, and figs could be purchased for meals. Unimpressed, the French Romantic novelist Chateaubriand judged *khans* to be "utterly devoid of civilized life."

Coffeehouses in towns also rented out beds, and sometimes lodgings were available in shepherds' huts. Travelers praised the generous and hospitable Greek character, so "vivacious and possessed of a natural subtlety of wit," remarked George Wheler in 1675.

Everyone was eager to try coffee, a specialty of Ottoman-ruled Greece. While some visitors complained about the minuscule cups and the dregs, others enthusiastically compared it to the "nepenthe" drunk by Helen in Homer's *Iliad*. All agreed that it "serves as a charm to pass the hours," and that it "encourages pleasant conversation." Another *kafenion* pastime was smoking Persian tobacco from elaborate *nargilehs*, hookahs or water pipes. A guidebook of the 1890s noted the "somewhat stupefying effect, similar to opium." The same guidebook went on to explain that the strings of beads that all Greek men twirled in their hands had no religious significance: this was a "mere restless habit." Rustic retsina was a shock. Nearly every traveler concurred with Spon and Wheler, who wrote one of the first modern Greek travel books in the late 1600s. They remarked that the flavor of the local wine was not enhanced "by a large admixture of tar," which rendered it "disagreeable to foreigners at first," although they admitted that most grew accustomed to the taste. The 1854 *British Handbook for Travellers in Greece* noted that the "resinous *vin du pays*" is scarcely drinkable, as it savors of vinegar and sealing wax."

The French were the most outraged by the *vin* and Greek cuisine in general: grumpy traveler Chateaubriand claimed in 1817 that every sip of the "ill-flavoured wine made one grimace." His French compatriots complained that Greek bread was "insipid," Hymettan thyme honey tasted "medicinal," the fruit was "only tolerable," the meat "overcooked to rags," and the olive oil "fit only for soap!"

In the 1600s, 1700s, and early 1800s most tourists traveled by horse and camped out, as did Spon and Wheler at the ancient sites of Eleusis and Delphi in 1669. The pair found the unmarked and unexcavated sacred site of Delphi with a great deal of difficulty, stopping along the way for goat's milk, roast chicken and lamb, and cups of retsina chilled with snow.

Lord and Lady Elgin journeyed to Corinth in May of 1802 and passed an uncomfortable night in leaky tents. In contrast, camping on the banks of the Eurotas River near Sparta, with his saddle for a pillow, Sir William Gell described a pleasant night sleeping under the constellation of Leda's Swan in August of 1806. And in the summer of 1810, Byron and his friend John Cam Hobhouse camped in a tent on the beach of Aegina. They feasted on "entire limbs of roast lamb with our fingers *à la turque*." Their supper was finished off with yogurt mixed with rice, preserves, and almonds, and enlivened by dancing, accompanied by many toasts from their hosts and much exuberant firing of pistols.

Camping out in Greece could be idyllic. Guidebooks of the 1800s assured travelers headed for Greece that much of the pleasure would arise from the "sheer hardship and privation," and that by traveling on horseback one could avoid the "languor and feverishness that result from traveling on wheels." For protection against the sun ("the glare and heat can scarcely be imagined!") guidebooks advised bringing a puggaree (sun helmet with a green gauze veil), a parasol, and a "wide-awake" (wide-brimmed hat). Sun-spectacles of smoked or blue-green tinted glass could be purchased from an optician on Hermes (Ermou) Street in Athens. "Though they feel strange at first, these will be a great relief to the eyes." Other supplies for the Grand Tour included ammonia for insect bites, Peruvian bark (quinine) for malaria, and, for fever, "Jesuit's drops," a tincture of balsam of copaiba, guiacum, and sassafras oil in alcohol. Travelers also required a canteen, a knife, a compass, a stout cane for "repelling shepherds' dogs," candles, a hunting gun, some curry powder and cayenne, a cooking kit, a pocket spyglass, walking shoes, and light but sturdy clothes.

The 1800s version of the "safari jacket" or "photojournalist's vest" so beloved of tourists today was the all-purpose red "Windsor" uniform. This was an official-looking outfit with brass buttons, which was believed to impress the locals. Double-sewn yellow trousers, three dozen shirts, and heavy boots completed the *milordi*'s wardrobe. By 1850, guidebooks were frowning on assuming native costume: "Simply ridiculous unless you are a PERFECT master of the language and customs!"

A tent was optional, but the *Baedeker* of 1894 suggested bringing one's own bedding—a linen sleeping bag that could be secured tightly around one's neck. The authors warned that "pests render the night hideous for even the most enthusiastic traveler." One could expect to be assailed by *psillous* (fleas), *koreous* (bedbugs), *psiraes* (lice), *kounoupia* (mosquitoes), and "other disgusting insects winged and wingless."

Edward Clarke, touring with Thomas Malthus (of birth control fame) and John Cripps (the man who introduced kohlrabi to Europe), wrote home in 1799, "While our guide cuts up an old goat for dinner, I'll sketch for you the luxuries we enjoy here in Greece: danger, fatigue, disease, filth, thirst, heat, storms, rocks, lice all over your body, fleas, bugs, cockroaches, rats. . . ."

Such privations and "musquîtoes" never bothered Byron: he complained about another sort of annoyance, the hordes of tourists! "Athens is infested with them," he wrote, "and Attica swarms with travelers. Our fair countrywomen ascend the rocks of the Acropolis" in droves. Like many tourists eager for a unique experience, Byron may have been oversensitive—one historian estimates that only about two hundred English tourists visited Greece between 1800 and 1830.

They came to immerse themselves in the glorious sights. One of the first visitors to Greece in the early 1600s recounted his excitement upon discovering that the actual buildings of Athens's golden age had not disappeared in the mists of time: "I was taken with a universal shivering all over my body. We fancied that every step we took was in the footsteps of Theseus or Socrates or Pericles."

Spon and Wheler marveled at the Parthenon before the Venetian bombardment in 1686: "Absolutely the most beautiful antiquity remaining in the world . . . we stood for hours in unwearying contemplation." They found the landscape and villagers charming. Many visitors, like Byron, were enamored of the Aegean sky, "darkly—deeply—beautifully blue." After Athens and the Makri sisters, the Mycenaean fortified city of Mycenae was the major draw, its Lion Gate almost obscured by vines and the inscribed names of travelers. Lady Elgin bravely scrambled into the subterranean "Treasury of Atreus" there, but on the island of Antiparos she was aghast at the treacherous descent into the famous grottoes. Her countrywoman, Lady Craven, had accomplished the feat in 1785, by torchlight, slipping and sliding on dubious rope ladders down the perpendicular passageways, but Lady Craven was a notorious adventuress, taking the Grand Tour to get over a divorce. Lady Craven's travel uniform was an English riding habit, and she once impressed her companions and guides by taking over the helm of their ship in a storm on the Black Sea. She planned her own route home through the Balkans, packing two pistols against bandits.

Early travelers were thrilled by the great festivals and dances held at the Temple of Theseus in Athens at Easter, when thousands of people filled the plain around the Agora, in brilliant costumes "like a field of anemones agitated by the wind." Whirling dervishes performed on Fridays at the Tower of the Winds in Athens (see chapter 33). Tourists strolled up to the Parthenon for sunrise, then to the Pnyx, Plato's Academy, the Kerameikos, and the Temple of Zeus, ending with a return to the Acropolis for sunset.

Gustave Flaubert's diary entry for 10:30 p.m., January 23, 1850, recorded his last night in Greece: "I went to say adieu to the Parthenon. The wind was strong, the sun was setting, the sky was all red above Aegina, turning the columns of the Propylaea egg-yellow." As he left, "two large birds flew out from the façade of the Temple and departed for the East, for Smyrna." As Flaubert headed back to his lodgings, below the Acropolis near the Herodes Atticus Theater, he stopped to talk to a man offering to sell him a figurine for two drachmas. Flaubert glanced back at the Acropolis and glimpsed "a ragged old woman in black climbing up to the citadel." (See chapter 40 for Flaubert's Carthaginian expedition eight years later.)

Sigmund Freud, who would name his psychological complexes after characters from Greek mythology, might be called the first truly modern tourist in Greece. Freud's reactions to his long-awaited dream of visiting the land of Narcissus and Oedipus in 1904 were summed up in an article he entitled "A Disturbance of Memory on the Acropolis." "When finally I stood on the Acropolis, a surprising thought entered my mind. So all this really *does* exist, just as we learnt in school!"

The rest of Freud's account is appropriately self-psychoanalytic, with a long, turgid discussion of his "conflicting emotions" upon viewing the Parthenon, a free association on his recent bout of depression during the voyage to Greece, his ambivalence about actually achieving his lifelong desire of beholding Athens, his anxiety over fulfilling such "an impossible wish," and his guilt about feeling superior to his father, who had failed to attain his own goal of visiting Athens.

For the first Renaissance travelers, too, it was astounding to discover that the "stuff" of Greece's illustrious history still existed, that one could actually tread the same paths as Pericles, Socrates, and Plato, sit in the very theater where the great tragedies had their debuts, touch statues of ancient Athenians and their gods and goddesses.

The Grand Tourists who made the scene in the nineteenth century, with their tinted sun-spectacles, newfangled mosquito nets, and copies of the ancient traveler Pausanias's second-century *Guide to Greece*, braved rocky roads, vermin, pirates, and fever to find an exotic experience among the romantic ruins. This description, which drew travelers in the 1850s, rhapsodizes about the same delights that draw today's visitors: "Travelers wearied by the artificial and overcivilized side of modern hotels and means of locomotion find extraordinary charm in wandering the less-sophisticated byways of Greece: majestic cliff-girt shores, deep bays and azure sea, calm bright isles resting on the horizon, olive-clothed slopes, dark tracts of pine, and snowy peaks, the silvery asphodels glittering in valleys, the anemones and poppies waving on mountains and shores, the fragrance of the orange groves, the azure morns, the lucid light. . . ."

Then, as now, the memory of sunset from the Acropolis was perhaps the finest souvenir. In the words of an early French traveler: "The whole horizon is flooded with rays of intense red, the clouds take on a vermillion hue, and the sea sparkles with fire . . . the mountains separate into deeply shadowed colors of vivid purple to darkest green . . . and the Greek moon far surpasses our poor moon. This white light, so pure and tranquil, imparts to the great ruins a language worthy of their meaning; all ignoble ideas flee and the observer has the impression of knocking at the door of eternity."

Who Were the First Recreational Mountain Climbers?

MOSES CLIMBED MOUNT SINAI to receive the Ten Commandments, and he ascended Mount Nebo (Jordan) to gaze on the land he would never reach. Jesus took three disciples to a mountaintop to commune with the ghosts of Moses and Elijah. Empedocles, the ancient Greek philosopher, climbed the active volcano Mount Etna on Sicily and leaped into the flaming crater in 430 BC. According to legend, Empedocles intended to become an immortal god; the volcano ejected one of his sandals turned to bronze by the heat.

Ascents of sacred mountains were spiritual journeys for emperors and monks in ancient China. Scholars have traced more than three thousand years of ritual worship at Tai Shan, just over five thousand feet, in Shandong Province. Emperors and feudal lords would climb to the heavenly summit and leave offerings of food and jade, and more than eighteen hundred inscriptions. Mountain worship contributed to the development of Taoism and Buddhism in China.

In Japan, according to legend, in about AD 663, the mystic ninja sorcerer En no Ozunu (En no Gyoja) ascended (some said he flew up) Mount Fuji (12,300 ft.) more than a thousand times to meditate. His feats inspired Shinto mountain worship by ascetic hermits.

During the Punic Wars, Hannibal and his army crossed the Alps to invade Rome in 218 BC, and in about AD 569 the Lombards invaded Italy by trekking over Kings Mountain, Matajur (5,387 ft.), in the foothills of the Alps.

But these military and religiously motivated peak experiences cannot be described as purely recreational mountaineering. No one knows why Ötzi, the mummified Copper Age Ice Man, was crossing the Alps (at 10,500 ft.) in about 3300 BC with an arrow embedded in his shoulder and other wounds. But his journey cannot be imagined as pleasant either. Nor can the journeys that resulted in the earliest documented reports of high-altitude sickness be considered pleasure trips. In 37–32 BC, the Chinese envoy Too Kin described crossing what were called "The Headache Mountains," arduous routes over high passes in the Pamirs and Hindu Kush, about 15,000 feet. Vivid descriptions of mountain sickness also appear in the writings of the Spanish explorer José de Acosta. He recounted his difficult crossings of mountain passes at 15,750 feet, in the Andes of Peru, in 1570.

Who were the first mountaineers to climb for pleasure? Romantic Chinese poets like Li Bai, who climbed Mount Tai to meditate on the scenery, in the eighth century AD, surely count. The wandering poet Li Bai (ca. 701–62) embraced Taoism's harmony with nature. Many of his poems are lyrical appreciations of the peace and serenity he found in the Zhongnan Mountains (about 8,500 ft.). The peaks were a favorite dwelling place for Taoist hermit sages as early as the third century BC. One of Li Bai's poems begins, "Down the blue mountain in the evening / Moonlight was my homeward escort / Looking back I saw my path / lie in levels of deep shadow." Another poem tells how "Ledges of cliff and winding trails lead to blue sky . . . I climb to the top. I survey the whole world. I see the long river that runs beyond return; yellow clouds that winds have driven hundreds of miles and a snowy peak."

In Europe, the Italian scholar Petrarch claimed to be the first person since antiquity to climb a mountain simply to take delight in the view. Petrarch said that he was inspired by Philip V's ascent of a mountain in the second century BC. With his brother and two servants, Petrarch ascended Mont Ventoux (6,270 ft.) in Provence in about 1336, and "stood like one dazed" gazing down upon clouds, mountains, and the Rhone.

Petrarch had read the account of Philip's ascent by the ancient Roman historian Livy, who wrote in the first century BC. Livy tells us that King Philip V of Macedon undertook a mountain-climbing expedition to admire the spectacular view from Mount Haemus in Thrace. This high peak (ca. 7,000 ft.) is in the Balkan Mountain Range of Bulgaria. In antiquity, it was a popular belief that one could see two different seas—the Adriatic and the Black—from the summit. In fact, on a clear day, one might see the Black and Aegean seas from the top, but not the Adriatic. Philip, recently retired from ruling his kingdom (involuntarily, owing to the Roman conquest of Macedonia in 197 BC) was keen to see this celebrated panorama. According to Livy, as Philip and his crew of climbers "approached the summit everything was so covered with fog that they were slowed down just as if they were on a night march." When Philip's party descended, writes Livy, the Macedonian mountain climbers "said nothing to contradict the general notion of the fabulous view of oceans, mountains and rivers that one could view from the peak." Livy then rather nastily insinuates that Philip and his friends hoped "to prevent their futile expedition from providing material for mirth." Why the cynicism? Livy and the Romans doubted the recreational nature of Philip's expedition. They suspected that his goal was military reconnaissance, part of a strategy to make war on Rome.

Saint Augustine wrote that "men go abroad to admire the heights of mountains [and] the mighty waves of the sea." Perhaps he had in mind another ancient instance of recreational mountain climbing that occurred in AD 126. The Roman emperor Hadrian had heard that sunrise over the Mediterranean from the active volcano Mount Etna was breathtakingly beautiful. The emperor's team ascended Mount Etna on the east coast of Sicily (ca. 10,900 ft.) when the volcano was quiescent, but smoking. Roman historians had recorded violent eruptions in 396, 140, 122, and 44–32 BC, and AD 40. Most of the forests on the slopes had disappeared by Hadrian's day, so the landscape, wrought by lava and ash, was desolate. The imperial team slept on the summit and arose at dawn to admire the sun's multicolored rays like a rainbow as it rose over the sea. The iridescent effect would have been due to the volcanic smoke and particulate matter in the atmosphere.

I wish I could learn more about the early ascent in AD 905 of the daunting snow-covered volcano Damavand (18,400 ft.) in the Elburz Range south of the Caspian Sea. The narrative was recounted by the popular Arab storyteller-traveler Abu Dolaf Kazraji, who amused Persian courtiers in Iran with colorful tales.

Another intriguing medieval mountaineering marvel was that of Peter III of Aragon, who scaled Mount Canigou (9,130 ft.) in the Pyrenees in AD 1275. At the time it was believed to be the highest peak in the range; it was visible to sailors as they approached the coast. The only account of his ascent is frustratingly terse. According to his chronicler, Fra Salimbene, it was the heart's desire of "stout-hearted" Peter of Aragon to see what was at the summit of the peak. His companions, two trusted knights, flagged and took shelter during a great hailstorm, dreading the crashing thunder and lightning. The king persevered alone. At the top, Peter tossed a stone into a tarn. A "horrible dragon of enormous size" flew up from the deep glacial lake "darkening the air with its breath." Without further ado the king descended.

CHAPTER 44

Ancient Tattoos

I will tattoo you with pictures of the terrible punishments
suffered by the most notorious criminals in Hades
I will tattoo you with the white-tusked boar

VIOLENT IMAGERY promising gruesome harm to rivals or
faithless lovers is common in Hellenistic curses, but the above
poem stands out because it threatens revenge by tattoo. The
author of this curse, on Egyptian papyrus fragments discovered in 1962 and 1991, is unknown, but a strong candidate is
the poetess Moiro of Byzantium, who wrote in about 300 BC.
A similar punishment turns up about the same time in a scene
by the Greek playwright Herodas. In *The Jealous Woman*, the
scorned Bitinna summons Kosis, a professional tattooer of
slaves, criminals, and prisoners of war, to bring his needles
to punish her unfaithful slave-lover.

While today tattoos are primarily decorative, in antiquity
they also had punitive, magical, and medical functions. In
Greece, the use of penal tattoos may have been introduced
from Persia in the sixth century BC. According to the historian Herodotus, the Persian king Xerxes, on his way to invade
Greece (480 BC), was so infuriated when the sea swept away
his bridge at the Hellespont that he ordered his soldiers to en-

slave the disobedient body of water by tossing iron fetters into the sea. Then he had men flog it with three hundred lashes. "I even heard," writes an amused Herodotus, "that Xerxes commanded his royal tattooers to tattoo the water!"

Another Herodotean tale tells us that in about 500 BC, the Ionian tyrant Histiaeus of Miletus was imprisoned by the Persian king Darius. In an effort to inspire his son-in-law Aristogoras to revolt, Histiaeus hit on a clever plan. He secretly shaved the head of his most trusted slave and pricked his scalp with pin and ink. "Histeaeus to Aristagoras," the message read, "incite Ionia to revolt!" In a few weeks the slave's hair grew over the tattoo, and Histiaeus dispatched his living letter. On reaching his destination, the slave shaved. Aristogoras read the instructions written on the man's scalp and launched an ill-conceived revolt that ended in the Persian invasion of Greece.

Tattooing captives was common in wartime. After defeating the wealthy island of Samos in the fifth century BC, the Athenians tattooed the foreheads of prisoners of war with an owl, Athens's city emblem. When Samos in turn defeated the Athenians, the Samians tattooed their prisoners with the image of a Samian warship. The historian Plutarch was appalled by the "unthinkable indignity" inflicted on seven thousand Athenians and their allies captured at Syracuse, Sicily, in 413 BC. Their foreheads were tattooed with an image of a horse (the Syracuse insignia) before they were sold as slaves to work the quarries.

A legal inscription from Ephesus indicates that during the early Roman Empire slaves exported to Asia Minor were tattooed with the words "tax paid." Acronyms, words, sentences, and even doggerel were gouged on foreheads, necks, arms, and legs of slaves and convicts, either as routine identification marks or as punishment. "Stop me, I'm a runaway" was a typical motto etched on the brows of Roman slaves. The Roman practice dehumanized social inferiors by turning their bodies into texts that forever recorded their captivity, servitude, or guilt.

The Greek philosopher Bion of Borysthenes (ca. 300 BC) described the brutally tattooed face of his father, a former slave, as "a narrative of his master's harshness." That some cruel slave owners tattooed their chattels without cause is suggested by a fragmentary Greek legal code of the third century BC that allowed masters to tattoo "bad" slaves but forbade the tattooing of "good" ones. In Rome, the emperor Caligula (AD 38–41) "defaced many people of the better sort" with tattoos and condemned them to slavery, according to his biographer Suetonius (see chapter 46). Gladiators were tattooed as public property, and in the later Roman Empire soldiers were tattooed to discourage desertion. Roman authorities also punished early Christians with forehead tattoos that condemned them to the mines, according to research by historian Mark Gustafson. In AD 330, the first Christian emperor, Constantine, banned the practice of tattooing the faces of convicts, gladiators, and soldiers. Because the human face reflected "the image of divine beauty," he declared, "it should not be defiled."

Punitive tattoos were not carefully or artistically applied. Ink was poured into crude letters carved into a captive's flesh with iron needles; three needles bound together made a thicker line. Copious bleeding was common, and the procedure was sometimes fatal. "Without hygiene, tattooing must always have been dangerous [which] contributed to its value as a form of punishment," notes classicist Christopher Jones. Marco Polo's vivid description of the ordeal of willing victims in thirteenth-century Central Asia gives a sense of traditional methods. To be tattooed with designs of elaborate dragons, lions, and birds, an individual was "tied hand and foot and held down by others, while the master craftsman pricked out the images with five needles." The "victim suffered what might well pass for the pains of Purgatory!"

Roman doctors developed techniques for removing tattoos, but the methods were painful and risky. A typical procedure described by the medical writer Aetius reads, "Clean the tattoo with niter (saltpeter), smear with resin of terebinth (turpentine), and bandage for five days." On day six "prick out the tattoo with a sharp pin, sponge away the blood, and cover with salt. After doing some strenuous running to work up a sweat, apply a caustic poultice; the tattoo should disappear in 20 days." Caustic preparations worked by ulcerating the skin, thereby obliterating the tattoo (see chapter 7 for ancient Chinese tattoo removal with toxic beetle juice). A safer expedient, mentioned by other writers, was to hide shameful tattoos under long bangs or a bandana. Some have suggested that pirates' traditional bandana headbands were originally a way of covering punitive or slave tattoos.

The demeaning use of tattoos in their own cultures made it difficult for Greeks and Romans to understand why the Thracians, Scythians, Dacians, Gauls, Picts, Celts, Britons, and other "barbarians" willingly tattooed themselves. In Thrace, according to Herodotus, plain skin signaled a lack of identity, and men and women with tattoos were much admired. One third-century account of the Scythian defeat of the Thracians notes that the victors incised symbols of defeat upon the losers, but that the Thracian women hit on the idea of embellishing the rest of their bodies with tattoos as a way of turning "the stamp of violence and shame into beautiful ornaments." Similarly, early Christians tattooed themselves with religious symbols to counteract those inscribed on them by their Roman persecutors. Among the Mossynoikoi of the Black Sea region in the fifth century BC, the historian Xenophon observed that "the chubby children of the best families were entirely tattooed back and front with flowers in many colors." For many ancient peoples, tattoos signaled bravery, ensured magical protection, and impressed enemies.

Romans were amazed by warrior cultures that seemed to gather psychological strength from tattoos. The historian Herodian records the first encounters with the wildly illustrated natives of the British Isles about AD 200, "ferocious fighters [who] tattoo their bodies with myriad patterns and all sorts of animals." The historian Claudian (ca. AD 400) described a skirmish with the natives of Scotland. The Roman soldiers, themselves tattooed against their will by the state, lingered after the battle to stare at "the strange devices on the faces of the dying Picts."

Despite their misgivings about the practice, the Greeks were fascinated by the idea of tattoos as exotic beauty marks. In the fifth and fourth centuries BC, a series of popular vase paintings illustrated the murder of the musician Orpheus by tattooed Thracian women wielding spears, daggers, and axes. Anthropologists have noted that tattoo designs are often used to accentuate musculature and motion. On these ancient Greek vases, the geometric and animal tattoos on the women's arms and legs draw attention to their athletic strength and flexing muscles. On a red-figure column krater, two women running barefoot display fully tattooed arms and legs. One of the women has designs from ankle to knee: parallel lines, zigzags, a sunburst, and a deer. Other vase paintings show women with chevrons, circles, vines, ladders, spirals, and animals.

The most technically and artistically brilliant tattoos from antiquity are preserved on frozen bodies discovered near Pazyryk, southern Siberia. The Altai region was home to the nomadic horse people known to the Greeks as the Scythians. There, in 1948, Soviet archaeologist Sergei Rudenko discovered a fifth-century BC tattooed warrior preserved in permafrost. Imaginary and real creatures swirled across the man's body, the sophisticated compositions conforming to his anatomy. Since then many more animal tattoos have been discovered on the skin of naturally mummified Scythian men and women.

Ancient Scythian tattoo designs. Drawings by Michele Angel.

A tattooed body was found at Pazyryk in 1993 by Natalya Polosmak of the Russian Institute of Archaeology and Ethnography. The woman was wrapped in fur and buried with six horses, all perfectly preserved in solid ice. She was about twenty-five at the time of her death some twenty-four hundred years ago. On her wrist and shoulder were exquisite tattoos of deer with fantastic antlers, recalling the deer tattoos of the Thracian women on ancient Greek vases. The tattooed mummy of a young horseman, found in 1995, wore his hair in braids and was buried with his horse around 500 BC. A large tattoo of an elk in the distinctive Scythian style spans his chest, shoulder, and back. Since then, even more tattooed Scythian men and women have been discovered, with some tattoos invisible until illuminated by infrared cameras. Some of these recently revealed tattoos show Chinese influence (see chapter 45).

How were the Scythian tattoos made? Rudenko speculated that a sure-handed artist had "stitched" the skin with a very fine needle and thread using soot as the coloring agent. Freeze-dried Inuit mummies found at Qilakitsoq, Greenland, examined by the Danish National Museum in 1978, provided evidence of stitched tattoos on six women who had died in the late 1400s. Scientists determined that the tattooers had made the designs by drawing a thread through the skin with a bone needle. Chemical analysis revealed ink made from soot, ash, and plant juices. But Scythian tattoos are much deeper than the stitched tattoos of the Inuits.

Recent archaeological excavations of Scythian burials have uncovered tattoo kits of ink and needles, and a leather stencil of an elk tattoo on a Scythian male's body was found among the man's grave goods. The tattooed animals may have had magical meanings, or they may have recorded important personal experiences such as hunting successes, vision quests, and perilous adventures.

Rudenko was intrigued by fourteen dots along one Scythian warrior's spine and six on his ankle. He knew that present-day Siberians believe such tattoos alleviate pain. Therapeutic tattooing is still practiced among Tibetans and peoples of the Arctic and Middle East. Like cauterization or acupuncture, such tattoos are thought to stimulate nerves or release toxins. This folk remedy is very ancient: blue marks on the Eleventh Dynasty Egyptian mummy of Lady Ament (ca. 2400 BC), for example, have been interpreted by French archaeologists as a therapy for chronic kidney disease.

Ötzi the Iceman, who died in an Alpine blizzard some five thousand years ago, has several tattoos: parallel lines on the right foot and ankle, bars along the lower spine, lines on the left calf, and crosses inside the right knee and left ankle. Noticing that they were concentrated at joints, and recalling Rudenko's medical interpretation of the dots on the Pazyryk warrior, Konrad Spindler of the University of Innsbruck ordered X-rays of Ötzi. Sure enough, they revealed chronic degeneration of bone and cartilage in the spine and arthritic wear and tear of the knee and ankles. The "precise draftsmanship" indicates that an experienced tattooist scored the marks with a sharp point; the bone awl found in the Iceman's pouch "would have been ideal for the task," wrote Spindler.

Ancient painted frescoes in Egypt depict both men and women with tattoos of animals or religious symbols. In 2014, anthropologist Anne Austin discovered a group of heavily tattooed female mummies, from about three thousand years ago, in Deir el-Medina, Egypt. Many of the tattoos were revealed with infrared technology. The designs include flowers, hiero-glyphs, baboons and other animals, and religious symbols. Austin speculates that the women were priestesses or healers.

History shows that humans have had themselves tattooed for myriad reasons—for magical protection, to relieve pain, for vengeance, or to declare victory over an enemy. Tattoos could beautify, shock, or humiliate. They proclaimed valor, religious belief, group solidarity, or personal independence. Their messages could be hidden or in plain sight. Tattoos have always been complex and mutable. What other lifestyle decision could draw into the same circle such diverse people across the millennia as Ötzi, Eurasian nomads, ancient slaves and prisoners of war, Roman gladiators and soldiers, Egyptian priestesses, murderous Thracian women, and tattoo enthusiasts of our own era?

Tattoos in Ancient China

IT IS INTRIGUING that the earliest Chinese word for writing, *wén,* referred to tattoos (*wen shen* means to "puncture skin"). Archaeologists find artistic representations reflecting tattooing practices in China in archaeological sites from the Shang to Han dynasty periods (1500 BC to AD 220). Accounts of the tattooing customs among the nomadic steppe cultures of Central Asia can also be found in many early Chinese chronicles.

Several ancient Chinese literary sources described tattoos as common body adornments among the "barbarian" nomads of the Northern and Western Wilderness, on the steppes beyond the imperial borders of China. For example, in the Warring States and early Han period (about 475 BC to 87 BC), the *Liji* (Record of Rites,) reported on the "wild" tribes of mounted archers of Inner Asia. These nomads ate only meat, wore animal skins, and tattooed their foreheads. In the third to first centuries BC, the *Zhan Guo Ce* (Intrigues of the Warring States) stated that the Western Wilderness horse-archers engraved their left shoulders with tattoos. The *Nan Shih* (History of the Southern Dynasties) of AD 630 refers to the Central Asian steppes as the "Land of the Tattooed." These "uncivilized" people marked themselves "with stripes and spots like wild beasts." The *Nan Shih* also noted that Siberian peoples of "gigantic" stature wore tattoos that signified their courage and signaled their marital status.

In antiquity, the powerful confederation of nomad tribes of the West became known to the Chinese as Xiongnu. A Han history by Sima Qian (*Shiji*, Records of the Historian, 147–85 BC) recounts the Han emperor's negotiations with the aggressive Xiongnu coalitions who exerted continuous pressure on China's western frontier. The nomads held the upper hand from the fifth century to the third century BC. To mollify them, Chinese rulers often sent lavish tributes and Han princesses as brides to seal treaties. When Chinese ambassadors arrived with gifts, however, the nomad leaders demanded that the envoys be tattooed (*me [mo] ch'ing*, "to tattoo with black ink") before they could meet the *Shan-yu* ("The Greatest," the chieftain).

The early Chinese, like the ancient Greeks and Romans, considered tattooing a form of punishment, the mark of a slave or criminal. Even so, ancient Greek vase painters portrayed beautiful barbarian women decorated with geometric and animal tattoos (see chapter 44). Permanent body markings evoked ambivalence among cultures that did not practice decorative tattooing. Among the Chinese, the lines began to blur between understandings of tattoos as shameful marks, as heroic badges of honor, as signals of derring-do, and as beautiful decorations of the body. As Chinese familiarity and exchanges with steppe nomads increased, some of steppe customs—such as riding warhorses, wearing tunics and trousers, and tattooing—began to influence Chinese culture.

Acceptance of tattoos became more common, especially among Chinese travelers, traders, explorers, and envoys who interacted and lived among the nomads to the west. Evidence for this comes from "The Mission to the West" in the *Han Shu* by Zhang Qian (Chang K'ien). Zhang Qian was a Chinese imperial diplomat who made many expeditions across Central Asia in 138–126 BC. He reported that some Chinese envoys, for example Wang Wu, who was himself a northerner familiar with Xiongnu customs, readily agreed to receive tattoos in order to meet with nomad leaders. One can imagine that some merchants and envoys could show off tattoos from each of the tribes they did business with, and that these marks may have served as guarantees of trust and safe travel, something like a passport.

Within China, some ethnic groups had long-standing traditions of tattooing. Women of the Dulong people in southwest China, for example, wore elaborate facial tattoos. In the same region, the Dai women tattooed the backs of their hands and foreheads, while the Dai men preferred images of dragons and tigers to accentuate the muscles of their arms, legs, and backs. The Li women of Hainan Island tattooed their necks, faces, arms, and legs. In ancient times, the Baiyue fishermen of South China were known for tattoos of sea monsters to protect themselves at sea. Sacred snake patterns decorated—and defended—the bodies of Minyue people of Fujian Province, also in the south of China.

By the time of the Tang dynasty (AD 618–907), even more Chinese people were decorating themselves with tattoos. *Youyang Zazu*, a fascinating miscellaneous collection by Duan Chengshi (written in AD 800–863), describes many different types of tattoos, including full body patterns. The most popular Tang-era designs were images of nature and lines of poetry. The association between writing and engraving the body is driven home by Duan Chengshi's disturbing notation that traces of tattoos could be discerned on the skulls and bones of the dead, so deeply had the needles penetrated.

There are many versions of the story of the famous tattoo of Yue Fei, the great general and cultural hero of the Song dynasty (AD 960–1279). Born in AD 1103, Yue Fei rose from poverty to lead the southern Song forces against the northern nomads of the Jurchen (Jin) dynasty in the twelfth century. Engraved across his back were the four large Chinese characters for "Serve the Realm with Utmost Loyalty."

I set out to learn more about the life of General Yue Fei and his illustrious tattoo after visiting his elaborate tomb and temple near West Lake, Hangzhou, China. I found that the historicity of Yue's tattoo is documented in texts and inscriptions. But his tattoo was also featured in many folk legends. Some said that Yue got the tattoo as a young man when the Jurchen nomad armies first invaded China, as a commitment to remaining faithful to the Song emperor. He would flash the tattoo whenever his village friends suggested running away to join rebel bandits in the mountains. Later, when General Yue was falsely charged with treason, he proved his innocence by displaying the tattoo, which became a cultural icon of loyalty to the state in China.

When Yue was a youth, exciting folktales circulated about the historical bandit-hero Song Jiang, who was leading uprisings against the Song emperor's troops. Outlaws were often tattooed, by choice to show bravado and/or as punishment for crimes. It was the Song dynasty that introduced sentencing robbers and other criminals to *wen* (or *ci*) *pei*, the punishment of "tattoo and exile." Law books of the era devoted many pages to specifying the words or marks, their size, and the placement of tattoos on criminals' faces. The classical fourteenth-century Chinese novel *Water Margin: Outlaws of the Marsh*, often attributed to Shi Nai'an, describes the tattoos of dragons and flowers on some members of Song Jiang's men. Song Jiang himself wrote poems while he was imprisoned; in one verse he tells how he was forcibly tattooed on both cheeks and exiled.

As for Yue's renowned "Serve the Realm" tattoo, most sources said it was his mother who tattooed his back. This was after the rebel pirate captain Yang Yao invited young Yue to become one of his commanders. Yang Yao's pirates were terrorizing the Hunnan lake region in 1130–35. Yue rejected the offer and denounced the pirate as a traitor. But his mother worried that Yue would face other temptations to join the enemies of the Song dynasty. She tattooed the motto on his back as a permanent reminder. The process reminds us of why ancient tattoos were employed as punishment, signified courage, and were recognized as works of art. Yue's mother painted the characters with a calligraphy brush on his back. Then she pricked them with a needle and rubbed in black ink and vinegar to make the characters permanent.

There are countless popular and official illustrations of this legendary scene of maternal tattoo artistry signifying national loyalty. One colorful, detailed painting, from 1750, is in the sumptuous Summer Palace in Beijing. Illustrations of the tattooing scene are also prominent in Chinese propaganda posters from the 1950s. Despite the patriotic message of Yue Fei's legendary tattoo, tattooing today in China evokes edgy ambivalence, associated with gangsters, criminals, and foreigners. Penal tattoos initiated by the Song dynasty continued until the early 1900s in China, and tattoos still retain a forbidden aura. Mao Tse-tung outlawed decorative tattoos when the Communist Party took power after World War II.

Today, tattoos are rarely seen in public in China. But the Internet, tattooed foreign celebrities, and local rappers—as well as the romance of tattoos in China's own history, art, and

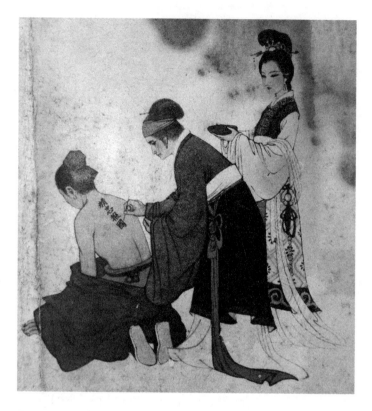

Yue Fei Tattooed by His Mother. Chinese propaganda image, 1950s.

literature—are giving the marks a secret cachet among the young. Despite social and government disapproval, Shanghai has hosted tattoo expositions since 2015. In the shadow tattoo subculture of China, large back pieces of vividly colorful dragons, demons, and phoenixes are favorite images. But some of the most popular designs illustrate the swashbuckling bandit-heroes of yore, like Song Jiang and his men in the classical novel *Water Margin: Outlaws of the Marsh.*

Caligula

LET THEM HATE, SO LONG AS THEY FEAR

CALIGULA (AD 12–41) has an image problem from hell. In-cest, murder, torture, mayhem, depravity on a grand scale—Caligula's reputation as an evil psychopath has persisted for nearly two millennia. Reviled for his grotesquely decadent lifestyle (gold-encrusted food, dissolved pearl cocktails à la Cleopatra, a consulship for his favorite racehorse) and cruelty (vicious practical jokes, executions, forced suicides), Caligula has long attracted sensationally bad press. Few tyrants, for example, achieve the distinction of being identified as one of the models for the Antichrist. In our own time, Caligula's de-monic spirit so infected the Hollywood movie *Caligula* (1979, rereleased 1981–2007, financed by *Penthouse* porn mogul Bob Guccione) that the film was universally abhorred as utterly vile and execrable, the same adjectives hurled at Caligula by historians since the first century BC.

Some modern Roman historians have tackled this ancient PR nightmare by explaining the historical and political con-text of the criticism. They probe hidden motivations under-lying Caligula's "imperial madness," sometimes uncovering a diabolical intellect behind the emperor's seemingly irrational

The Roman emperor Caligula, copperplate engraving, 1827. Alamy Stock Photo.

behavior. Previous historians' rationales for Caligula's bizarre excesses have included physical ailments, such as epilepsy or overactive glands, and various types of mental illness. So far no one has calculated the emperor's score on the modern "psychopath personality checklist." In most modern considerations, Caligula still emerges as loathsome and power mad, but not insane in the ways that Suetonius and other ancient Roman historians might have us believe.

One question raised by the character assassination perpetrated by Caligula's ancient biographers asks, What happened after the first two happy years of his short reign (AD 37–41) to make Caligula so hated? How did Caligula alienate the aristocratic Romans who later painted him as a monster? Reports of Caligula's malevolence were exaggerated, but terrible things did in fact happen under Caligula. What was the backstory, the Roman context by which Caligula's acts of "madness" should be judged? How did Caligula destroy the delicate façade of senatorial-imperial relations in Rome?

Augustus, the first emperor of Rome and victor in the bloody civil war that annihilated the old Republic, had devised an intricate dance—with the compliance of the Roman elites. This dance or game maintained a pretense of political friendship and cooperation between the old aristocratic class and himself as a dictator with unlimited powers. Governed by strict, unwritten rules of mutual hypocrisy, this dangerous charade required obsequious flattery on the part of aristocrats and fake modesty on the part of the emperor. Notably, Augustus also took great care to ingratiate himself with the common folk. The stakes were extremely high. Rome in this period was a treacherous place, teeming with intrigue, conspiracy, backstabbing, murder, assassination. Augustus's own playacting in this drama was so flawless that he took a bow from his deathbed (AD 14) and requested applause for the perfection of his performance.

But Augustus's successor, Tiberius, hated the incessant insincerity required to lubricate imperial politics. He finally withdrew into voluntary exile, holing up in his luxurious villa on Capri. Tiberius's departure from the city enraged the aristocrats as well as the masses. In his absence Rome was misgoverned by his corrupt lieutenants. Tales circulated about the louche lifestyle of the emperor-roué, whispers of murder and sexual perversions. So despised was Tiberius for his aloofness and refusal to play the "game" (among other crimes) that Roman mobs howled for his corpse when his death was announced (AD 37). There were rumors that Tiberius had been smothered in his bed by his young nephew and successor, Caligula. This story actually enhanced the popularity of the new emperor.

Caligula's own life had been in danger since boyhood. Some members of his family were murdered in political plots, while other relatives conspired to kill him. A survivor—thanks to his emotional control and sardonic wit—young Caligula spent his teenage years as a kind of hostage under the protection of his reclusive Uncle Tiberius on Capri. Whether or not he participated in the rumored debaucheries, he certainly learned to despise the hypocrisy and façade of imperial modesty. The young man also honed his literary and rhetorical skills. But the socialization he received on Capri was definitely not what Augustus would have prescribed for a future emperor.

The first years of Caligula's reign as emperor were marked by cautious political policies. But he soon began to pursue extravagant projects. He built colossal floating palaces, ten-story-tall ships adorned with priceless gems and purple silk sails, with spacious baths, banquet halls, even fruit orchards and grapevines planted on the ships' decks. Archaeologists have dredged up some spectacular bronze artifacts that decorated Caligula's pleasure fleet, sunk in Lake Nemi, in the Alban Hills near Rome.

In another flamboyant feat, the emperor, wearing armor taken from the tomb of Alexander the Great, led a parade across a three-mile-long bridge of ships. He had commanded the ships to form a bridge over the Gulf of Baiae, boasting that he had turned the sea to land. Ancient Roman historians called him mad for striving to accomplish "whatever men believed to be impossible." But his real motive was to demonstrate his fantastic personal wealth and unlimited power over his subjects, his so-called friends, and his enemies. His penchant for flouting traditional rules of decorum and rank in public and private also evoked anxiety in the senatorial class—just as it was meant to.

An assassination plot was discovered. Executions followed. But the close call tipped Caligula into an irrevocable course of action. In AD 39 he delivered a shocking speech. Caligula accused the aristocracy of masking their murderous hatred of imperial rule with flattery and false compliance. With this speech, Caligula publicly shredded the web of mutual hypocrisy spun by Augustus. Ripping off his already-slipping mask, snatching away the fig leaf of sham that had hidden the impotence of the aristocracy, the young emperor now bluntly asserted the fact of his own absolute power.

Proof of a cold-blooded, cynical intelligence? Yes, but perhaps not evidence of psychosis. After smashing this crucial political illusion with words, Caligula proceeded to inflict sadistic humiliations on the upper class. He intended to hammer home the message no one had yet dared express: Rome was now an absolute monarchy and the aristocrats were powerless. The idea of bestowing consular status on his horse Hotspur and similar outrages have been cast as sure signs of insanity. But they could have been vicious jokes, shrewdly devised to rub the aristocrats' faces in the fact that Caligula owned them.

The method to Caligula's calculated "madness" is revealed by his favorite saying, "Let them hate, so long as they fear me." But here he underestimated the motivating power of evoking such seething hatred and fear. There were many who conspired against the tyrant who had overturned the political game board—the delicate dance of pretense devised by Augustus and so despised by Tiberius. Caligula was making important men and women appear ridiculous. It is really little wonder that Caligula would become the first Roman emperor to be assassinated.

The Roman biographer of emperors, Suetonius, provides material evidence of the lingering toxicity of Caligula's reign. "After Caligula's death," Suetonius reports, "a huge chest full of various poisons was discovered," intended for Caligula's enemies. The new emperor, Claudius, ordered that the chest be thrown into the sea. The massive dump of poisons polluted the sea along the coast. Many fish died and were discovered washed up by the tide on the nearby beaches. The early Christian father Orosius (d. AD 420) recounted this incident to reveal the mercy of God. Orosius declared that the number of fish killed demonstrated how many innocent men had been marked for death by the evil emperor Caligula.

CHAPTER 47

A Mountain of a Man

MAXIMINUS THRAX

IN AD 235 a giant became the most powerful man in the Roman Empire. Maximinus of Thrace (Bulgaria) was a simple shepherd of unknown ethnicity. Some said he was a Goth-Alan, others that he was of Thracian-Roman stock. It was also said that he was the leader of a gang of bandits.

The young man's impressive size and strength attracted the attention of the Roman emperor Septimius Severus in AD 202, who tapped him for wrestling contests. Maximinus grappled with sixteen of the emperor's burliest soldiers, one on one. Then, only slightly winded, he raced the emperor's horse and went on to overcome seven more hefty legionnaires. The barbarian colossus was inducted into the Roman army on the spot.

Maximinus Thrax rose through the ranks. He proved to be such a beloved leader of the soldiers that he was given supreme command of the imperial army. In AD 235 the army assassinated Severus Alexander, and the Praetorian Guard and the Senate proclaimed Maximinus emperor of Rome. With neither senatorial nor equestrian background, Maximinus was the first "commoner" to become emperor. By the way, his name derives from the Latin *maximus*, "mighty, large, powerful, and glorious."

Ancient Roman writers claimed that Maximinus stood about eight feet tall. His sandals were said to be twice the size of regular army issue. He wore his wife's bracelet as a thumb ring. It was said that he devoured forty pounds of meat and eighteen bottles of wine at each meal. They claimed he crushed rocks in his fists, outpulled a team of horses, and dropped a mule with one punch. These are all exaggerations, of course. Similar sensational "facts" circulated in ancient Greece about the superstar Olympic wrestler Milo of Croton. That giant of a man was said to dine on bulls after lifting them in the air, drink two gallons of wine, and eat twenty pounds of meat and twenty pounds of bread each day. Unless Maximinus's skeleton is discovered someday in a coffin, his exact size remains unknown. But the man must have towered over the Romans of his day, whose average height was about five feet, six inches (see chapter 39).

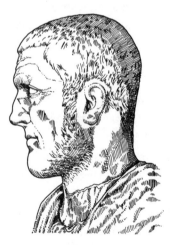

The Roman emperor Maximinus. Drawing of bust in Musei Capitolini, Rome, inv. MC473, by Michele Angel.

The detailed descriptions of his appearance and portraits in sculpture and coins suggest that the emperor may have had a form of giantism or acromegaly. Ancient sources said he was of "frightening appearance and colossal size," a "mountain of a man." Portraits of Maximinus display a prominent forehead, large nose, and lantern jaw. These are some typical symptoms of pituitary gland overproduction of growth hormones.

An intriguing archaeological discovery of a Roman-era "giant" was reported by *National Geographic* in 2012. The bones belong to a young man who lived in the third century AD, around the same time as Maximinus. He stood about six feet, eight inches tall and died between the ages of sixteen and twenty. He was buried in ancient Fidenae, a few miles north of Rome. This is the first skeleton from antiquity with clear signs of giantism.

Most sufferers of gigantism do not live long lives, but Maximinus died at age sixty-five in AD 238. He might have lived longer, but during his reign his popularity plummeted. Of humble origins, he hated Roman aristocrats and became paranoid and brutal. The public turned against him, taunting him with the nickname "Cyclops." During an unsuccessful siege, his soldiers mutinied. Maximinus was assassinated by his own Praetorian Guard as he slept on his immense cot in his big tent.

King Midas

GOLD AND BULL'S BLOOD

BEHIND THE TALE of the mythical King Midas with his "golden touch" and ears of an ass, there was a real King Midas. Midas appears in the records of the Assyrian Empire as "Mita of Mushki" (eighth century BC). The kingdom of Mushka (in Phrygia, west-central Turkey) reached its height under Midas. The kingdom's great wealth might have inspired the tragicomic Greek story of Midas and his wish for ever more riches, which became a curse. The story is one of many tales with the traditional folklore motif of a greedy plutocrat's divine comeuppance.

Archaeological excavation of the great royal tumulus at Gordion, Phrygia, constructed in about 700 BC, revealed the body of a powerful ruler, perhaps King Midas himself, who reigned in about 740 BC. The king was buried with fine wooden furniture and the remains of a lavish banquet. There was a beautiful inlaid table set with two hundred bronze dishes, cups, and plates, all containing residue of food and wine. A reconstruction of the king's face based on the skull found in the tomb is displayed in the Ankara Museum. In 2019, a Turkish farmer discovered a stele inscribed with ancient Luwian hieroglyphs in an irrigation canal. The stele announced

Tomb of Midas, king of Phrygia (738–695 BC), at Gordion, wood engraving, 1880s.
Interphoto / Alamy Stock Photo.

a victory by a Hittite army over the army of Midas of Mushka, further confirming that Midas was a historical king.

Many tales are told about Midas, drawn from a variety of Greek and Roman sources. In one tale, the king meets Silenos, oldest and wisest of all satyrs, lusty companions of Dionysos, god of wine. Satyrs were notorious for their wisdom and their love of wine. King Midas, eager to understand the meaning of life, spikes the fountain in his lovely rose garden with wine in the hope of luring a satyr. Midas manages to capture the venerable satyr Silenos when he comes to take a drink. For ten days, the king and the wise old satyr drink together and discuss the human condition.

The Roman poet Ovid adds a further twist to the story: Dionysos, grateful for the satyr's safe return, grants Midas a wish. The king wishes that everything he touches will turn to gold. At first Midas dashes about, exulting in his golden touch, tapping a twig, stone, clods of dirt, marble columns, and an apple, delighting in transforming them all to gold. But then he sits down to dinner and watches aghast as his bread and olives turn into golden lumps on a golden plate. As soon as his lips touch the wine, it becomes molten gold in a golden goblet.

Nathaniel Hawthorne's 1852 version took Ovid's story further and described how Midas's beloved daughter was transformed into a golden statue by her father's embrace. Tortured now by his world of gold, parched and starving, Midas begs the god's forgiveness. The king is finally cured of his golden touch by a plunge into the River Pactolus, whose stream has ever since carried gold sand. But that is not the last of Midas's legendary escapades.

One day Midas happens to be passing by when Pan and Apollo are holding a musical contest. Pan plays his rustic pipes and Apollo strums his refined lyre. All agree that Apollo's melody is sweeter—except for Midas, who pipes up in favor of Pan. Divine punishment is swift. Apollo causes the king's ears, so attuned to Pan's crude music, to become those of an ass, the ancient symbol of stupidity.

Anxious to hide his embarrassing disfigurement, Midas takes to wearing purple turbans. Only his barber knows what is under the royal headgear, and the barber is bursting to tell the secret. The man whispers the secret to the earth, which tells the reeds. The reeds reveal Midas's shameful secret whenever they rustle in the breeze.

A folklorist considering the tales surrounding the historical figure of Midas would note several common folk motifs: capturing a nature spirit with wine; contests between rival gods; the ill-advised wish that comes all too true. The ancient

Greeks' disapproval of autocratic Asian rulers and an aversion to extreme materialism certainly influenced the Midas legend. The Midas traditions expressed ambivalence about wealth and greed for Greek and Roman audiences over the centuries.

Aristotle (in the *Politics*) wrote that Midas died of starvation owing to his great greed. But Hyginus, a later Roman author, claimed that Midas committed suicide by drinking bull's blood. Here is a bit of a mystery. Other mythic figures were said to have died by drinking bull's blood. Examples include Jason's father, Aeson, and Helen of Troy, who contemplated suicide by bull's blood. Real historical people were rumored to have died by drinking bull's blood, too, such as Smerdis of Persia, Themistocles of Athens, the pharaoh Psamtik of Egypt, and Hannibal of Carthage. Was there any scientific reality underlying the belief that bull's blood was deadly to drink?

The ancients, from Aristotle to Pliny, had noticed that ox blood congealed more quickly than the blood of other animals. This observation led to the notion that drinking it would clog the throat and result in death by choking. In fact, drinking the blood of a bull would not be fatal, but it is interesting to note that quickly coagulating bovine thrombin (the blood-clotting enzyme) has been used in surgery since the 1800s. In fact, the quick-clotting bovine thrombin sometimes carries the risk of a "fatal cross reaction."

The Midas legend was a popular subject for Greek vase painters. The earliest example is a black-figure cup (about 560 BC), showing two hunters capturing a satyr labeled "Silenos" and a wineskin. Other vases depict Midas and Silenos in conversation. There is no known illustration of Midas wielding his golden touch, but his donkey ears are obvious on several fifth-century red-figure vases depicting the Phrygian king.

Home in a Body Bag

CLASSICAL PARALLELS FOR A PERSIAN GULF URBAN LEGEND

DURING THE 1991 GULF WAR and the 2003 Iraq War, many rumors and urban legends circulated, among Americans and Iraqis alike. During the US occupation of Iraq after Saddam Hussein's defeat in 2003, for example, some Iraqis believed that American soldiers' wraparound sunglasses gave them X-ray vision, and that their helmets and armored vests hid personal air-conditioning units. There were also Iraqi conspiracy theories that Saddam had been a CIA puppet. Meanwhile many Americans believed that their soldiers would be welcomed by flower-waving crowds of grateful Iraqis, and veterans told tales of giant man-eating camel spiders and Saddam's human-shredding machines.

As a classical folklorist, I was struck by the urban legend that circulated in March 1991, just after Saddam's defeat in the first Gulf War. The gruesome story about Saddam Hussein's response to an Iraqi woman who pleads for the return of her soldier husband was reported in *FOAFtale News* 22:8 (FOAF = Friend of a Friend, the typical method of perpetuating urban legends). The elements of the tale are remarkably similar to two separate incidents reported about two other rulers of Persia and Mesopotamia (Iran and Iraq) by the ancient Greek historian Herodotus, in the fifth century BC. The commentators on Herodotus, How and Wells (2:145) remarked in 1964 that the two "parallel" ancient stories in Herodotus have "the look of a legend." The stories' folklore status seems to be confirmed by the reappearance of such a similar tale immediately after the 1991 Gulf War, in the same geographic region.

About twenty-five hundred years ago, Herodotus (4.84) described the great Persian king Darius I's invasion of neighboring lands in 512 BC. Darius had ignored his advisers' arguments against the enterprise and commanded his vast army to march. A Persian man named Oeobazus approaches the king and says that his three sons are all in the army. He begs Darius to let one of them stay behind. According to Herodotus, "Darius, acting as though he is answering a modest request from a personal friend, assures the man that he will happily leave all three sons behind." The father is delighted. But Darius then "orders his officers to put all three young men to death. So the brothers were indeed left behind—with their throats cut."

In book 7 (39) Herodotus described the ill-fated invasion of Greece by the Persian king Xerxes in 480 BC. After amassing the greatest army in recorded history against the advice of his friends and advisers, Xerxes was approached by an old man whose five sons were in the army. He requests a small favor. Xerxes agrees, since the man had contributed great sums to the war effort. The man asks that his eldest son be released from service. Angered, Xerxes at once orders that the son be cut in half and the two halves be placed on opposite sides of the road, so the Persian troops could march out between them.

In a modern urban legend about the Gulf War, told in 1991, Saddam Hussein is the autocratic ruler. In a version of the story that circulated in Huntsville, Alabama, an Iraqi woman with starving kids approaches Saddam after one of his war speeches. She begs him to return her soldier husband home as soon as possible. Saddam listens patiently, then asks the man's name. He pats her gently on the shoulder and assures her that her plea will be answered soon. The very next day her husband is delivered to the front steps of her home, chopped into pieces and in a body bag.

All three stories are told by Westerners about a tyrannical Eastern despot (in each case, a ruler of Mesopotamia), who musters a large army to invade a neighboring land. Each ruler decides to invade after rejecting strong arguments against the plan, and all three military endeavors fail. In the two ancient versions, the fathers approach after the war deliberations, and the wife in the modern Gulf War version approaches "after one of [Saddam's] speeches." In the three tales, the person requests that a son or husband serving in the army "be left behind," "released from service," or "returned back home as soon as possible."

In each case, the cruel ruler seems to agree to grant the plea. But then he deliberately misconstrues the request, in good folklore fashion, by taking the wording too literally. The sons are left behind but with throats cut; the eldest boy is released from service but sliced in two; the husband is returned home but "chopped into pieces." Interestingly, cutting and chopping figure in all three versions, and the rulers' orders are carried out swiftly and publicly.

In their commentary on Xerxes's order that the army march out between the halves of the bisected boy's body, How and Wells point out that it was a Persian custom to protect people from harm by having them "pass between two parts of a sacrificed animal" (compare Genesis 15.10–17 and Jeremiah 34.18–19). The more valuable the victim, the stronger the protection. The anxiety produced by Xerxes's decision to invade with huge forces, against expert—and perhaps popular—opinion, might lend support to the "propitiatory sacrifice" motive for cutting the boy in half.

But it is significant that the same anxieties applied to the circumstances of Darius's war and Saddam's invasion, which occurred decades earlier and centuries later, respectively. Notably, all three tales are *postwar* stories, told by Westerners about authoritarian foreign leaders of doomed invasions in the Middle East. The fact that the victims are the rulers' own subjects is also important, since all three versions circulated, and probably originated, in Western societies. An interesting contrast to these stories is recounted in the 1998 war film *Saving Private Ryan*, loosely based on a true story, in which the US Army works to save a family's last remaining son after the first three brothers have died in action in World War II.

The recurrence of the ancient legend in the aftermath of the 1991 Gulf War demonstrates the perceived nature of dictatorship, and the relationship between the ruler and the ruled, from the points of view of modern Americans and ancient Greeks. These three stories were told among people who considered themselves free citizens of a democracy, in contrast to the enslaved subjects of an absolute ruler, whose arbitrary power led him to slaughter his own people while pursuing an unjust war.

CHAPTER 50

Perfumes of Power

THE SCENT OF LEADERS

"BUCEPHALUS," A MEN'S FRAGRANCE launched in 2020 by Armaf Niche, is named for the magnificent stallion who accompanied Alexander the Great from his boyhood in Macedonia to his conquest of India. One of the most renowned war horses in history, Bucephalus attained legendary status. He is said to have sired countless foals and fillies in his long career from Macedonia across Eurasia until his death in Punjab, in 326 BC, where the great steed was buried with honors in a city named for him. Warm, spicy, and ozonic, Bucephalus cologne is redolent of pepper, ginger, amber, saddle leather, and apples, a fitting tribute for such a noble equine celebrity.

In his biography of Alexander the Great, Plutarch claimed that Alexander's body naturally emitted a pleasant, honeyed fragrance enjoyed by his closest companions. Historians reported that when Alexander defeated the Persian king Darius in 333 BC, he discovered a casket of precious perfumes in his enemy's royal tent and tossed them aside with disdain. But over the next few years as he made more conquests across Asia, Alexander grew fond of lovely perfumes, sprinkling his floors with aromatic flower petals and spices, and he often burned myrrh, frankincense, and other fragrant resins to perfume his tent (see chapter 21).

The powerful ruler of Egypt Queen Cleopatra (69–30 BC) took a keen interest in perfumes. She not only maintained a large perfume-making laboratory near the Dead Sea, but she wrote a famous recipe book for perfumes and cosmetics, now lost but often quoted by ancient writers. Romans of the Republic were not yet connoisseurs of fine perfumes, but Cleopatra's lovers Julius Caesar and Mark Antony fell under her spell, enhanced by strangely seductive, exotic fragrances that suffused her body, clothing, palaces, and ships—even the sails of her ships were drenched in perfumes. (See chapter 27 for her fishing expedition with Mark Antony.) An amusing scene in the HBO TV series *Rome* (2005) has Cleopatra sniffing the rough Roman soldier Lucius Vorenus before inviting him to her bed: "Leather! Olive Oil! Not bad!"

By the time of the Roman Empire, Roman elites were enthusiastically awash in fabulous perfumes made from sweet- and spicy-smelling flowers, seeds, roots, and resins from plants and minerals of Africa, Asia, and Arabia (see chapter 1). Costly perfumes from afar served as personal and public propaganda demonstrating imperial power. Nero (AD 37–68), for example, bathed in rose-infused wine, dusted his feet with perfume, slept on a bed of rose petals, and filled his fountains with rose water—and he demanded that those around him do the same. Nero spent a fortune on perfumes, piping scented water into his palaces and misting his guests with refreshing fragrances. But it was the notoriously decadent emperor Elagabulus (AD 204–22) who anticipated the modern rise of celebrity perfumes marketed to the masses. Elagabulus and his courtiers bathed in a large pool filled with wine and perfume and then bottled their bathwater and distributed it to the Roman plebs as a special gift.

Long before the discovery of pheromones and their role in sexual attraction, handkerchiefs suffused with perfumes or the odorous bodily essence of the beloved were treasured keepsakes. It was said that Henry VIII, for example, kept a handkerchief in his armpit and presented this perspiration-infused token to women he fancied as a flirtation ploy.

The notion that an intoxicating smell of power and success wafts from the bodies of alpha males continues today. A new men's fragrance went on sale in Moscow's luxury department stores in January 2015. Called "Leaders Number One," the cologne was inspired by Vladimir Putin. The creation of perfumer Vladislav Rekunov, Putin's power scent comes in a sleek black flask decorated with the Russian autocrat's distinctive profile. Selling for about six thousand rubles for 3.3 ounces (about eighty-two dollars in 2021), the fragrance is described by *Business Insider* and others as "firm but not aggressive, warm, down-to-earth, and natural." Reuters, on the other hand, reported that it reeked of "cheap perfume." *Gentlemen's Quarterly* joked that the scent of raw meat and grizzly bear would be more appropriate. Smelling of pinecones, lemons, bergamot, musk, black currants, and mung beans, the cologne is intended to reflect Putin's personality, if not his personal body odor.

Donald Trump had marketed his own celebrity scent in 2004. "Trump," a woody aromatic with cucumber, mint, and pepper notes, was followed by an eau de toilette spray called "Success," launched in 2011 and advertised thus: "Donald Trump represents the quintessential American success story to many, and his name could be considered a brand of its own.

Fragrances inspired by Bucephalus, Putin, and Trump.

The famed real estate developer, deal-maker, business magnate, television personality and celebrity introduces his new fragrance, appropriately named Success. The classy masculine juice is housed in a simple bottle."

Trump's third fragrance, "Empire by Trump" (notes of apple, musk, tonka bean) was launched during his presidential campaign in 2015, selling for about eight dollars an ounce. Trump's perfumes for men were concocted by master perfumers Annie Buzantian and Yann Vasnier. The website Fragrantica® Trends tracks popular interest in perfumes. Their graph shows that interest in "Empire by Trump" peaked in January 2017 and plunged in November 2017, never to recover. A similar fate was met by Putin's fragrance: interest spiked, then plunged by July 2015, with a brief flare in 2017, and it has flatlined ever since.

Meanwhile, a venerable Soviet revolutionary perfume made a surprising comeback in 2010 and is still going strong in 2022. Widely popular in Russia, "Red Moscow" (Krasnaya

Moskva, Moscou Rouge), was created by Auguste Michel for Henri Brocard's perfumery in Moscow, which was nationalized and given the Soviet name "New Dawn" in the 1920s. The launch date of the perfume is debated—was it 1917 or 1925? The fragrance, still sold on Nikolskaya Street in Moscow, is described by Fragrantica as "rife with emotional associations," emitting "cool, almost metallic notes and floral and woody accords, pleasantly hefty and a bit tangy."

Today's men can select masculine, apolitical colognes named "Egoiste," or "For Him" by Narciso Rodriguez, described as smelling "like cement but in a good way." A more outré choice would be Antoine Lie's "Secretions Magnifique" launched by Etat Libre D'Orange in 2006, reputed to have olfactory hints of blood, seaweed, milk, iodine, sweat, and semen. It is described by reviewer-noses at Fragrantica as "piercingly metallic," "picked scab," "sour milk," "vulgar," "rust," "repulsive yet attractive." After its initial launch in 2006 popularity was flat until it suddenly took off in 2020.

It is unknown whether Trump dabs himself with his own celebrity colognes. Putin reportedly prefers the cologne called "Tsar," said to smell "seductive and exhilarating," with notes of leather, caraway, juniper, and musk. Tsar was released by Van Cleef and Arpels in 1989, during the collapse of the Soviet Union. Russian perfumist Anna Askarova describes Tsar cologne as "the scent of responsibility."

With such a venerable history, and the bold debuts of Trump and Putin colognes, is the world ready for more essences inspired by male heads of state in the "Leaders Number One" perfume line and other celebrity scents? The possibilities are heady.

NOTES

Page

25 Greek and Latin translations in this and other chapters are generally based on those in Loeb volumes. Sources: Herodotus 2.59, 2.63, 2.75, 2.155, 3.107–10. Aelian, *On Animals* 2.38, 16.41. Strabo 15.1.37, 16.4.19. Isaiah 6.2.6, 14.29, 30.6; Deuteronomy 1–11. Pliny 11.30. Cicero, *De natura deorum* 101. Josephus, *Jewish Antiquities* 2.10.2. Pomponius Mela, *De chorographia* 3.82. Solinus, *Mirabilibus mundi* 32.32–33. Ammianus Marcellinus, *Rerum gestarum* 22.15.25–26. Phlegon of Tralles, *Book of Marvels* 15. Further reading: Karen Radner, "The Winged Snakes of Arabia and the Fossil Site of Makhtesh Ramon in the Negev," *Wiener Zeitschrift für die Kunde des Morgenlandes* 97 (2007): 353–65. William Ayers Ward, "The Four-Winged Serpent on Hebrew Seals," *Revista degli studi orientali* 43, 2 (1968): 35–43.

36 Further reading: Daniel Ogden, *The Dragon in the West: From Ancient Myth to Modern Legend* (Oxford: Oxford University Press, 2021).

40 Further reading: A. Okrostsvaridze, N. Gagnidze, and K. Akimidze, "A Modern Field Investigation of the Mythical 'Gold Sands' of the Ancient Colchis Kingdom and 'Golden Fleece' Phenomena," *Quaternary International* 409, pt. A (2016): 61–69.

58 Our voyage on the glamorous *Sea Cloud I*, the private ocean-sailing yacht originally built for Marjorie Merriweather Post in 1931, was thanks to an invitation from Robert and Callie Connor and the National Humanities Center, in the summer of 1996. Further reading: Craig A. Williams, "When a Dolphin Loves a Boy: Some Greco-Roman and Native American Love Stories," *Classical Antiquity* 32, 1 (2013): 200–242.

74 Ancient sources: Aelian, *On Animals* 4.36, 4.41; Ctesias frag. 57.17; Aristotle, *On Plants* 820.6–7; Pliny 10.33, 25.3–7, 29.5; Nicander *Thēriaca* ("Antidotes against Poisonous Bites") and *Alexipharmaca* ("Antidotes"); Aulus Gellius, *Attic Nights* 17.16; Philo, *Geoponics* 14.24 and *Special Laws* 4.120–31; Lucretius, *On the Nature of Things* 4.639–40; Galen, *De temperamentis* 3.4; and Sextus Empiricus, *Outlines of Pyrrhonism* 1.57; Exodus 16.11–12; Numbers 11.31–34. Maimonides, *Commentary Epidemiarum* 6.5; Ibn Sina, *The Canon* 2.2.2.5; Qazwiny, *Kitab Aga'il* 2.250 also described coturnism. Further reading: *Dikai-ron*: W. Geoffrey Arnott, *Birds in the Ancient World from A to Z* (London: Routledge, 2007), 37. Pederin: J. H. Frank and K. Kanamitsu, "Paederus, Sensu Lato (Coleoptera: Staphylinidae): Natural History and Medical Importance," *Journal of Medical Entomology* 24, 2 (March 1987): 155–91. Avian toxicity: R. Ligabue-Braun and C. Regina Carlini, "Poisonous Birds: A Timely Review," *Toxicon* 99 (June 2015): 102–8.

111 In 2013, legislation was introduced, while Arnold Schwarzenegger was governor, to allow ferrets, which had been banned since 1933 in California. But as of 2022, pet ferrets are still illegal in California. Ferrets are legal in New York State, but in 2002 Mayor Michael Bloomberg defended Guiliani's ban on ferrets in Manhattan. Mayor Bill de Blasio recommended lifting the ban in 2014, but New York City's Board of Health voted to maintain the ban in 2015.

153 Further reading: "F Is for Fake," *New Scientist*, February 19, 2000; "Fake Trilobites" by Jens Koppka, Heiko Sonntag, and Horst Burkard, 2003, https://timevaultgallery.com/fake-trilobites-how-to-identify/.

161 Thanks to Philippe Taquet and Dan Edelstein for help in deciphering Cuvier's notes. Further reading: M. Michael Adams, "XXIII. Some account of a journey to the frozen sea, and of the discovery of the remains of a mammoth" (translated from the French}, *Philosophical Magazine*, ser. 1, 29 (1807): 114, 141–53. Louise E. Robbins, *Elephant Slaves and Pampered Parrots: Exotic Animals in Eighteenth-Century Paris* (Baltimore: Johns Hopkins University Press, 2002).

165 Many editions are available of *Geronimo, My Life, as Told to S. M. Barrett* (New York: Duffield, 1906). For more Apache fossil-related traditions, see my book *Fossil Legends of the First Americans* (Princeton, NJ: Princeton University Press, 2005), 161–63.

175 David Julius and Ardem Patapoutian received the 2021 Nobel Prize in Medicine for discovering the chemical process for temperature receptors.

249 Astronomer Andrew T. Young has compiled an amazing resource for the history of atmospheric physics: an ongoing annotated bibliography (seven hundred pages so far) of descriptions of atmospheric refractions, green flashes, and mirages, from antiquity up to the present, available online here: https://aty.sdsu.edu/bibliog/who.html.

271 Further reading: Arthur Boylston, "The Origins of Inoculation," *Journal of the Royal Society of Medicine* 105, 7 (2012): 309–13.

281 For an alternative cause of the Pythia's altered state, see William Broad, *The Oracle: The Lost Secrets and Hidden Message of Ancient Delphi* (New York: Penguin Press, 2006), describing archaeologist John Hale's discovery of toxic fumes emanating from the earth at Delphi.

285 For more on nineteenth-century foot fetishists, see Charlotte Ribeyrol, "'The Feet of Love': Pagan Podophilia from A. C. Swinburne to Isadora Duncan," *Miranda* [online] 11 (2015). On ancient podophilia, Daniel B. Levin, "ERATON BAMA ('Her Lovely Footstep'): The Erotics of Feet in Ancient Greece," in *Body Language in the Greek and Roman Worlds*, edited by D. Cairns (Swansea: Classical Press of Wales, 2006), 55–72.

336 Further reading: Tony Perrottet, *Pagan Holiday* (New York: Random House, 2009); Fernando García Romero, "Sports Tourism in Ancient Greece," *Journal of Tourism History* 5, 2 (2013): 146–60.

353 Further reading: Francis Gribble, *The Early Mountaineers* (Unwin, 1899).

362 Further reading: Lars Krutak and Aaron Deter-Wolf, *Ancient Ink: The Archaeology of Tattooing* (Seattle: University of Washington Press, 2020); A. Mayor, "Skin: Tattooed Amazons," chapter 6, in *The Amazons: Lives and Legends of Warrior Women across the Ancient World* (Princeton, NJ: Princeton University Press, 2014).

374 Further reading: Aloys Winterling, *Caligula, a Biography* (2003, in German, English translation University of California Press, 2011).

377 Further reading: Paul Pearson, *Maximinus Thrax: From Common Soldier to Emperor of Rome* (New York: Skyhorse, 2017).

CREDITS

SOME ESSAYS grew out of brief sketches for the Wonders and Marvels history of science website, active 2011–17. Chapter 2 is a revised, expanded version of "A Triton Pulled My Leg: Greek Mermaids and Sea Monsters," *The Athenian*, September 1985; reprinted in *Archaeology Odyssey*, March–April 2002. Chapter 5 expands on "Delfinia!" in *The Athenian*, May 1986. Chapter 6 is a revised version of "The Musical Racing Turtles of Greece," *The Athenian*, December 1989. Chapter 9 is a longer version of "Pet Birds through the Centuries," *Bird Talk*, May 1987. Chapter 10 draws in part on "Dog Food before Gravy Train," *Sports Afield*, September 1984. Parts of chapter 11 appeared in "Grecian Weasels," *The Athenian*, February 1989, reprinted in *Omnibus* 25 (January 1993); and *Modern Ferret: The Ferret Lifestyle Magazine* 3, 3 (1995). Parts of chapter 12 appeared in "The Modern Ferret Lifestyle," *Weekly Hubris*, May 2017. Chapter 13 is a revised version of "Colossal Fossils, Part 1," *The Athenian*, October 1983. Chapter 14, "Hunting Griffins," appeared in the literary journal *Southeastern Review*, Spring 1990. Chapter 16 is inspired by "The Folklore of Dinosaur Trackways in China: Impact on Paleontology," by Lida Xing, Adrienne Mayor, Y. Chen, J. Harris, and M. Burns, in the journal of trace fossils, *Ichnos* 18 (2011): 213–20. Some sections of chapter 20 appeared in "Slaves First Identified Elephant Fossils in America," *Weekly Hubris*, July 14, 2020. Chapter 21 draws in part on my interview on cannabis and Scythian warrior women with Colleen Fisher Tully for *Leafly*, August 5, 2020. Chapters 24 and 25 appeared as "Did Amazons Roam in Ancient Rome?" and "Especially in the Use of Weapons: Plato and the Amazons," respectively, in *Antigone*, October and March 2021. Chapter 30 is a revised version of "Libation Titillation," *Studies in Popular Culture* 16, 2 (April 1994): 61–71. Chapter 31 revises and updates "Derelict Ships," *Sea Frontiers* (International Oceanographic Foundation/Nature America) 38, 4 (August 1992); reprinted in *Mariners Weather Log*, 1992. Chapter 31 is an updated version of "Marine Mirages," *Sea Frontiers* 34 (1988); reprinted in Grolier's *Popular Science* annual (1989) and *Mariners Weather Log*, 1993. Chapter 33 is a revised and updated rendering of "Blowing in the Wind," *The Athenian*, February 1987. Chapter 37 appeared as "Mad Honey," *Archaeology*, November–December 1995. Chapter 39 is a revised version of "Giants in Ancient Warfare," *MHQ: The Quarterly Journal of Military History* 2, 2 (1999): 98–105. Parts of chapter 40 appeared in different form in "Pacesetter," *London Review of Books* 32, 12 (June 24, 2010): 30–31. Chapter 41 appeared as "The Travels of Ancient Tourists," *The Athenian*, August 1987. Portions of chapter 42 come from "Grand Tourists from Cyriac of Ancona to Sigmund Freud," *The Athenian*, August 1988; reprinted in *Chandris Hotels Magazine*, Summer 1992. Chapter 44 is a revised version of "People Illustrated," *Archaeology*, March–April 1999. Chapter 48 expands on my "Legendary Midas" sidebar for *Archaeology*, July–August 2001. Chapter 49 updates and revises "Home in a Body Bag," *FOAFtale News* 24 (December 1991).

INDEX

Note: Page numbers in *italic* type indicate illustrations.

Abenaki Indians, 155

Abishai, 291–92

Abkhazians, 37

acetylandromedol, 275

Achilles, 33, 59–60, 187, 191

Acosta, José de, 350

Acrisius (Argive king), 263

acromegaly. *See* gigantism

Acropolis, Athens, 254, 328, 339, 344, 346–48

Adams, Michael Friedrich, 158–59

Aeacus, 33

Aegina, 60–61

Aelian: Dikairon, 68, 74; flying snakes, 15–16, 22; fossils, 122; Griffins, 7, 128; military tactics, 312; talking birds, 82; turtles, 66; weasels, 93, 97

Aeneas, 187–89, 311

Aeolian harp, 260

Aeolos, 250, 256–57

A. Ernest Mills (schooner), 232

Aeschylus, 63, 129

Aeson, 381

Aesop: Boreas, 252; dolphin and monkey, 54; tortoise and hare, 59; weasels, 94–95, 97

Aetius, 357

Africa, 16, 22, 27, 46, 69, 72, 73, 82, 98, 114, 115, 168, 257, 306, 307, 311. *See also* Carthage; enslaved Africans

Agamemnon, 257

albatross, 233

Alcmene, 95–96

Alexander of Myndus, 76

Alexander the Great, 53, 90, 120, 189, 204–7, 239, 292–94, 372, 386–87

Amanirenas (Nubian queen), 189

Amarant, 304

Amazons: Ares worshipped by, 200; Athenians vs., 188; battle skills of, 176, 193, 194–96; beauty secrets of, 174–79; characteristics of, 193; clothing of, 173; debates over existence of, 205, 209–12; Dionysos's slaughter of, 119;

Amazons (*continued*)
Herodotus's accounts of,
192; images of, 173, *199*, 200,
209–10; Plato and, 194–97; as
single-breasted, 210; in Trojan
War, 187–88, 206; in Virgil's
Aeneid, 187, 189–93
Ambrones, 75, 298–300
Ambrose, John T., 276
Ament, Lady, 361
American Museum, New York, 160
American Museum of Natural
History, New York, 84, 247
American School of Classical
Studies, Athens, xiii, 5–7,
119–20, 122, 125, 130, 134
Amman, Jost, 218–20
Ammianus Marcellinus, 22, 183,
294–95, 303
Amphitrite, 53
Anakim, 289
Ancylotherium, 114, 123
Andrea Doria (ship), 235
Andrews, Roy Chapman, 137–38
Andromeda, 263
andromedetoxin, 275
Andronikos of Kyrrhos, 250
Anemone, 255, 261
Angelucci (priest), 236–37, 244
Antaeus, 287
Antarctica, 245–46, 248
Anthony, Saint, 239–40
Antiope (Amazon queen), 187
Anti-Vaccine Society, 269
Antony, Mark, 201–3, 282, 323,
328, 387

Apeliotes (East Wind), 254
apes, 112, 113, 115, 123, 147
Aphrodite, 95, 199, 284. *See also*
Venus (goddess)
Apollo, 64, 221, 261–62, 278, 333,
380
Apollonius of Rhodes,
Argonautica, 37
Appian, 38, 312
Apsyrtos, 37
Arabia: flying snakes in, 13–25,
18; legends of, 41, 229, 352;
winds, 257
Arab warrior queens, 180–82
archaeology: Amazons, 197, 209;
ancient giants, 289, 296, 377;
author's encounters with, 3,
5–6, 130; Caligula's riches,
372; Carthage, 309–10, 314–
16; Cyriac as father of, 337–38;
fossils, 152–53; Griffins, 118,
125, 132, 134–35; Midas, 378;
Scythians, 135–37, 359–60;
turtles, 63–64; vapor baths,
177; weasels, 98–99. *See also*
paleontology
Archaeology (magazine), 2, 3, 6–7
Archaeoraptor, 149, 151
Arctic, 244–48
Ares, 200
Areus (Spartan king), 200
Argos/Argive women, 198–200
Arion of Lesbos, 52
Aristeas, 7, 128
Aristaeus, 258
Aristogoras, 355

Aristophanes, 50, 93
Aristotle: Carthage, 310; dogs, 91; dolphins, 51; fossils, 122; *History of Animals*, 264; imagination, 124; Midas, 381; mirages, 240; physiognomy, 264; poisonous creatures, 69–70, 71; *Politics*, 310, 381; portraits of, 338; sea monsters, 28–29; wind, 260, 262
Armaf Niche, 386
Arrian, 90, 294
arrows, poisoned, 69
Arruns, 191
Artabanes (Persian king), 292
art deco, 217
Artemis. *See* Diana
Arthur (legendary king), 304
art nouveau, 217, 306
Asclepius, 329
Askarova, Anna, 390
asses, 181
Assyria, 17
Atalanta, 89, 193
Athena, 254
Athenaeus, 312
The Athenian (magazine), xiii, 4, 6, 395, 396
Athens/Athenians: Acropolis, 254, 328, 339, 344, 346–48; Aegina conquered by, 61; Amazons vs., 188; and Boreas, 252–53; defeat of Persians by, 61; dolphin anecdote about, 54; Parthenon, 334, 335, 338, 340, 345–47; tourism in, 324,

327–28, 332, 344–48; Tower of the Winds, 250–55, *251*, 346; winds in, 252–56
Attilius Regulus, 30
Augustine, Saint, 312, 352
Augustus (Roman emperor), 98, 124, 192, 328–29, 370–71, 373
Aunus, 189, *190*
Austin, Anne, 361–62
avian toxicity, 68–74
Avvim, 289
Axolotl VIII (fictional Mexican king), 220
azaleas, 274, 275, 277, 279–80
Aztecs, 82
Azwar, Dhiraar bin al-, 181–82
Azwar, Khawlah bint al-, 181–82, *182*

Baal, 311, 312, 315–16, 319
Bacchantes, 217
Balsdon, J.V.P.D., 302
Baluchitherium, 137
Barents, Willem, 245
Barnum, P. T., 27
Barrett, Stephen Melvil, 163–64
Barton, Benjamin, 276, 278
Baruch, book of, 292
Bate, Dorothea, 116
bats, 14, 19, 24
Batten, Lord, 81
Beardsley, Aubrey, 307
Beaufort scale, 261–62
Bebop (parakeet), 78
Beck, Horace, 235
Bede, Venerable, 42

bee-oracles, 279–80
bees, 5, 71, 262, 272, 274. *See also* honey
beetles, poisonous, 69–70, 73–74
Bee World (magazine), 275
Behn, Aphra, 208
Benaiah, 291
Benaki Museum, Athens, 340
Beowulf, 141
Bergen, Edgar, 85
Beringer, Johann, 147, *150*
betel nuts, 69
Beulé, Charles, 309
Bible. *See* Old Testament
Biddle, Nicholas, 341
Bill and Coo (film), 86
Binder, Judith, 130
Bindi (cat), 111
Bion of Borysthenes, 356
Birdcage Walk, St. James Park, London, 80
The Birdman of Alcatraz (film), 85
birds: anecdotes about talking, 78, 80–82, 87; author's, 78; banding of, 75–77, *76*; exotic, 80; honors given to, 84; inappropriate language from, 81–82; lifestyles of rich and famous, 84–85; in literature, 78–79, 86; as messengers, 77, 83–84; in the movies, 85–86; as pets, 78–87; poisonous, 68–74; of royalty, 82–83; as speakers of lost languages, 87
The Birds (film), 85
bison, 111, 116, 169

Black Death, 229
black ibises, 15–16, 22
Blade Runner (film), 62
Blaine, Mahlon, 307, *308*, 309
Blanche (ferret), 109–11
blister beetles, 70, 73
Blondie (band), 101
Blue-Capped Ifrita, 73
bluefin tuna, 203
Boccara, V. E., 239
Bol, Manute, 288
Bora (Northeast Wind), 253
Borchgrevink, Carsten, 248
Boreas (North Wind), 251–53, 254, 258, 260
Boston Museum, 27
Boudicca (British queen), 183, 297
Brassicaceae mustard, 174–75
breasts, drinking vessels associated with, 2–3, 213–21
British Museum, 41, 46, 47, 90, 116
Britons, 294, 297, 358
Brocard, Henri, 390
Bryas, 200
Bucephalus, 386, *389*
Buddhism, 349
buffalo, 46
bull's blood, 381
Burton, Robert, 218
Buto, 16–17, 19, 23
Buzantian, Annie, 389
Byron, Lord, 55, 140, 254, 260, 337, 339–41, 343–45; "The Maid of Athens," 341

cabbage, 174–75

Cabinet des Médailles, Paris, 44, 48

cabinets of curiosities, 27, 43, 49, 148

Caesar, Julius, 294–96, 329, 387

Calais, 252

Caligula (film), 369

Caligula (Roman emperor), 356, 369–74, *370*

Cambrensis, Giraldus, 240–41

Camilla, 187, 189–93, *190*

Campbell, Arthur, 168–69

canaries, 79–80

cannabis, 69, 136, 176–78

Cape Matapan, 52

capsaicin, 175

Carthage: archaeology of, 309–10, 314–16; child sacrifice in, 309, 312, 315–16; culture of, 317–19; Flaubert's *Salammbô* and, 306–14, 319–20; and Hercules/Heracles, 317; maritime expeditions and trade of, 317–19; Mercenary Revolt, 311–12, 313, 315; Rome and, 306–7, 310, 311, 313–14, 316–17, 319–20

cassia, 14

Catesby, Mark, 166–67

Catherine of Portugal, 80

cats: author's, 111; Egyptian, 92, 108; folklore about, 96; as pets, 92–93, 99

Catullus (Roman poet), 78

Catulus (Roman general), 301

Caulon/Caulonia, 188

cedar, 178

Celts, 42, 183, 293–97, 299, 302, 303, 357. *See also* Gauls

Centaurs, 124

Center for Hellenic Studies, Washington, DC, 131–32

Chalicotherium, 123

champagne glasses, 213–17, 220

Champlin, Caroline, *Life Blood*, 107

Chapman, J., portrait of Thalestris, queen of the Amazons, *205*

Charlemagne the Great, 41, 44–47, 49, 303

Charles I (English king), 339

Charles II (English king), 80, 204, 207, 219

Charles the Bald, 46, 49

Charlie McCarthy (dummy), 85

Charlotte (parrot), 83

Chateaubriand, François-René de, 341, 342

Ch'en, 70

child sacrifice, 309, 312, 315–16

China: dinosaur footprints in, *144*; foot binding in, 284–85; fossil forgery in, 148–49, 152; fossils in, 141; medicine, 70, mountain journeys in, 349–51; rhinoceroses in, 143–46; and tattoos, 360, 363–68; variolation in, 268

Chiomara, 183–86, *185*

Choresine beetles, 73

Christians, tattooing of, 356, 358
Cicero: Carthage, 312; flying snakes, 22; Greek tours of, 327, 332, 334; physiognomy of Socrates, 265
Cimbri, 75, 294, 297, 298, 301–2, 304
Circassians, 37
Circe, 37
Clark, William, 169
Clarke, Edward, 344
Claudian, 358
Claudius (Roman emperor), 292, 334, 373–74
Cleomenes (Spartan king), 198
Cleopatra, 201–3, 282, 323, 328, 387
cobras, 15, 19–21, *20*, 25
cocktails/cocktail dresses, 220
Cocktel (fictional Mexican princess), 220
Coeranus, 54, 57
coffee, 342
Colbrand, 304
Colchis, 38–40, 272
Coleridge, Samuel Taylor, 244; "Kubla Khan," 244; *The Rime of the Ancient Mariner*, 233, 244
colewort, 174–75
Colossus of Rhodes, 329–30
Columbus, Christopher, 82
Columella, 89, 298
Conan Doyle, Arthur, 32–33
Conklin, John, 142
Connor, Robert and Callie, 391n58
Constantine the Great, 258, 356
Conway, Martin, 49

Corinna, 78
Cornelius, Saint, 46–47
Cos, 329
Cotton, Robert Bruce, 48
coturnism, 72–73
coupes (glasses), 215–17, 221
Cowper, William, 79
cowpox, 267, 269
Crabbe, George, 81
Craven, Lady, 345
Crete, 34, 116, 153, 253, 269
Cripps, John, 344
Crocker Land, 246–47
crocodiles, 31
Croker Mountains, 246
Crusades, 43, 236, 258, 337
cryptozoology, 133–34
Cryptozoology (journal), 6
Ctesias, 68, 74, 128
cups. *See* drinking vessels
Cuthbert, Saint, 41–43, 47–48
Cuvier, Georges, 154–61, 167, 169
Cyclops, 121, 287
cypress, 178
Cyprus, 133–34
Cyriac of Ancona, 337–38
Cyrus the Great, 189

Dahoul (pirate), 229
Dames, Wilhelm, 113
Damostratos, 27, 28
Danae, 263
Darius (Persian king), 355, 383, 385, 386
David (Israelite king), 260, 286, *287*, 291–92

Dawson, Charles, 147–48
Dead Sea Scrolls, 289
Defoe, Daniel, *Robinson Crusoe*, 86
Dei Gratia (ship), 230
Deklugie, Asa, 163–64
Delphi, Delphic Oracle, 53, 263,
    272, 278, 280, 330, 332, 339,
    342, 343, 393n281
"Delphinokoritso" (song), 36
Demosthenes, 324, 327
Denise (ferret), 101–6, *102*
derelicts (abandoned ships),
    225–26, 230–35
desert long-eared bats, 19
Diana, 191, 192–93, 284
Dickens, Charles, 84
Dido, 187, 311
Dikairon, 68–70, 74
Dinotherium, 114, 123
Dio Cassius, 297
Diodorus of Sicily (Diodorus
    Siculus), 183, 240, 294–95, 312
Dionysius, 53
Dionysos, 52, 119, 122, 221, 273,
    280, 328, 334, 335, 379
Dioscorides, 275
discus, 261–63
Disney, Walt, 85
Divine Lucky Rhinoceros, 143–
    46, *146*
Dog and Cat Painter, 99
dogbane, 279
dogs: barking, 91; choosing, 88;
    feeding, 90–91; Greek image
    of, *89*; hunting, 31, 88, 99, 129,
    325; naming, 89–90; as pets,

99; physical characteristics of,
    88; treatment of, 90
dolphins: fishers' use of, 55; love
    of music, 50–52, *51*, 57–58;
    name of, 50; rescues by, 51–
    57; sociability of, 51, 54–58;
    trained, 56
dragonflies, 21–22
Dragon of Klagenfurt, 131
dragons: fake fossils of, 149; fossils
    as models for, 131, 141–42, *142*;
    in Germanic/Norse legends,
    140–42; Geronimo and, 164–
    65; sea monsters as, 29–31
drinking vessels, breasts
    associated with, 213–21
Drisko (schooner), 232
Druillet, Philippe: *Salammbô,
    Carthage, Matho* (trilogy),
    307; *Salammbô: Battle for
    Carthage* (video game), 307
Dryden, John, 204
Duan Chengshi, *Youyang Zazu*, 365
ducks, poisonous, 71
Duffy's Tavern (radio show), 85
dung beetles, 69
Durham Cathedral, 41, 43, 48
The Dying Gaul (sculpture), 297

eagles, 63
East India Company, 80
Edes, Samuel Barrett, 27
eels, 31, 32
Egypt/Egyptians: cats in, 92, 108;
    crocodiles in, 31; fishing scene
    in, *202*; flying snakes in, 13–25,

Egypt/Egyptians (*continued*) *18*; giants in, 287–88; physical stature of, 288; tattoos of, 361–62

Egyptian Execration Texts, 289

Egyptian foot, 282–83

Elagabulus (Roman emperor), 219, 387–88

Eleazar, 292

elephants: ancestors of, 113, 114, 123, 154–55, 158, 166–69; ancient habitats of, 115, 116, 145; Dionysos and, 119, 122; exoticism of, 46, 129; foot, 155, 160; fossils of, 116, 122; military use of, 293, 311, 318; in United States, 160–61. *See also* mammoths; mastodons

Elgin, Lady, 343, 345

Elgin, Lord, 334, 339, 340, 343

Elhanan, 291

Elijah, 349

Elizabeth II (English queen), 83

Ellingsen, Kris, 7–8, 117

Elytis, Odysseas, 36

Embirikos, Andreas, 57–58

Empedocles, 122, 349

Empire (fragrance), 389, *389*

Enalus, 53

Encyclopedia Britannica, 274

En no Ozunu (En no Gyoja), 349–50

enslaved Africans, 80, 155, 166–69, 267–68

HMS *Erebus*, 226, 246

Ericaceae, 275–76, 279

Esarhaddon, 17, 23

Etat Libre D'Orange, 390

Etesian winds, 254, 258, 259

Eucharides Painter, 99

Euphronios Painter, 99

Euripides, 50, 280, 327

Euroclydon (Northeast Wind), 253, 259

Euros (Southeast Wind), 254

Eusebius, 312

excrement. *See* poop

Exodus, book of, 72

Fafnir, 140–42

fairy isles/castles, 241–43, 248

Fannie E. Wolston (schooner), 225

Fata Morgana, 236–39

feces. *See* poop

Fénelon, Philippe, 306

Ferdinand, King of Aragon, 82

Fermor, Patrick, 57

Ferragus, 303

ferret-legging, 104–5

ferrets. *See* weasels/ferrets

Ferrill, Arther, 299

Finch, Anne, 208

Finlay, George, 113

Fischer, Henry, 288

Fisher, Gwendolyn, 213–14, *214*

Flaubert, Gustave, 84, 346; *Madame Bovary*, 309; *Salammbô*, 4, 306–14, *308*, 319–20

Flora, 254

Florus, 184, 296

flutes (glasses), 215–17

flutes (musical instruments), 34–35, 50, *51*, 52

Flying Dutchman (ship), 226–27, 229–30

flying snakes: appearance of, 14; explanations of, 18–25; habitat of, 13, 16–17, *18*; Herodotean account of, 13–14; images of, 19–20, *20*; post-Herodotean accounts of, 21–22; predators of, 15–16; pre-Herodotean accounts of, 17; reproductive life of, 14

Folklore (journal), 6

foot fetishism, 282–85, 328

Forbes, Patrick, 216–17

fossils: ancient accounts of, 5–6; author's research into, 119–39; in China, 141, 143–46; dragons linked to, 131, 141–42, *142*; fake, 147–53; in Germany, 141; in Greece, 113–16, 119–26, 135, 137–38; related to notion of flying snakes, 23–24; related to notion of Griffins, 7–8, 44; related to notion of sea monsters, 31, 33

Fragrantica Trends, 389–90

Franchthi Cave, 116

frankincense, 13–14, 17, 19, 21, 23, 128, 178–79

Franklin, Benjamin, 233–34

Franklin, John, 226, 246

Fraser, Alistair, 237

Frazer, J. G., 30

The Fred Allen Program (radio show), 85

Frederick William I (Prussian king), 305

Free Library, Philadelphia, 84

French Revolution, 48

Freuchen, Peter, 230, 232

Freud, Sigmund, 285, 346–47

Frigorifique (steamer), 231, 232

Gabbaras, 292

Galatians, 184

Galba (Spanish governor), 227, 229

Galen, 71, 72

Galinthias, 95–96

Gaudry, Jean Albert, 113

Gauls, 183, 294–97. *See also* Celts

Gell, William, 343

Gellius, Aulus, 71

gender equality, 182, *195*, 206, 210, 212

Gent (magazine), 215

Gentlemen Prefer Blondes (musical), 215

George V (English king), 83, 227

Germani, 75, 293–94, 297–303

Germany, fossils in, 141

Geronimo, 162–65, *163*

Getty, J. Paul, 334

Getty Museum, Los Angeles, 209

ghost ships, 225–35, *228*, 248

giants: in ancient warfare, 286–305; bones, 5, 6, 116, 119–21, 124, 154, 166; Celtic and Germanic, 293–303; Greeks vs., 287, 288, 292–94; Israelites vs., 286–92; medieval, 303–4; Romans vs., 288, 294–303. *See also* Maximinus Thrax gigantism, 288, 376–77

Gillray, James, 269

Giuliani, Rudy, 109

glasses. *See* drinking vessels

gliding snakes, 18

goats, 4–5, 64, 71, 127, 180, 343, 344

goblets. *See* drinking vessels

gold, 4, 19–20, 37–41, 118, 126, 128–29, 136, 138, 140, 153, 263, 296–97, 318, 369, 378, 380

Golden Fleece, 27, 37–40, 252

golden ratio, 283

Gold Rush (America), 39

Goliath, 286, *287*, 289–90

Gonatas, Antigonus (Macedonian king), 200

Goodrich, Norma, 184

Gorgon, 139

Gozon de Dieu-Donné, 30–31

Grammer, J., 274

Grand Tours, 4–5, 148, 337–48

Graveyard of the Atlantic, 233

grayanotoxins, 275, 277–79

Greece/Greeks: anomalous information about, 5–8, 119–26, 132–33, 135–36; dogs in, 88–91; dolphins in, 50–58; earliest humans in, 116; fossils in, 113–16, 119–26, 135, 137–38; Persian invasions of, 28, 61, 255–56, 355, 383; prehistoric, 113–15; sea monsters and merpeople in, 26–36; tourism in, 323–48; travels of early, 37; turtles in, 59–67; weasels in, 92–100

Greek foot, 282–83

Green, Fitzhugh, 247

Gregale (Greek wind), 253–54

Griffins: ancient images and accounts of, 7–8, 41, 46, *118*, 124, 126–31; art history and literature scholars' explanations of, 125–27, 139; author's letter outlining speculation about, 117–19, 123–36; claws of, 41, *42*, 43–49, *45*, 128; cups made from claws of, 44–47, *45*, 128; eggs of, 41, 43–44, 47, 128, 138; feathers of, 44; features of, 7, 128; fossil evidence and, 7, 139; habitat of, 41

Guccione, Bob, 369

Gulf Stream, 233–34

Gulf War (1991), 382–85

Gustafson, Mark, 356

Guy of Warwick, 304

gypsies. *See* Romani

Hadrian (Roman emperor), 331, 352

Hale, Sarah, *185*

halinda (colewort), 174–75

Hamilcar, 312

Handel, George Frideric, *Water Music*, 57

Hannibal, 311–12, 315, 317, 350, 381

Hanno, 82, 312, 318

harps, 260, 333

Harry, Deborah, 101

Harun al-Rashid, 45–46, 49

Hauraki (ship), 248

Hawthorne, Nathaniel, 380
Hecate, 95–96
Hegesippus, 298
Helen of Troy, 221, 323, 325, 333–34, 342, 381
helicoid gastropod fossils, 153
Helladotherium, 115, 123
hemlock, 72
hemp, 176
Henry IV (French king), 77
Henry VIII (English king), 48, 388
Henry the Lion, 47
Heptakometes, 273
Hera, 95
Heracles/Hercules, 65, 95–96, 125, 187, 253, 287, 316–17, 333–34
Herakleides, 324–25
Hermes, 64–65
Hermias of Iasus, 56
Herodas, 354
Herodian, 358
Herodotus: Amazons, 192; Argive women, 198; cannabis, 69; Carthage, 312, 318; Cyrus the Great and Tomyris, 189; dolphins, 52; flying snakes, 13–25; fossils, 121, 122, 125; Griffins, 128; hemp, 176; *Histories*, 13; Persian kings, 383; Scythians, 136, 176–79, 196; sea monsters, 28; tattoos, 354–55, 357; travels of, 134, 324; wind, 257
Hesiod, 55
Hilton, Paris, 105–6

Himilco, 318
Hippocrates, 136, 210
Hippolyte (Amazon queen), 187, 333
hippopotami, 114, 123, 129. *See also* pygmy hippos
Histiaeus of Miletus, 355
Hobhouse, John Cam, 343
Holofernes, 204
Homer, 254, 260, 287; *Iliad*, 33, 37; *Odyssey*, 37, 250–51, 256, 282
Homeric Hymn to Hermes, 279–80
honey: poisonous, 71, 120, 272–81; tourists' experiences of, 323, 334, 337, 342; weasels' and ferrets' appetite for, 93, 94, 95, 102, 110
Hoopoes, 73–74
Horace, 327
horned vipers, 21
Horner, Jack, 7–8, 117
horse latitudes, 233
Houdini, Harry, 84
Humboldt, Alexander von, 86–87
hunting, xiii, 19, 49, 104, 109, 145
Hyacinthus, 55–56, 261–63
Hydra, 125
Hyginus, 381
Hypsicratea, 189
Hysmire, 54

ibises, 15–16, 19, 21–22
Ides, Ysbrand, 157
Incas, 82
incense, 13–14. *See also* frankincense

Incense Route, 136, 179, 180
India: Alexander the Great in, 292–93, 386; elephants of, 119, 122, 160, 292–93; flying snakes and gliding lizards in, 18, 19; poisonous beetles in, 69–70; variolation in, 268
Ino, 53
insects, fake fossils of, 148
International Society of Cryptozoology, 133
Inuits, 226, 360
Iphigenia, 257
Iraq War (2003), 382
Iris, 254
Irving, Washington, 233
Isabella (ship), 246
Isabella, Queen of Castile, 82
Isaiah, 17
Ishbi-benob, 291–92
Israelites, 71–73, 289–92
Isthmus of Corinth, 53

Japan, mountain journeys in, 349–50
Jardin des Plantes, Paris, 161
Jason and the Argonauts, 27, 37–39, 252, 258, 381
Jefferson, Thomas, 168–69
Jenner, Edward, 267, 269, 271
Jesus, 349
John and Mary (schooner), 225
John the Baptist, 204
Jonathan, 291
Jones, Christopher, 356
Jones, David, 184–85

Josephus, 22, 240, 289–92
Joshua, book of, 290
Journal of the Optical Society of America, 249
Jovian (Roman emperor), 302–3
Judith, 204
Jurassic Park (film), 7

Kadmos, 333
Kaffa, 229
Kafka, Franz, 8
Kazraji, Abu Dolaf, 352
Keats, John, 260, 284
Kedar/Kedarites, 180–81
Kelly, Don, 133–34
Khawla bint Al Azwar Military School, Abu Dhabi, 182
Killigrew, Anne, 204–8, *205*
Kindergarten Cop (film), 101
Kingdom of Kongo, 168
Kingsley, Charles, 254
Kircher, Athanasius, 237
Kirchner, H., 141
Kirkpatrick, Cletis, 305
Klete, 188
Kokotos, Linos, 36
Kolbert, Elizabeth, 155
Kondouriotis, Lazaros, 33–34
krex (bird), 15

Lahmi, 291
Lalique stemware, 217
Lambert, René, 157
Lamour, Dorothy, 85
Lampe, Kenneth, 277
Laocoön, 29

Lartet, Édouard, 113
laurel, 275, 278–79
Lawrence, T. E., 257
Leach, David, 277
Leaders Number One, 388, 389, 389
Leakey, Louis, 66
leatherback turtles, 29–30
Leda, 323, 325
Leigh, Gerard, 44
Leonardo da Vinci, 108
Lewis, Meriwether, 169
Li Bai, 350–51
Libyans, 287–88
Lie, Antoine, 390
Life (magazine), 85
Liji (Record of Rites), 363
Lindisfarne, 42–43
Lindisfarne Gospel, 42, 48
Linus, 65
Little Shrike-thrush, 73
Livy: Carthage, 311, 312, 316; Celts/Gauls, 296; Chiomara, 184; Philip V's mountain ascent, 351–52
lizards, 18–19, 31
Lobell, Jarrett, 3
locusts, 21–22, 24
Loew, H. F., 148
Lombroso, Cesare, 265
London Review of Books (magazine), 2
Longfellow, Henry Wadsworth, 260
Longus, 276
looming mirages, 245–48

Louis (macaw), 84–85
Louis the Pious, 46
Lucian (historian), 198
Lucian, Saint, 55
Lucretius, 71
Lusitania (ship), 235
Lycophron, 188
lyres, 52, 59, 61, 64–65, *64*, 67, 330, 380

Macaulay, Rose, 280–81
macaws, 84, 86–87
MacMillan, Donald B., 247
mad honey, 272–81
Madonna (singer), 105
maenads, 280
Magenta (ship), 315
magic lanterns, 237
magnification mirages, 245–48
Maiasaura, 138
Major, Charles I. Forsyth, 115
Makri, Theresa, 341
malmsey, 338
Malta, 152–53
Malthus, Thomas, 344
Mamluks, 229
mammoths, 122, 125, 141, 154–61, *156, 158,* 166–69, *167.* See also mastodons
Mann, Thomas, 306
Mao Tse-tung, 367
Marathon, 61, 98, 122–23, 333, 341
marches, 2
Marie-Antoinette (French queen), 215
Marine Observer (magazine), 248

Marius, Gaius, 75–77, 298–302

Mary Celeste (brigantine), 230

Mary of Modena, Duchess of York, 204

Masefield, John, 260

mastodons, 115, 116, 123, 154–55, 157, 167–69

mastoi (breast cups for wine), 219, *219*

Mather, Cotton, 267–68

Mâtho, 311

matriphagy, 14–15

Mavromichalis, George, 33

Maximilian I (Holy Roman emperor), 303, 304

Maximinus Thrax, 375–77, *376*

Maxwell, Elsa, 85

Medea, 37, 258, 273

Medusa, 263

Mela, Pomponius, 22

Melikertes, 53

Melqart, 317

Meltemi, 254, 259

Menander, 327

Menelaos, 258

Mercenary Revolt (Carthage), 311–12, 313, 315

mermaids, 27, 35–36. *See also* Nereids; sea monsters; Tritons

Metabus (Volscian king), 192

Metcalf, Theodore, 82

Methymna, 53

Michel, Auguste, 390

Michelangelo, *David*, 282

microbats, 19, 24

Midas (Phrygian king), 378–81

Miles, Richard, 307, 309, 313–14, 316, 319–20

Military History Quarterly (journal), 2

Milo of Croton, 376

Minasi (friar), 238–40, 244

Mingo, 80–81

Minotaur, 124, 269–70

Miocene Greece, 113–14

mirages at sea, 226, 236–49, *242*

Mirivilis, Stratis, 36

misogyny, 94, 193

missing link, 147–48

Mithradates VI of Pontus, 70–71, 189, 267, 273

Mithridatium, 267

Mitsopoulos, Hercules, 113

Modern Ferret (magazine), 109

Moiro, 354

Moloch. *See* Baal

Montague, John (Earl of Sandwich), 340

Montague, Mary Wortley, 44

Morgan le Fay, 236, 249

Morocco, fake fossils from, *150, 151,* 152

Morrissey (ship), 245

Morritt, John, 340

Morro Castle (ship), 235

Mort the Triceratops, 8

Moseley, Benjamin, 269–70

Moses, 22, 290, 349

Mossynoikoi, 358

mountain climbing, 349–53

Mount Parthenion, 61

Mucha, Alphonse, 306
Muhammad, 182
Mummius, L., 334
Museum of the Middle Ages, Paris, 49
Museum of the Rockies, Bozeman, Montana, 7–8, 137–38
mushrooms. *See* Reishi mushrooms
music: dolphins' love of, 50–52, *51*, 57–58; turtle shells used for lyres, 59, 61, 64–65, 67; wind and, 260. *See also* flutes; harps; lyres; pipes
Mussorgsky, Modest, 306
mustard, 174–75
mynahs, 80, 85
Mytilini, 123, 127–30, 135

Nan Shih (History of the Southern Dynasties), 363
Narcissus, 333
narwhals, 49
Nashnush, Suleiman Ali, 288
National Geographic (magazine), 149, 377
National Humanities Center, 391n58
National Museum of Natural History, Paris, 156
Native Americans: and fossils, 154–55, 159, 162, 164–65; and poison honey, 278; sweat-lodge ceremonies of, 177
Natural History Museum, London, 148

Nawanagar, maharajah of, 85
Neïdes, 119, 122, 135
Nemesianus, 88
Nephilim, 290
Nepos, Cornelius, 312
Nereids, 33–35. *See also* mermaids
Nereus, 33
Nero (Roman emperor), 221, 227, 330, 331, 332, 387
Nerodia water snakes, 15
Neumayr, Melchior, 113
Newton, Helmut, 213–14, 216, 218, 220
New York Times (newspaper), 213–14, *214*, 220
Nibelungenlied (epic), 140–42
Nicander, 69–70
Nicholas, Saint, 258
Nile perch, 202–3
Noah's Flood, 147, 166
Nobel Prize, 36, 393
Normandie (ship), 235
North Pole, 246
Northwest Passage, 246
Notos (South Wind), 254, 257–60
Novaya Zemlya (New Land), 245
Numbers, book of, 72, 290

oarfish, 29
Ober, Josiah (Josh), 4–5, 7, 50, 101–3, 107–8, 110, 254
Odysseus, 54, 89, 121, 250–51, 253, 256, 260, 287
Oeobazus, 383
Oesterreich, T. K., 278
O'Flagherty, Roderick, 241

Og of Bashan, 290–91

Ohio Monsters, 169

okapi, 115

Old Bet (elephant), 160

Old Testament: ancient giants, 289; Arab warrior queens, 180; Carthage, 311, 315; flying snakes, 17; poisonous quail, 71–72. *See also individual books*

oleander, 274, 275, 278–79

Olga of Kiev, 273

Olympia, 130–31

Ombiaux, Maurice des, 221

onagers, 181

Onesimus, 267–68

Opis, 191

opium, 69, 276, 342

Oppian, 58

Oreithyia, 252

Orestes, 330

Orientalism, 309, 313, 320

Orosius, 374

Orpheus, 65, 358

Ortiagon, 183–84, *185*

Osbourne (yacht), 31

Ötzi, 350, 361

Ovid, 78, 89, 254, 325, 379

Oxford Journal of Archaeology, 7

Oxford University Museum, 147

Paederus beetles, 70

painted carpet vipers, 21

paleocryptozoology, 133

paleontology: author's interest in, 3, 5–8, 117–39; Cuvier as

father of, 154; in Greece, 112–39; hoaxes involving, 147–52. *See also* archaeology

Pan, 61, 380

parachuting lizards, 18–19

parakeets, 78–79

Paramount Pictures, 85

Paris (Trojan), 191, 221

Parkening, Christopher, 101

parrots, 78–87

Parthenon, Athens, 334, 335, 338, 340, 345–47

Parthian shots, 193

Pasiphaë, 269–70

Paul, Saint, 253, 329, 335

Pausanias: Alcmene, 96; Argive women, 198–200; *A Description of Greece*, 331–36, 347; dolphins, 56; fossils, 121, 122, 124; Greek tour of, 331–36, *331*; sea monsters, 30; Tritons, 26; turtles, 61; wind, 258

Pawnee Indians, 156, 159

Pazuzu, 254

Peabody Museum, 27, 65, 67

Peacock, Edward, 45

Peary, Robert E., 246–47

pederin, 70

Pegasus, 124

Peleus, 33

Penthesilea (Amazon queen), 187–88, 191, 206

Pepys, Samuel, 80–81

perch, 202–3

perfumes, 46, 282, 333; Alexander the Great and, 386–87;

Arabian trade in, 24, 180; Cleopatra and, 387; dolphins' dislike of, 56; ingredients of, 13, 178; men's fragrances, 386, 388–90; Romans and, 387–88. *See also* frankincense

Perseus, 139, 263

Persia/Persians: Griffin claw gift to Charlemagne from, 41, 45–46, 49; invasions of Greece by, 28, 61, 252, 255–56, 355, 383; and poison from Dikairon's feces, 68; and Romans, 303

Peter III of Aragon, 352–53

Peter the Great, 157

Petit, Pierre, 205, 209–12, *211*

Petrarch, 351

phantom ships. *See* ghost ships

Pheidippides, 61

Philip V (Macedonian king), 351–52

Philistines, 289

Philo, 71

Philostratus, 122, 283

Phlegon of Tralles, 23

Phoenicians, 317–19

Phoenix & Arabeth, 3

phrenology, 265

physiognomy, 264–66

Picasso, Pablo, 220

Picasso, Paloma, 213–14

Picts, 358

pigeon, messenger, 83–84

The Pigeon That Took Rome (film), 85

Pikermi, 112–15, 123

Pikermi Ape, 112, *113*, 123

Pilot Charts, 231, 234

Piltdown Man, 147–48, 151

Pindar, 324, 327

pipes (musical instrument), 51, 380

pirates, 52, 229, 337, 347, 357, 367–68

Pitohui, 73

plague, 72, 229, 254

Plato, 54, 194–97, 210, 265; *Laws*, 194–97; *Republic*, 197

Plato's Academy, Athens, 265, 333, 346

Playboy (magazine), 215, 217

Pleistocene Greece, 114, 116

plesiosaurs, 33

Plessis, Edouard, 32

Pliny the Elder: Antony and Cleopatra, 201–2; Carthage, 312; dolphins, 56; fossils, 122; Golden Fleece, 38; Griffins, 128; Helen of Troy, 221; honey, 273–77; mirages, 240; poisonous Pontic ducks, 71; Rhodes, 330; scorpions, 21; sea monsters, 29; weasels, 98; wind, 257–58

Pliocene Greece, 113–16

Plugge, P. C., 274

Plutarch: Alexander the Great, 292–93, 386; Antony and Cleopatra, 201–3; bird banding, 76; Carthage, 312, 315; Celts/Gauls, 296;

Plutarch (*continued*)
   fossils, 119, 122, 135; Germani,
   297–98; Pythias, 278; Roman
   military, 299–302; tattoos,
   355; warrior women, 184, 200
Poe, Edgar Allan, 233; "The City
   in the Sea," 243–44
poison: beetles, 69–70; Caligula's
   collection of, 373–74;
   Dikairon, 68–70; ducks, 71;
   honey, 272–81; Mithradates
   VI's knowledge of, 70–71;
   quail, 71–73; various creatures,
   71–72; weapons utilizing, 69
polecats. *See* weasels/ferrets
Pollux, 89
Polo, Marco, 356
Polosmak, Natalya, 360
Polyaenus, 198–99
Polybius, 184, 309, 312, 313
Pompey the Great, 189, 273, 303,
   329
poop: bird, 68–73; dinosaur, 152;
   ferret, 102
Popeye (parrot), 81–82
Poroselene, 56
Porus (Indian king), 292–93
Post, Marjorie Merriweather,
   391n58
Powell, Eric, 3
Prial, Frank, 217
Prior, Matthew, 79
Procopius, 312
Prometheus, 129
Propertius, 327, 331
Protoceratops, 137–38, 139

Psamathe, 33
Psamtik of Egypt, 381
Pseudo-Plutarch, *On Rivers*, 174
Psylli, 257
Putin, Vladimir, 388–90
pygmy hippos, 125, 133–34
Pyrrhus of Epirus, 200
Pythia, 278–80

Qedar/Qedarites, 180–81
quail, poisonous, 71–74
Queen Eleanor (steamer), 32

Rabelais, 256–57
Rachmaninoff, Sergei, 306
Radner, Karen, 23
Raffles (mynah), 85
Rainbow Island (film), 85
Rakhianu (Damascene ruler), 180
Ramachandran, Vilayanur, 285
ram-birds, 39–40, *40*
Randy and the Rainbows, 101
Ras Shamra Texts, 289
ravens, 84
Red Moscow (fragrance), 389–90
Reese, David, 133–34
Reggio di Calabria, 236–39
Reishi mushrooms, 143–44, 146
Rekunov, Vladislav, 388
Remus, 192
Rephaim, 289
Republic Pictures, 86
Reresby, John, 44–45
Restoration (England), 204, 207
retsina, 342
Revenue Cutter Service, 235

rhinoceroses: ancestors of, 137; ancient images and accounts of, 129; in China, 143–46; fossils of, 113, 115, 123, 131; as model for strange creatures of literature and art, 124; uses of, 145

Rhodes, 30–31, 329–30

rhododendron, 71, 272–76, 278–80

Richardson, Philip, 230, 234–35

Richmond, Frances Theresa Stuart, Duchess of, 84

rinkhals (spitting cobras), 15

Roc bird, 41

Rochegrosse, Georges, 306

Rodger, A. F., 32

Rodin, Auguste, 306

Rodriguez, Narciso, 390

Roland, 303

Romani, 4, 131

Romanticism (art movement), 140, 244, 254, 341

Rome (television series), 387

Rome/Romans: and Amazons, 187–93; and Carthage, 306–7, 310, 311, 313–14, 316–17, 319–20; dogs in, 88–91; "giant" foes of, 288, 294–303; and Hercules/Heracles, 316–17; military training of, 298–99; and perfume, 387–88; physical stature of, 294; tattoos in, 356; tourism of, 323–36, *326*; and turtles, 61; vulture mascots of, 75–77

Romulus, 192

Roosevelt, Theodore, 163

rosebay, 279

Ross, Andrew, 148

Ross, James Clark, 246

Ross, John, 246

Rowley, Thomas, 270

Royal Meteorological Society, 245–46

Royal Meteorological Society Quarterly Journal, 243

Rubicon (freighter), 225

Rudenko, Sergei, 135–37, 359–61

Rudwick, Martin, 154

Rufus, Quintus Curtius, 239

Rumney (ship), 231

Rundel, Lord, 339

Russian Academy of Science, St. Petersburg, 159

Saddam Hussein, 382–85

Saint-Denis church, 44, 46, 49

Saintsbury, George, 216

Saki, 104

Salimbene, Fra, 353

Sallust, 303

Salmonson, Jessica Amanda, 185

Salome, 204

Samos, 115–16, 118–19, 122–30, 134–35

Samotherium, 119, 123, 130, 135

Samsi (Arab queen), 180–81

sand boas, 15

USS *San Francisco*, 232

San people, 69

Sappho, 204, 323, 330

Sargon, 28

Sauropods, 141, 143

Saving Private Ryan (film), 385

saw-scale vipers, 21

Schliemann, Heinrich, 310

Schwarzenegger, Arnold, 101, 391n111

Scientific American (magazine), 237

Scipio Aemilianus, 311, 312, 314, 319

Sciron, 29

scorpions, 15, 21, 24

Scott, Robert Falcon, 248

Scott, Walter, 227, 340

Scythia/Scythians: animal designs/tattoos of, 3, 135, 136–37, 178, 359–61, *359*; as archers, 194–97, *195*; burials of, 136–37; characteristics of, 173; gender equality among, 194–97, *195*; gold in, 39, 136; Griffins in, 118–19, 123, 126, 129, 135–36; Plato and, 194–97; trade practiced by, 179. *See also* Amazons; Siberia/Siberians

Sea Cloud I (yacht), 50, 391n58

Sea Frontiers (magazine), 2

sea monsters, 28–33, *28*, 125. *See also* mermaids; Nereids; Tritons

sea turtles, 29–30

Seferis, George, 35

Selznick, David O., 85

Sennacherib (Assyrian king), 181

Severus, Septimius (Roman emperor), 375

Severus Alexander, 375

Sèvres porcelain cups, 215

Sextus Empiricus, 71

sexual cannibalism, 14–15

Shakespeare, William, 260, 338

sharks, 28, 30, 120, 125, 152, 153, 168

Shi Nai'an, *Water Margin*, 366, 368

Shintoism, 350

Shoumachoff, Ossip, 158–59

Sibbecai the Hushathite, 291

Siberia/Siberians: mammoths found in, 157–58; tattoos of, 359–61, 363–64. *See also* Scythia/Scythians

Siegfried, 140–42

Silenos, 379, 381

Silk Routes, 39, 41, 44, 179

Sima Qian, 364

Simo (dolphin), 55–56

Simonides of Samos, 94

Sippai, 291

Sirens, 34

Sirocco (Southeast Wind), 254, 259

Skiron (Northwest Wind), 254

Skouphos, Theodore, 113

skunks, 93, 104

slavery. *See* enslaved Africans

smallpox, 204, 208, 267–71

Smerdis of Persia, 381

snakes, 97, 98. *See also* flying snakes

Society for the Investigation of the Unexplained, 133

Socrates, 265, *265*, 332

Solinus, 22

Solomon (Israelite king), 180

Song Jiang, 366–68

Sopater, 258

Souroko. *See* Sirocco

South Pole, 246

souvenirs, 323, *326*, 328, 330, 332, 335–36, 338–41

Sparta/Spartans: and Argive women, 198–200; Hyacinthus cult of, 262–63; tourism in, 324–25; windy encounter of, 254

Spendius, 311

Sphinx, 124, 333

Spike (ferret), 106–8

Spindler, Konrad, 361

Spon, Jacob, 339, 342–43, 345

Sports Afield (magazine), 2

Spur-Winged Goose, 73

Stanhope, Hester, 340

starlings, 80

Stella (ferret), 109–11

Stevenson, Robert Louis, *Treasure Island*, 86

Stewart, Zeph, 132

Stono Plantation, South Carolina, 155, 166, 168

Strabo: Amazons, 210; Britons, 297; Carthage, 312; flying snakes, 19, 21; Golden Fleece, 38; Greece, 330, 336; poison honey, 273; wind, 254

Strait of Messina, 236–39

Stuart, Frances Theresa (Duchess of Richmond), 84

Sturz, Lisa Aimee, 142

Stymphalean Birds, 126

styrax (resin), 13–14

Success (fragrance), 388, *389*

Sudanese, 287–88

Suetonius: Caligula, 356, 370, 373; fossils, 124; ghost ship, 227; Rhodes, 329

Sulla, 334

sunglasses, 337, *338*, 343

Svaneti, Colchis, 38

sweat-lodge ceremonies, 177

Swift, Jonathan, *Gulliver's Travels*, 289

Swinburne, Algernon, 284

Symon's Monthly Meteorological Magazine, 242

Tacitus, 296, 297, 299–302

Taenarum, 53

Tanit, 312, 315

Taoism, 349, 350

Taquet, Philippe, 156

Taras, 53

Tarentum, 53

Tatian, 199

Tatler (journal), 79

tattoos: barbarian, 3, 357–58, 363; of captives and slaves, 355–56, 364; Chinese and, 363–68; Egyptian, 361–62; functions of, 354, 357–58, 361, 362, 364; Greek images of, 358–59, 364; process of, 357, 360, 365, 367; as punishment, 354–57, 364, 366–67; removal of, 70, 357; Scythian, 3, 135, 136–37, 178, 359–61, *359*; therapeutic, 361

Te'el-hunu (Arab queen), 181

Telemachus, 54

Telesilla, 198–200

Temple of Hera, Argos, 200

Temple of Zeus, Athens, 334, 346

Terpander, 65

HMS *Terror*, 226, 246

Tertullian, 312

Teutobochus (Teutonic king), 301

The Teutonic Prisoners (sculpture), 297

Teutons, 75, 294, 297, 298–300

Teylers Museum, Netherlands, 147

Thalestris (Amazon queen), 189, 204–7, *205*

Thebes, 324–25

Themistocles, 256, 381

Theodore Metcalf (parrot), 82

Theophrastus, 122, 124, 312

Theropods, 141

Theseus, 187, 188

Thetis, 33, 284

Thornton, Robert John, "Effects Arising from Vaccination," *270*

the Thousand (tyrannical oligarchs), 200

Thracians, 357–58

Thucydides, 124

Tiberius (Roman emperor), 323, 329, 336, 371

Tiglath-Pileser III (Assyrian king), 180–81

Time (magazine), 86

Titanic (ship), 235, 245

Titans, 287

toasting, 218–19

tobacco, 342

Todorov, Alexander, 265

tomb of Midas, *379*

Tomyris (Massagetae queen), 189

Too Kin, 350

tortoises. *See* turtles

tourism: accommodations and meals, 324, 327–28, 331, 341–44; Europeans in Greece, 337–48; hardships of, 337, 344; Romans in Greece, 323–36; souvenirs, 323, *326*, 328, 330, 332, 335–36, 338–41; supplies for, 343–44; theft of antiquities, 334, 338–39

Tower of the Winds, Athens, 250–55, *251*, 346

Treasure Island (film), 85

Triceratops, 137, 139

trilobites, 149, *150*, 151

Tritons, 26–27, 250. *See also* mermaids; Nereids; sea monsters

Trojan War, 187–88, 206, 257, 287

Trump (fragrance), 388

Trump, Donald, 388–90

Tsar (fragrance), 390

Tucson Fossil and Mineral Show, 149

tulip champagne glasses, 215

tuna, 203

Tunisia, 307, 309, 310, 314

Turnus, 189

turtles: admired qualities of, 61; folklore about, 61–63; as food for eagles, 63; as food for humans, 63–64; Greek habitats of, 60–61; mating habits of, 65–67; and music, 59, 61, 64; as playthings, 61, *62*; and racing, 59–60, 61; as sea monsters, 29–30; vocalizations of, 66–67; Zeus and, 62–63

Unicorn horn, 49
United Nations Entity for Gender Equality, 182
United States: fossils in, 166–69; Gold Rush in, 39. *See also* Native Americans
universal antidote, 71, 267
University of California–Santa Cruz Slugs, 61
University of North Carolina National Center for Catastrophic Sport Injury Research, 263
Uraeus, 19–21, *20*, 25
urban legends, 382–85
US Army, 305
US Coast Guard, 225, 235
US Exploring Expedition (1838–42), 246
US Navy Hydrographic Office, 231

vaccinations, 208, 267–71
Valerius Maximus, 184, 312
Van Buchel, Arnold, 44
Van Cleef and Arpels, 390
Vanderpool, Eugene, 5, 122–23
Van Dijk, Pablo, 213–14, *214*
vapor baths, 175–77
variolation, 268

vase in the shape of a foot, 282, *283*
Vasnier, Yann, 389
Vegetius, 298
Venezis, Ilias, 35
Venus (goddess), 95, 204, 221, 284. *See also* Aphrodite
Venus (planet), 248
Verdun, Battle of, 83–84
Vermonnel (French government commissioner), 157
Verres, 334
vessels. *See* derelicts (abandoned ships); drinking vessels
Vikings, 248
Vinick, Larry, 214–15
Vinycomb, John, 47
Virgil, *Aeneid*, 29, 187–93, 311
Vitellius (Roman emperor), 292
Vorenus, Lucius, 387
Vulso, Gnaeus Manlius, 183
vultures, 75–77, *76*

Wadjet, 19, *20*, 25
Wagner, Andreas, 112
Wagner, Richard: *Flying Dutchman*, 233; *The Ring of the Nibelung*, 140; *Siegfried*, 142, *142*
Waldrapp (Northern Bald Ibis), 16
Wall Street Journal (newspaper), 105
Wang Wu, 365
Wars of Religion (France), 48
Washington, George, 160, 161, 168, 268–69
water nymphs, 33–35
Watson, George E., 65–67

weasels/ferrets: associated with sex, marriage, and birth, 95–97; author's, 3, 94, 101–11; bad reputation of, 93–94, 104; characteristics of, 94; folklore about, 92, 94–97, 104; food of, 94, 102, 103; Greek images of, 99, *99*; laws about, 109, 392n111; lifespan of, 103, 105, 109, 110; mating habits of, 103–4; mouse-hunting abilities of, 92–95; odor of, 92, 93, 104, 107; as pets, 94, 99–111; relatives of, 97–98, 104, 106; sleeping habits of, 103; slithering abilities of, 101, 102, 107; snakes as enemies of, 97, 98; teeth and claws of, 102–3, 109–10; thieving abilities of, 93, 106; uses of, 98, 104, 109; vet care for, 103; vocalizations of, 93

Wesley (minister of Epworth), 81

whaling, 49

Wheler, George, 339, 341–43, 345

White, Miles, 214–15

Wilkes, Charles, 246

Wilson, Victoria, 84

wind-lullers, 258–59

winds, 250–60

witches, 96

W. L. White (schooner), 234

women. *See* Amazons; Argos/ Argive women; breasts

Wonders and Marvels (website), 2

Woodward, Arthur Smith, 113

Wordsworth, William, 244

World War I, 83–84

worms, as dog ailment, 91

wormwood, 91

Wren, Warren, 232

Wu (Chinese king), 145

Xenophanes, 152–53

Xenophon, 89–90, 272, 312, 358

Xerxes (Persian king), 256, 354–55, 383, 385

Xiongnu, 364–65

Yang Yao, 367

Yatie (Arab queen), 181

York (enslaved member of Lewis and Clark expedition), 169

York, Duke of, 80

Young, Andrew T., 238

Young, Peter, 3

Yue Fei, 366–67, *368*

Zabibi (Arab queen), 180

Zeno of Elia, 59–60

Zephyros (West Wind), 254, 256, 260, 261–62

Zetes, 252

Zeus, 62–63, 95, 263, 323

Zhang Qian, *Han Shu*, 364–65

Zhan Guo Ce (Intrigues of the Warring States), 363

zooarchaeology, 125

Zopyrus, 265

ALSO BY ADRIENNE MAYOR

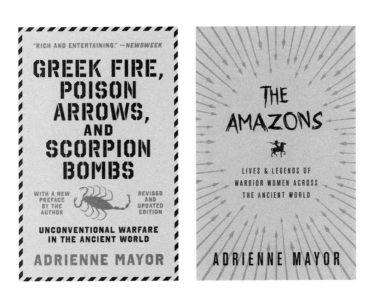

PRINCETON UNIVERSITY PRESS

Available wherever books are sold.
For more information visit us at press.princeton.edu